The Ground of Professional Ethics

Professionals are increasingly under pressure both to be responsive to their clients and to deny them certain services which neither they nor the public purse can afford. Balancing these pressures while maintaining a relationship of mutual trust with clients poses a difficult challenge to doctors, lawyers, the clergy and other professionals.

Daryl Koehn argues for a new kind of professional/client relationship in which the professional is not bound by the whims of the client but by a promise to serve the particular good (e.g. health, salvation, social justice . . .) which both parties must wish to promote. Only through taking on this role can professionals preserve their self-esteem and moral legitimacy.

The Ground of Professional Ethics also examines the difficult practical questions: What can clients justifiably expect from professionals? When may service to a client be legitimately terminated? Should professionals resist political pressure?

The Ground of Professional Ethics will help professionals and the public to re-think what professionals owe clients. It also explores the responsibilities of the clients to the professionals whose help they desire. This book will be of great value to professionals as well as to students and teachers of ethics.

Daryl Koehn is Assistant Professor of Philosophy at DePaul University in Chicago. She has published numerous articles in the field of professional and business ethics and regularly consults with corporations on ethical matters.

Professional Ethics
General editors: Andrew Belsey
Centre for Applied Ethics, University of Wales College of Cardiff
and Ruth Chadwick
Centre for Professional Ethics, University of Central Lancashire

Professionalism is a subject of interest to academics, the general public and would-be professional groups. Traditional ideas of professions and professional conduct have been challenged by recent social, political and technological changes. One result has been the development for almost every profession of an ethical code of conduct which attempts to formalise its values and standards. These codes of conduct raise a number of questions about the status of a "profession" and the consequent moral implications for behaviour.

This series seeks to examine these questions both critically and constructively. Individual volumes will consider issues relevant to particular professions, including nursing, genetic counselling, social work, journalism, business, the food industry and law. Other volumes will address issues relevant to all professional groups such as the function and value of a code of ethics and the demands of confidentiality.

Also available in this series:

Ethical Issues in Journalism and the Media
edited by Andrew Belsey and Ruth Chadwick

Genetic Counselling
edited by Angus Clarke
Institute of Medical Genetics, University of Wales College of Medicine

Ethical Issues in Nursing
edited by Geoffrey Hunt
European Centre for Professional Ethics, University of East London

The Ground of
Professional Ethics

Daryl Koehn

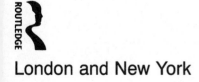

London and New York

First published 1994
by Routledge
11 New Fetter Lane London EC4P 4EE

Simultaneously published in the USA and Canada
by Routledge
29 West 35th Street, New York, NY 10001

Phototypeset in Times by Intype, London

Printed and bound in Great Britain by T J Press Ltd, Padstow, Cornwall

British Library Cataloguing in Publication Data
A catalogue record for this book is available from the British Library

Library of Congress Cataloging in Publication Data
Koehn, Daryl, 1955–
    The ground of professional ethics / Daryl Koehn.
      p.   cm.—(Professional ethics)
    Includes bibliographical references and index.
    1. Professional ethics.   I. Title.   II. Series.
BJ1725.K64   1994
174—dc20   94–9871
                                                               CIP

ISBN 0–415–11666–X
        0–415–11667–8 (pbk)

For my parents who have given me life;
For my teachers and colleagues who have
enriched my life;
For my husband and friends who have shared
that life.

Contents

Series editors' foreword

Professional Ethics is now acknowledged as a field of study in its own right. Much of its recent development has resulted from rethinking traditional medical ethics in the light of new moral problems arising out of advances in medical science and technology. Applied philosophers, ethicists and lawyers have devoted considerable energy to exploring the dilemmas emerging from modern health-care practices and their effects on the practitioner–patient relationship.

But the point can be generalised. Even in health care, ethical dilemmas are not confined to medical practitioners. And beyond health care, other groups are beginning to think critically about the kind of service they offer and about the nature of the relationship between provider and recipient. In many areas of life, social, political and technological changes have challenged traditional ideas of practice.

One visible sign of these developments has been the proliferation of codes of ethics, or of professional conduct. The drafting of such a code provides an opportunity for professionals to examine the nature and goals of their work, and offers information to others about what can be expected from them. If a code has a disciplinary function, it may even offer protection to members of the public.

But is the existence of such a code itself a criterion of a profession? What exactly is a profession? Can a group acquire professional status, and if so, how? Does the label 'professional' have implications, from a moral point of view, for acceptable behaviour, and if so how far do they extend?

By concentrating on the 'ground' of ethical practice in the

three 'liberal' professions of medicine, law and the ministry, Daryl Koehn is able to produce a new understanding of the professional–client relationship as one which is focused on a particular good which both parties wish to promote. This account, Professor Koehn argues, gives the relationship a moral legitimacy which other accounts fail to provide. In exploring the implications of her views, Professor Koehn throws new light on a wide range of issues in professional ethics.

This series, edited from the Centre for Applied Ethics in Cardiff and the Centre for Professional Ethics in Preston, seeks to examine ethical issues in the professions both critically and constructively. Individual volumes will address issues relevant to all professional groups, such as the nature of a profession, the function and value of codes of ethics, and the demands of confidentiality. Other volumes will examine issues relevant to particular professions, including those which have hitherto received little attention, such as journalism, social work and genetic counselling.

Andrew Belsey
Ruth Chadwick

Acknowledgements

This book would not have been written if it had not been for my friends and colleagues who patiently listened to me try out ideas about professional ethics for what probably seemed an eternity. I am particularly grateful to the following persons who carefully read and commented on earlier drafts of various chapters of this book: Paul Camenisch, Stephen Houlgate, Karen Hyman, Dr Leon Kass, Martin Marty, Leszek Kolakowski, Rebecca Roberts McCarthy, and Dr Mark Siegler. Extended and animated discussions with John Cornell and my colleagues Ken Alpern and Michael Naas regarding the nature and value of trust also contributed in many direct and indirect ways to the formation of my views on the professions expressed in this book. I hope and trust that the extensive notes reflect my large debt to the philosophers, sociologists, economists and historians who have written on the theory of the professions and to the practicing professionals who have taken time out of busy schedules to speak with me. Jill Lavelle provided invaluable production support. Final thanks go to my husband Julian who offered me unfailing support, as well as helpful criticism, during the years in which this book was written.

Chapter 1

Introduction

George Bernard Shaw once charged that all professions were conspiracies against the laity. No doubt many today would agree with Shaw's assessment. Professionals stand accused of craving only status and wealth and even of disabling, rather than helping, their clients.[1] In one sense, these modern accusations merely continue the long tradition of attacking professionals. Anti-clerical movements periodically have convulsed Europe. Elizabethans cheered Shakespeare's oft-quoted proposal, "First, let's kill all the lawyers." Patients of early Greek and Roman doctors carped that physicians overstated dangers to health in order to build their reputations.[2] Suspicion of individual professions clearly has a long pedigree and is not in and of itself particularly noteworthy. What *is* remarkable and decidedly uncommonplace is the increasingly voiced suggestion that all professional authority is inherently unethical and consequently illegitimate as presently constituted. This book is an attempt to confront and rebut this challenge to the authority and ethics of professionals by showing that this authority rests upon a secure and morally legitimating ground.

THE CHALLENGE

While adequately confronting this challenge will require developing and defending a full-blown account of the relations among professionals, their clients and the larger community, the challenge itself can be described in a few pages. The attack on professional authority has been mounted by three distinct groups. The first group of critics charges that there is nothing inherently good about professional practice. Although professionals have traditionally been seen as acting in the spirit of public service, these antagonists deny that professionals are benefactors.[3] On their view, the ancient Greek physicians erred in seeing themselves as "lovers of mankind."[4] Cicero was wrong to portray the attorney as a servant of the public whose house is "without doubt the oracular seat of the whole community."[5] At best, the professions are houses of trade. They may pretend to operate for the public good. But, at root, professions are just another form of commerce, albeit a particularly well-entrenched and well-organized species of it.[6]

This view has derived support both from recent Supreme Court decisions construing professions along the model of business and from changes in university disciplines. In America, the learned professions traditionally have been immune from certain antitrust proscriptions because they were not considered instances of commerce. Since the 1970s, however, courts have struck down lawyers' bans on the advertising of legal fees and services on the ground that such bans impede free commercial speech.[7] Professions are, on this view, not merely economic institutions but also effective monopolistic ones aiming at restricting trade in order to maximize professional income and power.

Changes in university disciplines, especially history and sociology, also have played a part in displacing the notion that professional practice serves the public's interest:

> The academic sociologists of the 1940's and 1950's were prone to emphasize as the central characteristics of professions their especially complex formal knowledge and skill along *with an ethical approach to their work* [emphasis mine]. These and other traits were used to set professionals off from other occupations and to justify the protective institutions and high prestige that also distinguished them. Writers from the late 1960's on, however, emphasized instead the unusually effective, monopolistic institutions of professions and their high status as the critical factor and treated knowledge, skill and ethical orientations not as objective characteristics but rather as ideology, as claims by spokesmen for professions seeking to gain or to preserve status and privilege.[8]

So viewed, professions have no inherent legitimacy. They are only a dominant ideology to be replaced, one infers, by institutions or practices that truly aim at the public good.

Unlike the historians and sociologists, the second group of

critics, composed mainly of philosophers, has been willing to grant that professions have a non-ideological ethic. For these philosophers, being a professional is akin to being a parent. The parental practice of child-rearing exhibits a distinctive ethos where an ethos is understood as a characteristic devotion to a particular good. This ethos tends to define the practice: parents who do not take care of their children are not parenting. When confronted with non-nurturing parents, the court acts *in loco parentis* and places minors with persons who it thinks will rear the children well. Professions such as medicine and law can be thought of as similarly defined by a distinctive commitment to benefit the client. If they are so defined, it follows that professionals are legitimately concerned about such things as the untoward effects of advertising upon their clients. True, attempts by professionals to prohibit advertising may be interpreted as an ideological effort to retain monopolistic power. But the philosopher will argue that one can re-describe any activity as narrowly self-interested. Rearing a child may be construed as an attempt to produce an asset which will generate cash for the parents' old age. It does not follow, however, from the fact that an activity can be so described that, in fact, it is no more than an economic ideology.

Most philosophers, then, accept that professions are not ideological monopolies. Their quarrel with professionalism lies rather with what they take to be the normative claims made by professionals. They charge that professionals understand themselves as ruled by ethical norms or standards which permit, and maybe even oblige professionals, to perform actions not permitted by the "ordinary" norms applicable to the rest of us.[9] Some doctors, for example, claim that they are entitled to lie to a patient if doing so protects the patient's health. This claim qualifies as an instance of an appeal to special norms because we are not ordinarily entitled to lie to others. That there are such special norms is precisely what philosophers doubt.

Again the analogy with parenting is useful. Professionals may, like parents, aim at genuinely aiding others. However, like parents, the professions are not allowed to do just anything in the name of helping another. Parents' commitment and professed willingness to nurture their children has limits. As a parent, I am not entitled to murder another child so that my daughter will become cheerleader. Any practice, be it that of parents or professionals, must abide by the norms governing all other members of the community. On this second view, no ethic can be self-derived, including a professional ethic sometimes thought to derive from a promise to assist others.

Even if professionals promise to use their expertise to benefit their clients, a promise must be accepted by the affected parties in order to be binding. Under ordinary morality, a promise to cut someone's hair is not binding upon the promisor if the party in question does not wish to have her hair altered. It would seem to follow that no professional could be bound to promote some good unless the client has accepted the professional's promise to further that good. And it is not obvious that any promises by professions have been so accepted.

Furthermore, the content of the promise enters into our evaluation of the morality of the promise. If I have promised to keep your confidence and you tell me of a plan to overthrow the United States government, many persons would question whether this confidence should be kept. Thus, while some doctors or lawyers argue that their medical or legal ethic binds them unequivocally to aid their client by preserving secrecy about what has been confided to them, the existence of an absolute unqualified duty to keep confidence seems unlikely.

Concerns such as these have led philosophers to conclude that for professional ethics to constitute legitimate norms or standards for governing professional behavior with respect to clients and non-clients, these ethics must either be derived from, be identical with, or be an intensification of ordinary morality.[10] By claiming for themselves the privilege of deriving their own unique ethic from a pledge to serve others, professions have forfeited legitimacy. According to the second group, professionals' ethics must be re-conceived as part of our general communal ethics if they are to regain legitimacy.

Yet a third group of critics – the organizational analysts – wonder whether there even are such things as professions. They note that there is no single list of professional traits upon which everyone agrees. According to these critics, it would be better to focus less upon whether an activity is professional and more upon whether people are effective at whatever they do. These critics remind us that the process of professionalization is not one of simply acquiring traits, whatever they may be, but rather one of developing skills and strategies for improving performance.

The process of professionalization is what matters most.[11] To understand professionalization we do not need an inquiry into the legitimating norms of the professions. Instead, we should use the empirical sciences of history, sociology, psychology, and political science to give us an accurate description of what professionals are actually doing. If we can become clear about the actions being performed by individual professionals in specific societies, we will have a better sense of what these agents and their clients want. Increased effectiveness will make the professional appear more expert, and this appearance of enhanced expertise will bestow legitimacy.

THE SERIOUSNESS OF THESE CHALLENGES

These challenges to professional legitimacy and authority should disturb professionals and clients alike. Professionals unquestionably have enjoyed prestige and privileges, such as the testimonial privilege of not having to disclose client-confided matters in court (unless the client so orders). But prestige and privilege have been theirs partly because they are thought to bear more responsibility and a heavier moral charge than other agents in society. J. Cardozo's claim that "[m]embership in the bar is a privilege burdened with conditions,"[12] applies not only to members of the bar but also to other practitioners like those in medicine and the clergy. By severing privilege from professionals' "atypical moral commitment,"[13] critics have ignited, if not fueled, public suspicion of professional activity, privileges and prestige. It is indeed hard to see why clients should trust the medical and legal professions with their lives and liberty if the latter are no more than ideologically driven institutional arrangements designed to gratify doctors and lawyers' lust for status and wealth. Like the fabled emperor, the professions appear to be bereft of any legitimate trappings of power.

While the nude emperor's state was merely comic, that of the professions borders on the tragic. We should not forget that professions represent the only mechanism we have for collectively providing ourselves with the goods of health, legal justice, and spiritual peace. If professionals are not trustworthy, whom should we trust? This question must be confronted. We cannot simply hope that the sick, the accused or injured, and the spiritually needy will provide adequately for themselves. Clients grant, or at least permit, professionals access to something of value (e.g. their bodies) precisely because they are unable to secure or promote a desired state of affairs (e.g. a return to health) by themselves or are better able to do so with assistance. Given that the critics are not proposing any alternative source of help, we will be left without recourse if we cease to believe that professionals merit trust under some conditions.[14]

The question of professional legitimacy merits our attention for a second reason as well. Professions represent our communally *chosen* response to the problem of delivering help to the ill, the injured or accused, or the sick in spirit. We could have endorsed alternative solutions to this problem. For example, some states have functioned as the church, managing a caste of state priests. Citizens of Western liberal democracies, however, have collectively preferred an arrangement in which the professions are in some sense and to some degree independent of state control. Before we follow the critics' lead in collapsing the distinction between professional and ordinary morality, we should press for clarification as to whose ordinary morality we are discussing. As I shall show in Chapter 8, it is part of Anglo-American "ordinary morality" to allow professions a rather high degree of autonomy, including the freedom to justify their actions by appealing to special promises professionals have made to patients, litigants, etc. Here I would merely emphasize that if the community begins to doubt the wisdom of permitting professionals to exercise their authority, this skepticism will have ramifications for whatever other democratic values are linked to professionalism. If we care about these values, we should attend to shifts in public support of professionals and responsibly think through any and all attempts to ground professional authority.

Finally, we should not deceive ourselves as to what is at stake in critics' seemingly innocuous insistence upon a purely descriptive investigation of professionalism. These demands emanate mainly from social scientists who try to describe what behavior is in fact accepted by a group and who eschew any attempt to establish what the norms of professions should be, preferring instead to treat the mechanics of the process of professionalization. While such research has its place, we must be clear that the choice of the descriptive method is itself an ethical matter with enormous consequences for the goods we pursue, the attitudes, practices, and ideas we embrace, and the conclusions we draw. Failure to address questions about the nature of a profession and its proper relation to other human activities can only result in singularly unsatisfying discourse about professionals. Either we will wind up discussing the process of professionalization but never clearly defining the end state toward which professions are allegedly evolving;[15] or we will accept as professional anyone who lays claim to the title and never ask under what conditions a claimant acts unprofessionally. Both methodologies amount to a practical refusal to try to delineate how the professional *qua* professional acts. While it might turn out that there are no distinctive professional norms, we should avoid the fallacy of assuming as true the very thing that needs to be demonstrated.

We must also bear in mind that it is a normative matter to assert that a profession has no inner meaning but rather consists of the sum total of what all or a majority of its members happen to be doing at a certain point in time. Taken to its extreme, this position will yield mind-boggling claims of the sort that Adolph Eichmann's lawyer offered in defense of that war criminal's actions: Eichmann was innocent of the killings by gas because gassing "was indeed a medical matter, since it was prepared by physicians; it was a matter of killing, and killing, too, is a medical matter."[16] Unless one is willing to say that doctors and mass murderers belong to the same profession and are equally good and worthy of respect, our practice of holding persons responsible for their actions will eventually force us to confront the question with which I propose to begin: what do professionals do, and what, if anything, legitimates their practice?

THE PROJECT

The argument of this book attempts to justify trust in the practice of professionals by showing that this practice is in fact morally legitimate. I will argue that professional practices qualify as morally legitimate because, and to the extent that, they are structured to merit the trust of clients. Contrary to the assertions of our first set of critics, professions are not mere ideologies but inherently ethical practices. Furthermore, each of these practices has its own special ethic, one deriving its peculiar and distinctive character from its end of engendering and preserving the trust of clients who lack a specific genuine good such as health or legal justice. While each of these professional ethics is not identical with ordinary morality, we shall see that they do not violate its dictates and therefore can escape the philosophers' charge that they are immoral. Finally, we shall see that the descriptive versus normative distinction dear to the hearts of our third group of critics – the social scientists – cannot be sustained when one is discussing the practice of professions. Since the professions are in their essence structures aiming at making the professional worthy of client trust, any discussion of professions inevitably will prove to be both descriptive and normative.

This project to justify trust in professionals is properly conceived of as an attempt to ground professionals' authority. "Ground" is a technical term, sometimes identified with the notion of a "source." But clearly not all sources are grounds.[17] The fountainhead of a river is the source of the flowing water, but it is not the river's ground. A ground is a special type of source. It is a source of standards or norms which are binding on a certain class or group of agents. Thus, we might argue, as some political theorists do, that the ground or ultimate source of a law's authority over a country's citizens is the law's conformity to a constitution (written or unwritten) to which the citizens of this country have given their consent. We have grounded legal authority when we have discovered and specified whether and why the laws are binding upon some group of people. In general, a grounding must reveal not only who is bound by what but also why what is binding constrains one party (e.g. citizens of state A) but not another (e.g. citizens of state B). In the case of consent theory, the law binds only those who can be said to have consented to it; others are not subject to it. Note, too, that the grounding discloses in whose eyes the agent is so bound. Under consent theory, consent binds the consenting agent in his eyes and in the eyes of all those who recognize consent as the source of the law's legitimacy.

By analogy, grounding professional authority entails specifying the source of the standards governing professional actions undertaken or authored on behalf of the client. The grounding must show why the norms bind professionals and only professionals. For if the norms bind all agents, citizens, or rational beings, then we will not have located the ground of professional authority *per se*. We will have offered instead a general theory of authority. In addition, since authority must exist in the eyes of the clients as well as the professionals, the grounding must reveal why clients voluntarily entrust these norm-governed professionals with the power to affect their lives. Although professionals and clients will turn out to be considerably more than correlatives of one another, the dictionary definitions are right as far as they go: professionals are persons who serve clients and clients are "individuals aided by professionals."[18] Consequently, any grounding of *professional* authority must legitimate the exercise of professional power in the eyes not only of professionals but also of clients, be they actual or potential.

Since the majority of clients served are thinking persons who do not repose trust indiscriminately, this grounding of professional authority is primarily concerned with specifying the conditions under which reasonable people freely allow professionals access to matters of great concern to them. In other words, the trust to be justified is that of competently reasoning men and women. The fondly foolish seek no ground for their trust; therefore, their expectations and behavior will not figure greatly in this argument. Yet they cannot be totally ignored either. The fact that some persons become clients as a consequence of reason-impairing conditions, such as brain tumors or overwhelming, paralyzing anxiety or grief, means that professional norms must be such as to make the actions undertaken on behalf of such clients legitimate in the eyes of the reasonable community members of society who commit the mentally ill, enfeebled, or undeveloped to the care of professionals. In such cases, someone other than the client has freely and voluntarily given access to the client's life. Not only clients' trust but also the trust of these clients' proxy agents or guardians must be legitimated. Unless one proposes to prohibit professional relations with reason-impaired clients – and I know of no historian, sociologist or philosopher who has endorsed such a proposition – the professional ethic must in some way authorize the doctor or minister to act on behalf of clients who are unable to communicate their wishes.

THE METHODOLOGY

It should be clear from this admittedly sketchy overview that any grounding of professional authority will and must be both a normative and a descriptive enterprise. The grounding is normative because we shall be trying to discover which standards or norms, if any, should regulate professional conduct. It is descriptive because we cannot know whether professional authority is illegitimate until we examine the character of the professions. The structure or character of the professions cannot be investigated without using materials from history, sociology, political theory, and economics to describe what *in fact* are the practices, expectations, and ends of professionals, clients, and the community in which the professions exist. Therefore, I shall freely draw upon these materials in arguing that professions are not arbitrary creations of the community or of power-hungry agents but are practices carefully structured to serve clients legitimately.

However, several caveats are in order. First, the descriptive argument I will advance does not make professionals immune to criticism. On the contrary, the argument provides a basis for criticizing individual professionals or whole subgroups of professional practitioners (e.g. cosmetic surgeons or spiritual leaders who promise God will heal the sick for a fee). When their acts do not conform to the legitimating structure of the profession they "profess" to practice, they deserve censure. Second, while the argument will explore what we mean by trust while simultaneously revealing the ways in which professions are structured to merit it, I make no attempt to look beyond trustworthiness for reasons justifying trust. In fact, I cannot say what it would mean to ground the norms embedded in the human phenomenon of trust in some other "more objective" ethic. The argument here advanced looks to what trust is. From the nature of trust, it derives necessary conditions for the existence of trust between professionals and clients. This argument is "objective" because trust is the "object" sought and because the argument will appeal to characteristics of trust to decide when and whether clients' decisions to entrust professionals with their health, legal rights, and spiritual well-being are justified.

Someone might protest that this type of argument confuses what people do with what they ought to do. To this objection, I can do no better than insist that:

> when the "facts" we are describing are societal or institutional facts, including various kinds of relationships individuals and groups enter into among themselves, then the oughts, the shoulds, the norms – in the forms of promises or other commitments made, the obligations willingly entered into, the expectations knowingly engendered – are often an integral and even

an essential part of those arrangements which must be included in any adequate description of those social realities."[19]

That is to say, if and when professionals voluntarily pledge to practice in a fashion structured by these same professionals to elicit client trust, then these professionals may justly be thought of as being bound by norms implicit in and derivable from trust-worthiness. Perceptions of what doctors or lawyers are doing inevitably appeal, either implicitly or explicitly, to commonly recognized norms regarding what they should be doing. Indeed, we routinely expect practitioners to conform to these norms and approvingly speak of these agents as "professional" when our expectations are met.

This is not to deny that sometimes the term "professional" is applied indiscriminately to anyone who exhibits a high level of style, skill, or even cunning.[20] As the sociologist Eliot Freidson has noted, the term has become confused in modern times as skilled occupations (e.g. the trades) have tried to increase their prestige and status by calling themselves professions.[21] This confusion explains why one often hears persons with particular skill or cunning described as "real pros." But we do not base our decision to trust professionals upon cleverness or skillfulness. Since a given skill may be perfectly compatible with harmful service, our judgments of professionalism ultimately look beyond skill to some trust-engendering feature of professional practice. Of course, individual professionals may or may not live up to this ideal of judgment. Membership of a profession does not somehow exempt one from greed, lust, and the other mortal and venial sins: "Sometime when the public good is pretended, a private benefit is intended."[22] Nor have I any illusions about the far from illustrious past of medicine, law, or the ministry. History abounds with examples of professionals adopting morally objectionable rules or procedures as a matter of policy. The argument of the following chapters describes the *essence* of a legitimate profession. My claim is not that any existent person or group fully exhibits that essence, but rather that professionals will be more legitimate the more fully they do so.

To anticipate a bit the argument of succeeding chapters, when nineteenth-century doctors in Cincinnati committed themselves to a treatment (bleeding) more deadly than the ills the cure was meant to rectify, patients were right to boycott these doctors.

These patients did no more than hold the physicians accountable *as professionals*. In these clients' eyes, the doctors' practice was not worthy of trust because it failed to fulfill the medical pledge to act for the benefit of the sick. The sick were routinely and as a matter of policy being made sicker. Under such circumstances, the ill had no reason to grant strange physicians access to their bodies. Faced with a dwindling number of patients, the Cincinnati doctors responded by adopting more homeopathic techniques designed to help the body heal itself. As this change in practice became known, patients returned to these doctors. While the profession of medicine might very well have ceased to *exist* if the doctors had not altered their techniques, its essence would have remained what it is today – a practice of trying to heal the sick. Indeed, it is this essence to which the Cincinnati doctors appealed in restructuring their practice to regain their authority. Looking to an ideology of making money or a general ethic of honoring people's rights would not have steered them in the direction of adopting the homeopathic techniques.[23]

SCOPE OF INQUIRY

This inquiry will focus on the activities of the so-called "learned" or "liberal" professions of law, medicine, and the ministry. These professions traditionally have long been seen as sufficiently similar to one another and different from other activities to warrant being grouped under the rubric of the "liberal professions."[24] Since we are trying to discover what, if anything, legitimates the activity of these seemingly special agents known as "professionals," we can hardly do better than look at those activities we have historically treated as different from other human practices. This narrow focus, though, should not be interpreted to mean that there are no professions apart from the learned ones. Those familiar with practices such as accounting, consulting, engineering, teaching, and architecture will find much of what follows applicable to these practices as well. If accountants or consultants think the analytical shoe fits, then certainly nothing in this analysis prevents them from wearing it.

There is a second reason for focusing on these three liberal professions. Their members understand themselves to be professional. No such agreement exists among other groups sometimes thought by outsiders to be professional. For example, while there may be a kind of distinctive craft ethic, and while artists may contribute enormously to the development of a culture, artists tend to reject the title of professional because, unlike professionals, they do not serve clients. They often create for themselves, not for a clientele. Furthermore, while artists may eventually entice some patrons to purchase their work, it may take years before patrons appreciate their accomplishments. Unlike the physician or lawyer, the artist has to rely upon his or her works to generate their own demand.[25]

Some journalists, like authors, refuse to be called professionals, preferring to conceive of themselves as "the trade." The history of newspapers supports this latter usage. In the United States, newspapers began as organs of political propaganda and aimed at selling papers to a wide enough readership to attract lucrative advertising. So, while some journalists think of themselves as the profession which afflicts the comfortable and comforts the afflicted, others look to their history to make the case that they and their publishers write and print stories to sell papers, not to benefit the public. Therein lies a significant difference between journalism and the three liberal professions. While doctors, lawyers, and ministers sometimes question whether a fellow member has acted professionally, these three groups never wonder whether their practices are professions or something else such as a trade or craft.[26]

Indeed, their claim to being professions is so well established that other occupations wishing to assume the title consistently attempt to assimilate themselves to law or, more often, medicine. For example, business journals are filled with articles in which authors argue for the professionalism of business because it, like medicine or the law, trains its practitioners in principles of science, establishes codes of conduct, organizes groups of managers who aim at continuing to educate peers in the latest techniques of business management, etc.[27] Taking its cue from the clergy, law, and medicine, business has agitated for and obtained its own professional school in many prestigious universities. Given that other practices treat the learned professions as paradigmatic, we can probably gain the most insight into well-established and new professions by following suit.

A FINAL REMARK

While I have taken pains not to misrepresent any professional practice, one certainly could say much more than I do about select topics, such as physician-assisted suicide or the conflicts of interest confronting lawyers, particularly corporate attorneys. In my defense, I will simply say that my interest here lies not in canvassing all such issues but rather in determining when, why, and to what extent professionals in general are morally entitled to use their knowledge and skills to act on clients' behalf. If we can clearly grasp the ground of professional authority, we will be in a better position to evaluate specific responses to more topical issues. At the very least, we will see more clearly which factors should be considered in thinking through the problems and what effects various solutions are likely to have on client–professional relations. Let us now see what we can discover concerning the ground of professional authority.

Chapter 2

The untrustworthiness of professional expertise

We have not yet defined just who a professional is. And with good reason. Since the concept is intrinsically normative, who qualifies as a professional varies according to the norms one thinks the professional is bound to obey. In other words, "professional" is a dialectical term. Inquirers who wish to discuss professional behavior must explore just who a professional is at the same time as they evaluate this behavior. Attempts to decide this issue of professional status by definition alone are not satisfactory because they wind up begging the question. For example, we might begin, as one prominent sociologist does, by defining professions as economic monopolies and peremptorily dismissing the ministry's claim to be a profession on the ground that ministers do not serve markets.[1] However, given that the clergy have long thought of themselves as professionals, they cannot be excluded without first establishing that serving markets is a defining trait of professionals. Failure to make such an argument merely assumes what needs to be shown.

I propose therefore to argue dialectically, beginning with a relatively uncontroversial observation. Sociologists, historians, and philosophers alike understand that professionals act on behalf of fellow human beings or clients. Since reasonable adults do not normally trust strangers with their health, freedom, or funds, there must be something about professionals that warrants clients' trust in them. What is it? Two answers to this question dominate the literature. Professionals are thought to be trustworthy agents of clients either (1) because they are experts; or (2) because they are service providers who, for a fee, obey clients' wills. The first view is supported by many professionals who believe that their superior knowledge and skill or expertise enables them to identify and then do the morally right thing. Clients and those who champion their rights, on the other hand, mistrust the power of experts. In order for the professional–client relation to be moral, the professional, in their view, must be empowered by the client to act on the client's behalf. The empowering occurs when both parties agree to the terms and conditions of a fee-for-service contract specifying what the professional is to do for the client.

Each of these views has its merits. Although we shall see that neither ultimately provides a satisfactory justification for client trust in professionals, each position is sufficiently serious to merit our attention. Furthermore, precisely because these views have a great deal of currency, they deserve careful consideration. We can gain insight into what does constitute an adequate understanding of the professions if we establish precisely in what respects the models fail to justify client trust. This chapter will explore the ethical implications of conceiving of professionals as experts. The next chapter will examine why the service provider model, like the expert model, does not justify trust but in fact makes the professional untrustworthy. Once we grasp why the expert and service provider are not genuinely trustworthy we will be better positioned to state how professionals should behave if they are to attract and retain clients to serve – i.e. if they are to be professionals.

THE APPEAL OF THE EXPERT MODEL

Many professionals will argue that they desire to use their skills to help people. In order to assist clients, they must have the freedom to exercise their skills as they, not their clients, see fit. If clients were able to help themselves, they would do so. But the fact that clients voluntarily come to the professional reveals that clients are unable to assist themselves and that they plan to accept the expert advice of the professional.

On this view, there is nothing immoral in the expert aiding clients who cannot help themselves. The expert does not make the client inept. Client inability is simply a fact; and clients are, from the expert's perspective, wise to allow the expert to make their decisions for them. It might be better if clients could learn to help themselves, but the knowledge they would need to do so is not easily acquired. Formal training and extensive practice are necessary to master many professional techniques. To knowledgeably interpret the word of God, the minister and rabbi must devote hours to learning Biblical languages and to studying commentaries on the text. Not all interpretations are equally good. Even those religions which hold that all men are priests (e.g. the Amish and Quakers) respect a need for leaders who are versed in presenting and judging interpretations advanced by their predecessors.[2]

Similar reasoning applies to the practice of law and medicine. Litigants possess the right to self-representation.[3] However, judges urge litigants to employ counsel because, to avail themselves of the protection the law affords, they would need a familiarity with cases, statutes, and court procedures most litigants do not possess and cannot readily acquire. Self-medication, like self-representation, is possible to some extent. But surgery is notoriously difficult. Brain surgery is so tricky that fully qualified neurosurgeons operate for years under the guidance of still more skilled surgeons. And even if your average Joe were to miraculously master the surgical technique overnight, he still would not be able to operate upon himself. In some cases, self-help is simply impossible.

Experts cite a second impediment to self-help as well. They contend that clients do not know what help involves. Yes, innocent persons unjustly accused of crimes know they want justice; patients suffering from back pain want it alleviated. However, in the professions, unlike the trades, "helping the client" is not identical with "securing the outcome the client is seeking." A tradesman performs a job, a task relatively well defined in advance of any discussion with the person contracting for the job performance. The tradesman has a list of standard questions and prices for different jobs. We speak of some tradesmen as "jobbers" because consistently producing a desired outcome is the aim of a trade. Professionals are not jobbers because the tasks they perform are defined in and through conversation with the client. In Chief Justice Warren Burger's words, legal services are not like a packaged consumer product because they "can rarely, if ever, be 'standardized' because potential clients rarely know in advance what services they do in fact need."[4] Service is always tailored to the client's particular situation, which is not known until the professional has skillfully interviewed the client. The interview may very well elicit information the client does not think is important but which proves, upon reflection and further inquiry, to be quite important. This inherent indeterminacy in the practice of helping means the client cannot know prior to speaking to the professional exactly what help is needed or desirable.

Nor can the client, the expert argues, adequately assess the service once it is rendered.[5] Plenty of clients are unhappy with good results or satisfied with bad ones. The client sometimes does not recognize, or will not admit, that her problem is not soluble, even with professional assistance. The satisfaction of the client with an outcome is not, therefore, the chief measure of whether the professional has acted in a trustworthy fashion. It is all very well for the patient losing her eyesight to wish for an operation to restore it. But she may have to settle for a surgical procedure that only retards the loss of sight. Given the current state of technology, a "good" outcome may be total blindness delayed for five years.

One can extend this argument and contend, as the sociologist Wilbert Moore does, that the client can neither judge whether a thing has been done rightly nor whether the right thing was done:

> The client is in no position to judge competence, except, possibly, at the extremes; what appears to be extreme competence may appear to colleagues as mere showmanship, and what appears as extreme incompetence may appear to colleagues as reasonable conduct in a situation fraught with difficulties and possibly bad luck. Even on ethical matters, it should surprise no one that complexity is more nearly the rule than the exception, and thus that judgment rather than merely routine compliance with unambiguous rules governs even the most scrupulous practitioner.[6]

THE WEAK LINK BETWEEN EXPERTISE AND TRUSTWORTHINESS

While it is certainly true that professionals must have something to offer if clients are to be enticed to seek their help; and while professionals' hard-to-acquire skills hold out a promise for real help clients cannot easily render themselves, expertise *per se* clearly does not merit our trust. The doctor can use his pharmaceutical knowledge to poison as well as to heal. No doubt it was his awareness of this moral neutrality of skill which led Justice Louis Brandeis to make the professional's motivations a defining characteristic of the professional. In a passage "quoted so frequently that it has taken on the dimensions of a classic,"[7] Brandeis characterizes a profession as:

> an occupation for which the necessary preliminary training is intellectual in character, involving knowledge and to some extent learning, as distinguished from mere skill; which is pursued largely for others, and not merely for one's own self; and in which the financial return is not the accepted measure of success.[8]

Notice that Brandeis insists upon a close connection between professionalism and a commitment to serve others' good. Brandeis' insistence is appropriate because the existence of such a commitment is central to trust. If we provisionally take trust to be an expectation by the trusting party A that A will be the beneficiary of the trusted party B's good will, then B's acts must not raise doubts regarding his or her good will toward A. If this concept of trust is applied to professional–client relations, it follows that professionals should avoid creating situations in which the question arises as to whether they are serving primarily the client or the economic self-interest of their members. Evidencing good will toward the client becomes difficult when the profession is pursuing an aim intrinsically incompatible with promoting client welfare. When these so-called conflicts of interest are present, trusting the professional is inherently problematic, irrespective of whether the party is an expert with preliminary intellectual training.[9]

There seems then to be a crucial link between professional motivation and client trust. But what precisely is the character of this link? Again the Brandeis definition is notable, this time for its failure to clarify precisely why the client should trust professionals and heed their advice. One might argue, as Brandeis seems inclined to do, that professionals need only profess some allegiance to a non-specific good in order to merit our trust. But a mere expression of altruism is not morally legitimating. Many people profess a desire to help me but I certainly do not trust those who proposition me on the street simply because they are interested in "helping" me. Mother's oft-repeated warning to beware of strangers does not suddenly cease to be good advice the moment one is in need of professional help. If then an altruistic commitment does not elicit or justify client trust, perhaps expertise coupled with altruism will. This hypothesis, though, is not sound either, because expertise by its very nature undermines client trust in at least five ways.

The first problem: the inherently untrustworthy character of expertise

It is important to be clear about the character of professional knowledge. The professions always have had a theoretical or scientific basis. They are not crafts which have developed and passed on habitual ways of doing things according to rules of thumb. Hippocratic medical texts, for example, reveal practitioners seeking causes of diseases and exploring why certain treatments work better than others. For their part, clerics such as St Thomas Aquinas have specified carefully how and in what sense knowledge of the divine and its relation to mankind's welfare is possible. Ethicists and sociologists are correct therefore to insist upon the theoretical and learned character of the professions.[10]

Nevertheless, the theoretical or scientific knowledge necessary to be a professional should not be confused with the relatively new phenomenon of expertise. Historically professionals have become such by professing. Professing has been understood as a public avowal to perfect one's life. Perfecting one's life, in turn, has been thought to require *scientia*. *Scientia* is "a passion or perfection resulting from the union of something intelligible and an intellectual power."[11] Such a union is possible when things are known through their proper causes. Like their predecessor Aristotle, medieval professors believed that every thing has its own integrity or being. Knowledge is possible only when the thing's own character guides the inquiry and determines the form it takes. The possibility of such guidance is what enables "the union of something intelligible and an intellectual power" to occur.

Thus, the science of theology derives its guiding principles from the nature of God, who cares for man. Since God must be known at least in part through revelation, it is sheer hubris from the disciplinary perspective to think that man can know God through unaided reason. Minister and laity alike are perfected and saved through the revealing word of God. Medicine, too, is a science. The professing doctor takes her principles from the thing she studies – the production and maintenance of health in the human body. Since the living organic body regulates itself, it is absurd, scientifically speaking, to think that medicine or the doctor is the cause of health. Health is itself the cause of health. The physician only helps the body to assist itself: "Medical science does not control health, but studies how to procure it; hence it issues orders in the interests of health but not to health."[12]

Students learn *scientia* from their professors. In those teaching, *scientia* "is properly called ... doctrine," while in the person learning it is known as discipline.[13] In both cases, the good, end or cause of practical *scientia* is knowledge of its object. Since the object the professional studies as part of perfecting his own life is the health of the patient or justice for the litigant, the client's good is the professional's object. This good is present "in" the knowledge. Furthermore, this good, like all objects of *scientia*, has the peculiar power and function of regulating the acquisition and application of the knowledge.

Not so with expertise. Louis Brandeis is more correct than he knows when he treats professional expertise as knowledge *which the practitioner puts in the service of an end*.[14] Unlike practical *scientia*, expert technique is not inherently purposive. Those who term today's professional knowledge "formal" speak volumes.[15] The acquisition of expertise is curiously lacking in purpose because expertise itself lacks an end or object until the knower supplies one. Expertise must always be put to use to do something. In the world of expertise, the knower chooses an end to his own liking. He then "learns," or equivalently, "becomes expert" by acquiring the ability to consistently produce a preferred outcome. The highest grade of marksman is thus rightly termed "expert," since the skill of marksman and expert alike consists in successfully and repeatedly executing a task the agent sets for himself or herself.

Almost as an afterthought experts add that their practice is altruistic. The expert must don the mantle of altruism in order to reassure the client. The client needs such assurance because expertise, unlike *scientia*, is not regulated by an order intrinsic to itself which contains the client's good within it. That which clients care about – health, justice, or salvation – rather than the private agenda of the expert, regulates the disciplines of medicine, law, and the ministry. Expert technique, by contrast, tends not to put welfare first because technique necessarily assumes a thing with no proper causes. Mastering or becoming better at a technique means exercising more control over what is being investigated and attempted. More control means, in turn, being more successful at making the thing (or client) serve the ends the expert establishes. By definition, then, the expert *qua* expert will always be pursuing a private agenda, and no amount of vague ramblings about a desire to help changes this fact. Clients may hope this agenda will secure their good. But expertise, unlike *scientia*, gives clients no reason to place much confidence in this hope. In terms of our provisional definition of trust, the reasonable client will not *expect* to benefit from the expert's good will and consequently cannot be said to trust the expert.

The second problem: the disappearing client

The consequences for clients of such expertise become readily apparent if we contrast the behavior of experts with that of agents who retain the original sense of themselves as beings who have publicly pledged, professed, or, in William May's phrase "covenanted,"[16] to promote the well-being of the bodily or spiritually ailing, the accused, or injured. These "professors" arguably have profession-specific responsibilities not incumbent upon private citizens.[17] For example, if I am a professing lawyer publicly committed to helping litigants obtain the legal justice they are seeking, then I have a responsibility to keep my promise and to counsel the accused man should he come to me for help. Indeed, it might even be argued that I have a responsibility to seek him out should I have reason to suspect he has not received the protection of the law. Certainly in the past we have seen lawyers take up the cause of prisoners whom they suspect of having been framed or having in some other manner suffered a miscarriage of justice. In any case, the particular end I have professed or avowed imposes a service obligation upon me: when an individual falls into the category of clients whose good I have promised to study and promote, I am bound to act on her behalf.[18]

But if the professional is only an expert he stands in no particular moral relation to the client. The expert is no different from a private citizen. As a private citizen, I have no obligation to rearrange my day to provide legal representation for a man accused of a crime. Even if I happen to know a great deal of law and am an expert on the inner workings of the United States court system (perhaps I have written several books on defending the indigent), I still would not have any obligation to represent this man.[19] Knowledge of how to do an activity does not create an obligation to perform that activity.

As we have seen, the expert as such need not even consider what the client's good is. Experts aim at perfecting their technique. Their technique is their object, the thing over which they are trying to exercise ever greater control. This object or end explains why the only professional duty all experts consistently recognize is the obligation to stay abreast of technical developments in their field.[20] The expert must do so if he is to retain the power of technical manipulation. Yet staying abreast of technical developments inevitably proves difficult, if not impossible, because the direction this takes depends only upon the *private* desires of the technician. New fields and techniques (liposuction; "shame-based" psychotherapy) can be and are invented at will. Remaining knowledgeable about these developments takes time, time which could be spent with the client. The client suffers a kind of benign neglect.

Nor is the expert under any obligation to rectify this neglect. Unlike the covenanting professional, the expert is not bound to take on clients. The client is no longer at the moral center of the professional–client relation. This displacement of the client is quite clear in the legal profession. As law professor David Mellinkoff has forcefully argued, by refusing to define the legal profession as part of the administration of justice, the American Bar has severed the vital link between lawyers and the interests of the client.[21] The lawyer is now little more than an expert counselor, negotiator, or drafter of documents. Yet these skills do not make him the helper of the accused or injured. A lawyer counsels people, but so do a minister and a banker. A lawyer negotiates agreements on an individual's behalf, but so do a real estate broker and a student ombudsman. A lawyer drafts documents affecting one's legal rights, but so do politicians, insurance agents, and legal secretaries. Only the function of representing in court individuals seeking legal justice belongs uniquely to lawyers. When lawyers refuse to acknowledge this function as their responsibility, clients necessarily suffer. Since no other group has the privilege of so representing persons, the accused have no alternative but to turn to a lawyer for help. But when they approach attorneys who define themselves by the "expert" techniques they possess rather than by an end they have publicly professed to serve, the accused find themselves denied help on the ground that the lawyer's technique is not well suited to the client's need.

If the expert does happen to choose to help a client, the client has little recourse if the professional harms him. The expert may be disciplined by fellow experts appointed to act as representatives of the profession. However, experts are loath to take time away from research to perform what amounts to a public service. Furthermore, the self-absorption of the expert tends to work against the client in those rare cases when disciplining does occur. Bizarre as it may seem, when the American Bar decides to investigate a lawyer for violating client trust, it does not bother to inform the client who complained of harm of where the proceedings stand or what the outcome is.[22]

Once again clients *may* receive service when they seek expert help. The defense of authority offered by the professionals, however, gives them no good reason to *expect* either attention or assistance. The client is an almost invisible person barely discerned by the expert,[23] unless of course the client's condition constitutes a test case against which doctors or lawyers can experiment with their techniques or in some other way advance technical knowledge.

The third problem: the disorganization of practice

When the attempt is made to ground authority in expertise, clients confront a third problem. The professionals who supposedly are serving them may wind up working at cross-purposes and even harming these same clients. This lack of co-ordination arises when a publicly stated, shared end or object to which all members of a given profession are committed vanishes. And disappear it must when professionals become experts, agents who are free to pursue private agendas.

Again it is useful to contrast the disciplined, covenanting professional with the expert. As long as all doctors aim at restoring and maintaining the health of their patients, physicians can specialize without harming the client. The cardiologist heals heart disease, while the ophthalmologist preserves and restores eyesight. The practice of all doctors is clearly organized around *parts of the patient's body to be healed*. In other words, the practice is disciplined in the original sense of the word. The thing studied – the human client – is the source and cause of knowledge and its divisions. Since the doctor studies the preservation and maintenance of health in the patient, he takes as his proper object things that exhibit health (organs in the case of specialists; the whole person in the case of general practitioners). This focus explains why medicine has no division of, say, cautery, even though many physicians cauterize tissue in order to restore health. The doctor does not heal cautery, so this process does not organize his practice.[24]

When the general practitioner refers her patient to the cardiologist, she can be confident that she and the specialist have the same object. The client, too, can trust that both doctors are working together in his interest. After all, strictly speaking, he is the object of their study. The character of the healthy person has informed their training and learning. When technical power and expertise, though, take the place of *scientia*, the organization of medicine disintegrates. It is no accident that in the twentieth century we find specialties studying disease entities such as cancer and viruses as well as the health of various parts of the body. Since cancer and viruses do not exhibit health, it is worth asking what exactly this new type of physician studies. Does the virologist protect the health of the human immune system by discovering how to destroy "bad" viruses or how to build "good" ones? And what would it mean to design a "good" one?

These questions are far from academic. They inevitably arise when the end of the practice is stated as a technical objective rather than as the client's good. A physician could, for example, aim at "controlling the spread of the AIDS virus" by making it more virulent than it now is. A deadlier virus would kill its carriers faster, thereby making it less likely that they would infect others. The physician would participate in the killing of some patients in order to save other people's lives. Executing such a plan (rumored to have been discussed at a 1988 medical conference in Denver) would constitute a technical advance. The physician would be able to control or manipulate a disease entity in a new way. It is unlikely, though, that AIDS patients would knowingly, voluntarily go to a physician for help under such circumstances even though the expert physician would undoubtedly argue that he was working to cure AIDS. (Note how even the language reflects the bias toward manipulation and away from the patient's good: the expert cures the disease, not the patient.)

Furthermore, the general practitioner now confronts a problem when she considers referring her patients. The generalist and specialist may not share a common object. The generalist aims at healing a patient; the expert specialist may very well study not health in the patient but rather properties of a disease entity, which may or may not inhabit a human body. Lacking an objective basis for assessing her colleagues' intentions, the generalist cannot make a "good" referral. Under such circumstances, the client clearly has no reason to trust the doctor's recommendations nor the profession as a whole. The generalist might be on his side; but the recommended specialist need not be.

Lest this example seem far-fetched, I cite a second piece of evidence for my contention that the professional practice loses its internal coherence and consequently its trustworthy character when it becomes an expertise. The medical profession is obviously uncomfortable with physicians practicing cosmetic surgery. Physicians generally insist upon distinguishing cosmetic from reconstructive surgery. They do so for good reason. As Plato shrewdly observed, the cosmetic art aims at producing the appearance of beauty and health while the medical art (understood as including "gymnastic" or preventive medicine) aims at the reality.[25] As a result, the cosmetician's art always threatens to undermine the doctor's practice.[26] The art persuades patients that they need not live an active life and consume a nutritious diet in order to be healthy but can instead rely upon a short cut. In effect the cosmetic surgeon says to the patient: "Are you too fat? Don't alter your eating habits. Just come in for liposuction and have the fat removed."

If cosmetic surgery is part of the practice of medicine (and medical doctors are the ones who are increasingly establishing such practices), then medicine is in conflict with itself. It aims both at making people healthy and at providing them with an illusion of health. The illusion is of a particularly pernicious sort because it results in people avoiding the practices which both make and keep them genuinely healthy. Medicine's insistence upon the difference between reconstructive and cosmetic surgery is a belated attempt to separate a practice which aims at a genuine good (e.g. rebuilding people's noses so they can breathe better and function more normally) from one which produces an illusory benefit potentially harmful to patients in the long run. However, as long as "organized" medicine tolerates expert, specialized practices at odds with its professed end, the profession itself will suffer credibility problems and remain curiously "disorganized."

The law profession appears equally in danger of losing its internal coherence as an increasing number of its members define themselves as experts. Here one sees such a proliferation of specialties (real estate law; marriage law) that the law profession can no longer give a coherent account of what constitutes legal practice. Instead, it settles for proclaiming it "neither necessary nor desirable" to define the practice of law or the role of the lawyer.[27] Law has become little more than a collection of specialties practiced by expert lawyers who, like expert doctors, are primarily dedicated to their field. I suggested in the prior section that this loyalty has displaced the client from the moral center of professional practice. Now I would add that this displacement has not only been caused by the rise of expert specialties but that such specialization has increasingly taken on a life of its own, driving an ever deeper wedge between the practice of law and the interests of the client and shifting authority away from the disorganized legal specialties to other institutions. Changes in the profession's own disciplinary rules document this dynamic.

In the past, as long as a lawyer did not have a conflict of interest, she was obliged to represent the client irrespective of whether or not the client's case fell within her specialty. In fact, the *Code of Professional Responsibility* did not allow a lawyer "to hold himself out as a specialist or as having special training or ability."[28] If a lawyer found he needed the assistance of someone who was particularly knowledgeable about the client's legal problem, he was obliged to associate himself with a lawyer competent in the matter at hand.[29] The individual lawyer had a positive duty to the client to be adequately prepared under the circumstances and not to neglect a legal matter.[30] Under the new *Model Rules*, the client's need for help triggers no obligation. Model Rule 1.1 states only that a "lawyer shall provide competent representation to a client."[31] The rule neither requires the lawyer to refer the client to someone who is competent to take the case nor binds the lawyer to whom the referral is made to take the case.

At least under the old rules the clients were served, albeit through a deceit. Despite the pretense to generality, lawyers have been specialized at least since the 1960s.[32] In the past, they simply hid this fact from the public. In large law firms, the lawyer would be " 'too busy' to take a case which [was] actually remote from his surreptitious specialty and [would] suggest an 'appropriate' attorney or firm."[33] Still, the client got an acceptable recommendation and obtained the help needed. Under the new rules, the professional's primary obligation is to himself. He is to be competent in his field. Whether clients are actually aided has become of secondary importance.

Note, too, that the new rules make the client responsible for finding competent counsel. This task is exceedingly arduous, given that expertise destroys disciplines, leaving experts free to organize however they want. Whole firms now may be specialized. Or the firm may contain a variety of different specialists. Or members of a partnership may all be generalists. The well-educated client with contacts among lawyers may negotiate the maze of specialties successfully. But what happens to the ill-educated defendant with no connections? We already know the answer – the court winds up appointing counsel for the defendant.[34] The client is served not because of the profession but rather in spite of it. In other words, expertise does not ground professionals' authority but rather shifts it from the profession to another institution (the court) as clients are forced to look from the profession to a third party for assistance.

The fourth problem: the destruction of distinctive professional roles

While clients do not and possibly cannot know everything professionals intend to do on their behalf, they certainly can and do form expectations concerning the character of the aid they will receive if they seek help from a doctor or a minister. Forming these expectations is part of deciding whom to trust. When we trust someone, as opposed to merely relying upon them, we act on a belief that the entrusted party will show us good will. The party may not live up to this expectation but "[trust] ... is accepted vulnerability to another's possible but not expected ill will (or lack of good will) toward one."[35] Expertise erodes trust by undermining the distinctive professional roles around which client expectations of help coalesce.

Consider today's ministry. Seminarians now receive "professional" training in counseling individuals. But advising people about their problems is not a skill unique to the clergy. Lawyers, marriage counselors, arbitrators, and financial planners are all adept at counseling individuals. In fact, the behavior of today's seminarians confirms the generic character of their skills. Many ordained ministers "move laterally into counselling firms" or "in several other professional directions."[36] A characteristic ministerial role ceases to exist in a world in which all ministers do is peddle generic counseling skills divorced from any particular end. The would-be client is left wondering whether she should take her marital difficulties to her minister, a psychoanalyst, fellow members of her support group, or a social worker. In a world of expertise, clients are left to sort through a host of competing claims they are ill-equipped to evaluate.

The theologian Martin Marty attributes professionals' desire to specialize to the fact that they must find a place among competitors such as "*Psychology Today* and Channel 38, . . . the encounter group and the classroom."[37] This claim is at best a half-truth. Ministers are in competition with these others in the first place only because and to the extent that they have made their authority depend on specialized expertise instead of deriving it from an end they alone profess to pursue (i.e. helping man stand in the proper relation to God). True, the professional must be responsive to clients, but only to a limited extent. It is misleading to claim as Mark May does that the minister "never knows where he will land or live or what *specific work* [emphasis mine] he will be called upon to perform."[38] While it is true that professionals do not control what clients will demand, ministers can and should know what they, as ministers, will and will not do. If they are unwilling to draw limits around their function, then it is hard to see how they will preserve any integrity or authority. Eventually May's minister will be able to stop worrying about what tasks people will bring him. Individuals bring "specific work" only to agents with "specific" functions. *Ex hypothesi* the professional will have no such function because he will have ceased to occupy a distinctive role. He also will have experienced a loss of authority since he will not be called upon by clients to originate or author actions on their behalf.

The fifth problem: destruction of an organic clientele

As I noted earlier, it is tempting to try to counter the delegit-imating effects of expertise by grafting an altruistic motivation onto the practice of experts. But even if we take the best case and posit experts who always skillfully put their knowledge to use benefiting clients, expertise still will not ground professional authority. This approach reduces the client to a party the pro-fessional chooses to help. It ignores other important features of the client, such as the client's membership of a family and of groups such as congregations. In particular, it fails to recognize that trust is held in common by what we call a "clientele," a word reflecting the organic character of those served by the professional.

Medicine has acknowledged this wholeness to a degree by creating the specialty of family practice. Since members of a family often infect one another or share genetically based dis-eases, family physicians treat the whole family as their client. It is the ministry, though, which has gone the furthest in recognizing the organic dimension. Pastors ministering to their congregations serve a group of which they are a part. Church members "though many, are one body in Christ, and individually members one of another."[39] Ministers cannot, therefore, teach, lead, and care for their congregation if they become experts in counseling indi-viduals. The minister might be successful at helping individuals overcome their difficulties, but this privatization of the help itself constitutes a problem. By putting their skills in the service of a single client, these ministers (whose Latin name literally means "servant"[40]) cease to be servants of the church, the body of Christ, the organic whole to which all members equally belong. Those counseled are not members of a body but rather beings whom the minister has happened to encounter in the church.

One can see this tension between professional authority and technical power put in the service of atomistic individuals quite clearly in the theologian Karen Lebacqz's analysis of ministerial ethics. A minister counseling a young pregnant girl about whether or not to have and keep the child will have, according to Lebacqz, sound theological reasons for involving the girl's parents in the decision:

> The commandment "Honor thy father and thy mother" reflects the structural importance of family ties and lineages. The

notion of the covenant, the image of the "body of Christ" –
many theological themes could be found that would suggest
that ... [the] surrounding community, and particularly ... [the
girl's] family, should be part of the decision.[41]

Having said all of this, however, Lebacqz opts for the position
that the minister is basically a counselor of individuals.[42] So conceived the minister does not differ from a psychiatrist or social
worker. She will neither have nor recognize any role-specific
responsibility to the girl as a member of the congregation.
Instead, according to Lebacqz, she owes her primary loyalty to
the girl. But this position does not withstand scrutiny. For how
did the girl come to be within the minister's care in the first
place? Through her membership of the congregation. If ministers
are "to be permitted special obligations that allow [their] loyalties
to be specific to some individuals,"[43] the question arises as to who
authorizes the minister to assume these special obligations. The
church has not done so. The minister must have unilaterally
appointed herself the church therapist. If the minister were not
already in a complex web of relations with other congregants,
this self-appointment might be acceptable. But, under the circumstances, it must appear both arbitrary and aggrandizing.

Given that the minister's loyalty is so highly subjective and
apparently arbitrary, the girl has little reason to place any confidence in this minister. The minister's loyalty may shift again when
tomorrow dawns. For their part, the parents have good reason to
distrust this minister. After all, the minister has not seen fit
to include them in the discussion of their daughter's problem. Yet
it is they who have granted the minister access to the daughter by
bringing her into this church and who will unquestionably share
in some form or fashion in the consequences of any decision
made. How will the pastor effectively serve the parents if they
need help in coping with these consequences? By casting herself
as the exclusive agent of the girl, the minister loses standing with
the parents and can no longer make any specific claim to help
them. In the long run, she may forfeit her chosen client's respect
as well if the girl comes to think the minister has encouraged her
to deceive her parents. Finally, the entire congregation may suspect the minister's authority because, when advising one member
of the congregation, she failed to honor other members' claims
to participate in decisions affecting them.

The ministry's analogy between the human and church body proves apt: like the human head, the church head (the minister) and church body (congregation) share a life, and the head cannot sever itself from the body without destroying the life of both. Ministers' decisions to serve just one member of their congregation violate their role as servant of the church and, in effect, abolish the vital bond of trust between minister and congregation. The authority of the minister is diminished, if not lost entirely, as a result of using counseling expertise.

I would not want to be understood as arguing for professional violation of confidence.[44] Rather, I am arguing that confidence in professional relations has a semi-public character to the extent that the professional serves a body of persons, a clientele. Discussions of what constitutes appropriate professional behavior, therefore, must consider whether a practice such as keeping client confidence is limited by the client's membership of the larger clientele. Construing professionals as experts cannot possibly legitimate authority because this model prevents this question from arising within discussions of client confidentiality. The model makes authority rest upon the technical use of power which the expert puts in the service of ends he or she selects. This approach must fail to ground trust because it ignores important traits of clients (e.g. their membership of families, other groups, and the community at large), traits which matter to the client and will enter into the client's decision regarding whom to trust.

FIRST DEFENSE OF AUTHORITY UNSUCCESSFUL

Expertise does not bestow authority: it destroys it by letting experts establish their own private agendas; by displacing the client from the moral center of the professional–client relation; by disorganizing professional practice; by destroying distinctive professional roles; and by ignoring the organic dimension of professionals' clientele. Of course, I am not claiming that professionals do not need skills in order to benefit the client. Rather the analysis suggests that, if professionals are to preserve client trust, their skillful practice must consider who the client is and must derive its principles from features of the client's good which professionals study and dedicate their lives to promoting. This possibility will be pursued in Chapter 4. But first we must see whether the contractual model favored by clients and many ethicists does a better job of providing clients with a reason to trust professionals.

Chapter 3

Delegitimating client contracts

As was noted in Chapter 1, philosophers and clients are often uneasy with the image of professionals as independent altruistic experts who use their discretion to provide the service they judge best for the client. The prior chapter's analysis suggests they are right to be concerned about this image. But does these critics' concept of professionals as service providers bound by a formal contract negotiated with clients do a better job of making professionals trustworthy?[1]

THE APPEAL OF THE CONTRACTUAL SERVICE PROVIDER MODEL

Those who support formal contracts correctly judge that professional expertise in and of itself provides no ground for trusting professionals. Expertise is, strictly speaking, ateleological.[2] It has no end until the private desires of the expert supply it with one. But when one trusts, one grants another access to that which one values on the basis of a belief that the entrusted party shares one's values or interests and can be relied upon to act upon these shared values.[3] Since nothing in the *private* (and often unexpressed) desires of the expert gives the client reason to think the two of them share values, the client quite sensibly refuses to trust the expert. The expert lacks legitimacy in such circumstances. By positing a contract in which the client's purposes control what the expert does, the contract theorist makes the two parties' purposes congruent. Such congruence seems necessary if the expert's actions on behalf of the client are to be accepted as trustworthy.[4]

Given that this congruence could equally be achieved by

making the client's purposes conform to the expert's, why should the client's purpose be the controlling one? To this the contractualist has several responses. First, the client's stake in the interaction is far greater than that of the experts. While a doctor or attorney may lose a bit of honor or some money if he fails to help the client, the client stands to lose life or liberty as a consequence of this failure. Using contracts to protect oneself in such high risk interactions is the standard way of coping with this risk. For example, as buyers, we routinely use contracts to bind the seller to the type of performance we desire when making a major purchase like a car or house. It seems reasonable therefore for clients to similarly rely upon contracts to further their ends when placing their lives in the hands of professionals.

Second, given that clients pay professionals, surely the clients are right to expect that the latter's expertise will be put to use in promoting their welfare rather than the expert's own end. A contract specifying which client's wants or needs the professional will serve in return for a certain fee seems an appropriate mechanism for regulating the delivery of service and ensuring that the client obtains help of the sort desired.

Third, while clients are not entitled to have every one of their desires honored, it does seem as though the professional must be sensitive to what a reasonable client would want if the interaction is to be perceived as fair. The contract theorist asks us to engage in a thought experiment in an effort to discover what makes an arrangement fair.[5] Assume for a moment that you know nothing about your condition except that you are an agent who is able to plan and execute a course of action for yourself. You do not know your age, wealth, status, sex, race, family connections and thus are free of any bias toward social arrangements promoting your particular combination of traits (e.g. white Anglo-Saxon female, etc.) In what kind of system would you desire to live? The contractualist claims that you would choose for yourself a system in which you had a guaranteed freedom or right to fulfill your desires in accordance with your own value orderings to the extent that such fulfillment is consistent with others exercising the same freedom.[6] You would, according to this argument, prefer a medical system in which you were given the kind of information about your condition that a reasonable person would want over a system in which you were not told your diagnosis or prognosis. Furthermore, since you do not know exactly what your position now is or may be in the future, you would also choose a system in which agents could fulfill their desires only to the extent that their acts do not unduly interfere with other agents' ability to act upon their ordered desires. To continue the analogy: you would prefer a medical system in which you get relevant information without violating others' right to privacy over an arrangement in which others' right to privacy was violated in order to provide you with information about your condition.

Given, then, that every thinking agent would always choose such a system in preference to alternative arrangements, this system and the norms and procedures which support it are the morally right ones. And, if so, it follows that professionals' actions are right if and only if the professional allows the client freedom to realize his or her ordered desires consistent with others being able to fulfill their desires. From this insight, it is but a small step to conclude that professionals and clients should negotiate a formal contract in which it is clearly spelled out in advance precisely what will be done as part of helping the client. Explicit agreement is critical because the only way one can know for sure that the client's freedom is not being infringed is for the client to knowingly consent to the proposed procedures.

The contractual service model as it has developed in professional ethics is supported then by a combination of at least three arguments. The professional should do what the client dictates in a formal contract because: (1) the client needs to control the professional's action in order to minimize risk; (2) the client is paying for the professional's service; and (3) the client's freedom and rationality must be respected if the two parties' relation is to be moral in the eyes of thinking agents. Although I do not think these arguments justify use of a formal contract in the professional–client setting for reasons I will give shortly, I do want to insist that they cannot simply be dismissed as an attempt to introduce a kind of crass consumerism into professional–client relations. Like the model of professionals as experts, this model derives some support from the practice of the professions themselves. Just as the experts defended their position by pointing to the fact that clients often cannot help themselves and do not know in what help consists, so the contractualist and client can cite the history of the professions to support their efforts to empower clients.

For example, it is a fact that all three of the learned professions acknowledge that clients' ends are in some sense and to some degree determinative of what counts as professional service. Medicine's Hippocratic Oath explicitly forbids the doctor to have sex with the patient.[7] Physicians are not permitted to proceed as though their desire for sexual gratification, rather than the patient's desire for health, lies at the moral center of the interaction. In fact, the client's desire for health is so controlling under the oath that early Hippocratic physicians gave clients ample opportunity to compare doctors' service. These physicians accepted and apparently even expected dismissal if the patient judged another physician better able to heal.[8]

In law, it is well established that "[b]oth lawyer and client have authority and responsibility in the objectives and means of representation."[9] The American Bar Association (ABA) *Model Rules* go on to say that within limits imposed by law and by the legal profession's own responsibilities, "[t]he client has ultimate authority to determine the purposes to be served by legal representation. . . . Within those limits, a client also has a right to consult with the lawyer about the means to be used in pursuing those objectives."[10] Clients do not control what legal justice is. Under the rules, however, they do determine the general strategy of a case by deciding whether to press charges, how to plead, etc.

In a similar fashion, the laity has the final say in whether they will be saved in accordance with a particular church's understanding of and rites of salvation. Except for those periods during which the Catholic church functioned as a state and used its powers to force people to comply with policies of its own devising, the clergy have treated the embracing of religion as a free act. The minister of each church explains the role that his sect's rites, sacraments, and precepts play in the soul's salvation, but the decision to participate in a rite or to follow a particular precept rests with the individual.[11] The minister, like Christ, stands at the door and knocks;[12] he does not force the lock to gain admission.

The professions themselves clearly are committed to giving scope for the voice of the client to be heard and to be at least somewhat controlling. However, it does not follow that professionals have no legitimate moral authority unless they conform to the wishes of the client expressed in a formal contract. As with the expertise model, the contractualist model loses much of its compelling quality the moment one thinks about it in relation to human trust.

THE TENUOUS CONNECTION BETWEEN A CONTRACT AND CLIENT TRUST

On the one hand, the contractualist is surely right to insist that professionals cannot be hostile to clients' interests and still maintain moral authority. Lacking any means of compelling people to become clients, professions would not have survived for centuries if they had not been perceived as responsive to client wishes. The sociologist Eliot Freidson is correct therefore to dismiss as naive the view that professionals have some great power to impose their wishes willy-nilly on clients.[13] On the other hand, to the extent that contractualists focus on extant, *ongoing* professional–client relations, they tend to forget that professionals first must be perceived as trustworthy if clients are to initiate relations with them. And when one shifts one's focus to the trustworthiness of professionals, the contractualist's attempt to build a theory of professional authority on a contractual foundation begins to collapse.

First, if the professional is indeed bound to do whatever the client wants as long as the client's desires do not interfere with others' desire satisfaction, then the professional is little more than a hired hand. The professional does whatever the client happens to desire at some point in time. Yet thinking agents do have second thoughts. Consider the case of Dr Kervorkian, the American physician who has been helping people kill themselves with his suicide machine. One reason the American public has been so concerned about Dr Kervorkian's trustworthiness is that Kervorkian does not seem to have any awareness that people change their minds. It now looks, for example, as though he went ahead and killed a patient who initially contracted to die but then later pleaded to be taken off Kervorkian's so-called "suicide machine."[14] Moreover, we know that people sometimes need assistance in sorting out what their real fears and desires are. While Janet Adkins, Kervorkian's first "patient," claimed that she wanted to die because Alzheimer's disease was leaving her disabled, her plea seems a bit odd in light of the fact that the day before her death she had beaten her teenage son at a vigorous game of tennis. One might wonder, as some psychiatrists did, whether Ms Adkins was pleading for some attention, not for death. The trustworthy agent would join with the client in exploring what the client really wants. If the professional simply abides by the terms of a contract in which the client states what he or she appears to want, then the doctor or lawyer is likely to be accused by the client of betrayal when this apparent good turns out not to be a good at all.

In other words, for the professional to be perceived as trust-worthy over the long haul, the professional must address the client's true needs, not just his or her apparent desires. The contract is static, fixing the client's agenda. Yet what the client really wants must be determined dynamically. For example, the client may insist upon a cancer treatment which is, in the short run, far more disabling than other available treatments. Since the client's desire does not violate anybody else's rights, the professional, according to the contractualist, must provide this treatment. But what is the professional to do if, as often happens, the client's own words and behavior send out a mixed signal? This same client may have confided at an earlier time that her greatest fear was of a loss of independence. From the perspective of trust, the professional needs the freedom to explore just what the client really wants. Yet the contract service provider has no ground to stand on in demanding this freedom. For as long as the client's actions do not impede anyone else's satisfaction, then even whims must be honored.

These few comments alone suggest that the contractualist has not devoted adequate attention to the nuanced conditions under which trust, a necessary part of a voluntary relation among strangers, develops and is sustained. At a minimum, treating professionals simply as hired hands does not engender an environ-ment in which trust can thrive. What I will show next is that the contract model is actively hostile to trust in numerous important ways.

The first problem: professional discretion is both desirable and unavoidable

The contract theorist advocates use of a contract because it ren-ders client expectations explicit. However, the contract theorist fails to establish that explicitness is a condition for trust. We routinely trust all kinds of persons with whom we have no con-tract. I do not trust the policeman to protect my safety because the two of us have negotiated a written contract spelling out our respective rights and responsibilities. If I trust the police I do so because I think they are committed to caring for those things about which I care: the personal safety of myself, my family, and my fellow citizens and safety of my household goods.

As trustors, we know in very general terms with what the various trustees are entrusted. We know to call the police when personal safety is being threatened by another person, but to call the fire department when a blaze poses the threat. We have such awareness not because we have a contract with the police but because we know of their public pledge or promise to serve us. It would seem therefore that a pledge would be at least as effective a mechanism for establishing trust as the contract. It might even be better since clients are more likely to comprehend a succinct pledge like the Hippocratic Oath than the four-page fine-print contract between the physician and patient favored by the professional ethicist.[15]

The contract looks like a better basis for trust than a general public pledge only if trust cannot exist without detailed specifications of who does what for whom, when and at what cost. Yet trust not only exists without contracts; contractual stipulation may actually be a good reason to *mistrust* the party with whom one is interacting. I say this because the contract provides clients with the illusion that their every wish is controlling in the relation. But, in reality, clients must rely upon professional discretion simply because no contract can anticipate every contingency. The attorney–client relation is necessarily fraught with surprise because parties to a dispute do not and need not tell the other side precisely what they propose to do. Moreover, as the American Supreme Court has noted, there are not enough hours in the day for attorneys to explain to clients the reason for every legal maneuver they undertake when representing the client in court.[16] Attorneys, and professionals in general, must deal with issues and problems as they arise in the manner the professional deems most in the client's interest.

Of course, this discretion is not unlimited. It is understood by both parties to have role-specific limits. The sick entrust the physician with their bodily health and expect the latter to do what should be done to promote health. They do not expect physicians to tell them where to send their children to school. Nor do physicians presume to counsel patients about matters unconnected with preserving or restoring health. If trust is present, it is because both parties understand the professional to exercise limited discretion. However, this discretion is not so limited that it deprives professionals of the crucial option of revaluing prior commitments in light of new contingencies. The fire department may have planned a charity costume ball. Nevertheless, if a gasline explosion results in a massive fire, the dance becomes of secondary importance. The community, the department's clientele, would deem its trust betrayed if members of the fire department did not reassess the prior commitment to attend the charity ball in light of the new development but instead mechanically adhered to some rule (e.g. all prior commitments must be honored in the order in which they are incurred).

Use of a contract eliminates or at least greatly restricts this professional discretion so crucial for trustworthiness. The mechanical character of the contracting professional's service becomes apparent the moment one considers how a contractualist handles emergency cases. Let us assume I am a party who has contracted with my physician to treat my common cold symptoms. Assume as well that I have honored my appointment and consented to pay a fee for the service I am about to receive. Now just when my turn to see the physician comes, you arrive at this same one-doctor hospital in need of an emergency tracheotomy. You do not have an appointment nor have you made or honored a contract to reimburse the physician for his service. If one construes the doctor's written agreement with me as a document akin to a legal contract (and clearly the contract theorist intends that we do so, for why else call the arrangement contractual and bother with a written agreement?), then the physician is bound to serve me even if it means letting you die. I have a contract with him; you do not.

The philosopher Robert Veatch, perhaps the most thoughtful of the contractualists, realizes there is a problem here with contract theory. He suggests that the physician should try to persuade me to allow him to attend to you. However, this is not a solution to the problem. I may refuse the physician's request. Now the physician is powerless, torn between providing emergency care and honoring a contract made with an unreasonable individual. Veatch circumvents this problem by building an escape clause into the patient–doctor agreement. In the case of an "emergency," the physician may break any agreement negotiated with any individual in order to attend to a "non-patient" who is in dire straits.[17]

This concession is curious on several scores. First, since Veatch does not specify in whose eyes the situation is an emergency, he simply has glossed over what must be decided: does the professional exercise controlling discretion within the relation or not? Second, the presence of the escape clause means that professionals have obligations to people with whom they have not executed a contract. Veatch calls such persons "non-patients" but such terminology is somewhat disingenuous because the sick are obviously not non-patients in the same sense as are those beings who never can be sick (e.g. the dead or God). The physician apparently owes help to the sick who come into his presence even if he has not negotiated a valid contract with these parties. Consequently, the contract cannot be doing the grounding work the contract theorist imputes to it. Ironically, the real ground of professional legitimacy appears to be something like the doctor's public oath to serve (the Hippocratic Oath), the very pledge the contractualist seeks to replace with a more explicit contract.

Third, even with the escape clause, the contract leaves professionals bereft of any principled way to exercise discretion in allocating their time between patients. This last point is non-trivial. As we saw in the example of the fire personnel, an agent must have the power to reassess priorities in light of what is owed to all trusting parties, if trust is to remain intact. Commitment to promoting a specific good (e.g. the health of the sick) enables the professional to do this reassessment. In our example, the physician has the flexibility to investigate what order of treatment would better promote health. Obviously treating you first and me second would do so. My cold can wait for treatment until you can breathe again.

Note, too, that if I have trusted the doctor on the strength of the medical pledge, I can hardly complain when he appeals to the pledge to set his priorities in a manner which will preserve trust. The contracting professional, though, has no such ordering principle operating in the interest of all clients. Using only contractual criteria, the physician will treat me and allow you to die. Under such constraints, the physician does not order his services; chance does. I just happened to book the physician before you chanced to fall ill. The contract thus seems morally suspect on the contractualist's own criteria because an arrangement which leaves both the professional and the client at the mercy of chance can hardly be said to protect the individual freedom and autonomy critical for self-realization.

Lacking an architectonic end, the professional's practice slides toward the untrustworthy. No reasonable person would want to trust a professional who does not care enough about her clients to give some thought as to how best to arrange service in order to maximize the opportunities for appropriately caring for what clients value.[18] Possessing an architectonic end obviously does not solve all problems of allocating time and energy. Difficulties always will arise in deciding how to allocate time and energy between a variety of needy clients. The existence of an overriding architectonic principle does not preclude the need for judgment in light of the circumstances. However, judgment is aided and legitimacy promoted by the existence of some guiding good, recognized and embraced by both professionals and clients. A controlling good of this sort is desirable yet it is precisely this that the contract model lacks. Lacking such a good, the model fails to legitimate professional practice.

The second problem: the impossibility of contracting with unequal clients

The contract theory's insensitivity to conditions for trust is nowhere more manifest than in its assumption that the professional and client are fundamentally equal.[19] While one might argue that professional and client are equal in deserving respect, one certainly cannot assume that both are equal in their ability to act upon well-formed desires or even to articulate their wishes. Babies and paranoids cannot negotiate a meaningful contract, yet they do come before professionals and must somehow be appropriately served. Either professionals must refuse to assist such parties or they must discover some ethically fitting way of aiding them. Since the contract theorist view provides no guidance for helping those who cannot negotiate the contracts which transform them into clients, professionals must either rely upon their private instincts to guide them in their interactions with this type of individual or they must fall back on responsibilities stemming from a role, prior pledge, or combination thereof.

The first option will not legitimate professional authority. No thinking individual would knowingly place the helpless or especially vulnerable at the mercy of persons whose principles and values are unknown. Some variant of the second option may very well legitimate authority; we have yet to consider how a pledge-based ethic might cope with non-competent clients. What we can say is that the contractual model treats the problem such clients pose in an oblique and perhaps somewhat disingenuous fashion. Knowing that some notion like a "duty of office" or a role-specific responsibility is necessary for dealing with these cases in which the client clearly is not the professional's equal, the theorist avoids rejecting the notion outright. Veatch, for example, claims to leave open the question of whether there are role-based duties. But contract theorists cannot have it both ways. If they are going to rely upon the oath-defined role to ground trust whenever the professional deals with an unequal client, then their assertion that the contract is the ground of professional legitimacy is itself morally bankrupt.

The contract theory fails to ground professional authority because it provides no ground for trusting the professional's motives in those cases which pose the greatest dilemmas for the professional – situations in which the professional's judgment does not inform the decision of the client but must stand in its stead. In these cases, where discretion is greatest and trust most critical, the contract theorist's argument is weakest. Moreover, the theory provides little protection for the unsophisticated or impaired client in the event that the professional proves untrustworthy. The client is to hold the professional responsible for fulfilling the terms of the negotiated contract, presumably suing whenever the contract is violated. Yet this expectation seems unreasonable. Licensing exists at least in part because not everyone is the well-informed, litigious consumer the contract theorist envisions. While young, urban professionals may be experienced negotiators, versed in dealing and litigating, most clients do not fit this profile. Some clients need help in assessing the claims professionals make. Professional organizations and the state provide some admittedly limited assistance by certifying practitioners as qualified and trying to prevent unqualified persons from serving clients. Certification and licensing exist because, in the words of Justice Hugo Black:

> The average individual called upon, perhaps for the first time in his life, to select a lawyer may happen to choose the best lawyer or he may happen to choose one of the worst. He has a right to rely at least to some extent upon the fact that a lawyer has a license.[20]

Under the contract model, vulnerable clients or their guardians cannot avail themselves of the guidance and protection licensing provides. For licensing is only possible when the profession knows in advance what is and is not acceptable behavior. Some standard of practice is necessary to establish licensing. Since the contract model sanctions all sorts of actions that many in a given profession would think of as "unprofessional" (e.g. the contract ethicist Veatch envisions permits unnecessary or non-therapeutic surgery),[21] it is hard to see how any guidelines for regulating professionals could be established under the contract approach. The contract-negotiating client will have to rely upon his or her own assessment of professional qualifications. And, as Justice Black observed, it was exactly this state of affairs that licensing was intended to remedy.

The third problem: weakened client discipline

Given contract theory's emphasis on client control of the end and strategy of medical treatment, legal argument, and salvific rites, it sounds somewhat paradoxical to assert that the theory endorses client passivity. Yet the theory does just that. It never explores the possibility of a client role with significant responsibilities. Rather it posits a customer-client with no duties apart from stating what service is desired, paying the fee and showing up on time to claim the product (i.e. the professional service).[22] These minimal responsibilities correspond to those one has in dealing with a tradesman or craftsman. After the customer has let the plasterer into the house, told him which walls need to be repaired, and signed a contract promising to pay him, the customer can depart, leaving the plasterer to do the specified job. The customer does not participate in the tradesman's activity. The tradesman "jobs" his job and that is that.

Client responsibilities, though, would seem to be considerably more onerous than those of a customer. For example, in those religions in which congregations choose their spiritual leaders (e.g. in many Protestant sects and in all Anabaptist sects), the laity must test the would-be leader's calling. A divinely inspired urge to undertake a religious career is not simply a private affair but is public, something professed to a church body which wants to ensure that its leaders are not suffering from hallucinations or delusions of grandeur. In most sects, the congregation has the responsibility for choosing wisely. Congregations are not allowed to dismiss ministers simply because the minister fails to please the congregation. Unless the minister can be shown to be guilty of some gross breach of responsibility, the minister cannot be discharged.[23] Accepting responsibility for their choice in leader is a step on the path toward salvation, since salvation requires a good faith effort to make one's purposes more one's own and not to cast oneself in the role of a victim.[24]

We should not overlook then any responsibilities clients assume if and when they ask the professional for help in furthering a particular end. Just as it can be argued that parishioners seeking salvation have some obligation to test the calling of their leaders, so it can be contended that patients, too, have an obligation to try to understand medicine to the degree they are able to do so. The patient who does not attempt to do so will fail to ask soul-searching questions of the sort which help make healing possible and which lead to a just evaluation of the physician's merit, questions such as: has this particular physician failed me or have I failed my physician? In what way have my own actions affected the success of treatment? Like the individual penitent who ultimately must repent on his own, the patient shares responsibility for the outcome of the professional's help. Professional authority and power depend upon the client wanting to do what is necessary in order to be benefited. If the patient will not follow the physician's advice, or if the penitent will not do penance, then specifying in a contract that the doctor or minister will take measures to help the client is at best useless and at worst misleading. Law might seem to provide a counter-example to the thesis that clients must involve themselves in securing their own good. After all, the client usually says nothing in the courtroom. The lawyer does all of the talking and case preparation. But a second look suggests that the client does have some responsibility not to abuse the court system through which she hopes to find redress. The temptations to abuse it are great. Plaintiff suits have a nuisance value. The defendant must always weigh the cost of payment to the plaintiff against the expenses likely to be incurred by litigating the matter. The defendant's litigation expenses afford the plaintiff a covert legal form of blackmail. A defendant, on the other hand, may appeal against a decision regardless of merit in an attempt to obstruct action and to force a plaintiff who may be short of cash to settle for less than the amount already awarded.

Seeing that the delivery of legal justice depends upon client responsibility, the English legal system mandates that the party losing the suit must pay both sides' legal fees. This requirement discourages parties from covert blackmail of the sort just described and encourages them instead to focus upon whether they have truly been injured. In the US, where the contractual model has had more sway, citizens are living with the lack of client discipline and the consequences thereof.[25] Frivolous court suits are more or less tolerated as long as the client pays the attorney's fees. The result, chronic court congestion, has diminished public hopes of obtaining legal justice. This reduced hope for action in turn undermines trust. For trust requires the trustor to believe that the entrusted party not only will recognize obligations to the trustor, but also will act upon these obligations. For example, if I did not believe that my husband not only thinks that taxes should be filed but also that he will in fact complete and mail in the appropriate forms, I would not trust him to file the forms. Similarly, when people stop believing that their cases at law will be considered and decided before they die, they cannot be said to trust their lawyers. Since getting cases decided is a large part of the *raison d'être* of the court system and legal profession, the legitimacy of lawyers necessarily becomes suspect as clients' hopes for timely resolution of their cases dwindle.

The fourth problem: service for fee obscures the end of the professional–client interaction and promotes an imbalance of power

The contractual model posits a professional who provides service for a fee. The "fee for service" terminology, borrowed from retailing, equates the professional with a tradesman whose expertise is strictly for hire. On such a view, professional fees are a form of consideration where consideration is understood as a thing of value which must be exchanged in order to render a contract legally valid. The client gives up valuable fees. In return, the professional provides expert service of equal worth.

As a descriptive account of what professionals do, the contractual model leaves much to be desired. If professionals are strictly for hire, they have no responsibilities until they enter into a mutually acceptable contract with a client. However, all learned professionals recognize a duty to serve a client on the ground that the client falls into the category of people whom they have promised to serve (the sick; the accused or injured; the spiritually needy). Thus, ministers speak of their duty to stop at the scene of an accident to see whether they, like the Good Samaritan, can be of assistance to a potentially lonely, frightened, helpless, hurting victim.[26] Doctors similarly believe they have a responsibility to provide emergency care to injured and sick individuals.[27] Even American defense attorneys, who increasingly are wont to argue that they have no responsibilities to a litigant until they have agreed to take the person on as a client, change their position when pressed. Yes, they admit, if they were the only defense attorney in town, they would have a duty to represent a local man accused of a crime.[28] They make this concession because they recognize a role-specific obligation to defendants in need of legal assistance, regardless of whether the defendant is party to an acceptable contract.[29]

In general, professionals understand themselves as having responsibilities connected with the specific function they perform, a function they alone have been entrusted by the community to fulfill. The longstanding equating of professions with "callings" captures something of the obligation professionals feel toward their clients. Client neediness "calls" or summons the professional to action. A recent discussion of *pro bono* defense of death row litigants illustrates the character of a professional calling quite nicely:

> Initially, large firms were reluctant to involve themselves in [death row] litigation that was usually far from their areas of expertise, where the stakes involved were literally life or death .... [But] large firms came to see that the question was not one of whether they were qualified to undertake the litigation, but whether if they opted not to, who would? The answer was painfully evident; no one would take the case, and an unrepresented prisoner with a potentially meritorious appeal would lose his life. Reluctantly, large firms began to take cases.[30]

If the professional were strictly for hire, there would be no felt obligation to assist indigent members of the community. Yet the notion of a calling testifies to just such a felt obligation. The "fee for service" or contract theorist's model cannot and does not account for this sense of responsibility. It simply pretends it does not exist.

Of course, we can alter the way in which we practice law, medicine, or the ministry and over time our conception of professional responsibilities will change as well. Why not then allow professions to base themselves upon a market contract? The answer is simple. The agent warrants confidence either because of a known commitment to a particular good which predates the writing of the contract; or because money has changed hands and the professional's service has been contractually engaged. The courts have been far ahead of philosophers in distinguishing and then evaluating these two possible grounds of client confidence. While the courts have recognized "employment contracts" between lawyer and client, they have held that retainer contracts "are not always enforceable in the same manner as ordinary commercial contracts."[31] The problem with equating a retainer contract with a commercial contract turns on a point of trust. Clients often repose trust and confidence in the lawyer *before* signing any contract. For example, the client must confide information about his case before the lawyer can decide whether to take it. If the relationship antedates the establishment of terms of service (and courts have held that it sometimes does),[32] then any arrangement with respect to fees is a *product* of trust in a profession rather than the *source* of it. In other words, the nature of professional practice will itself require professionals to employ some non-contractual standard to govern how they treat the clients before they sign a contract and during the negotiation of it. Talk of a professional–client contract is worrisome because it deflects attention from the need for a non-contractual standard.

The "fee for service" view obscures the ground of client trust in a second way as well. It makes the *pro bono publico* dimension of professional activity incoherent, thereby rendering client trust still more problematic. If professional service is contractual, then all *pro bono* work is really "paid for" service. It is just that in some cases the fee is set at zero. But this reasoning creates an obvious problem: if the service is normally provided *for the sake of the fee*, why does a professional choose on some occasions to waive the fee? Since this motive must differ from the contractor's end of providing service in return for a fee, the contracting professional's position is strange. She has, on the one hand, a public mission to aid only those clients with whom she has a valid contract; on the other hand, she possesses a private motive that mysteriously supervenes on some occasions and renders null and void the publicly stated reason for action. This protean professional may help the impoverished or incapacitated client. However, the doctor or lawyer may just as easily decide midstream to start charging for service or to abandon the client at hand for a more lucrative one. The *pro bono* client can only watch apprehensively and hope that the enigmatic supervening motive holds for as long as he is in need of help. The indigent client may have to depend on such a professional; but to say that the professional is trusted by the client would be a stretch of the imagination.

Lawyers traditionally have not been at liberty to sue for fees precisely because they have rejected any rule or procedure which turns them into agents for hire. In Britain, "a counsel can maintain no action for his fees; which are given, ... not as salary or hire, but as a mere gratuity, which a counsellor cannot demand without doing wrong."[33] Until recently, lawsuits for non-payment of fees were also discouraged by the American Bar. The *Code of Professional Responsibility* enjoins lawyers not to "sue a client for a fee unless necessary to prevent fraud or gross imposition by the client."[34] No minister can prosecute lay persons for failure to honor the tithes out of which the minister is paid;[35] it is well known that couples give a gift to the minister who performs the wedding ceremony in appreciation for service rendered but that the minister charges no fee. Physicians in impoverished rural areas know that, although they may earn the undying gratitude of these clients, they will not be paid much, if anything, by their patients. In the US, Medicare and Medicaid may pick up part of the cost but they probably will not pay the doctor as much as she might like to be paid.

While many professionals no longer think of themselves as bound by this historical view of the fee as gratuity, the question is whether or not they are right to abandon the perspective. There are at least two compelling reasons for fighting to retain something of the historical view. First, thinking of the fee as a gratuity given in thanks for service rendered reduces client uncertainty as to what will occur in the interaction with the professional. All professional activity, insofar as it is professional, is made to aim not at a fee but rather at the particular end or good of the practice in question. There is no question of who or what controls the relation. Service is for the sake of the good (e.g. health) of the relevant public (e.g. the sick). That is, all service is *pro bono publico*. Reference is made to this good when deciding issues such as who qualifies as a client, when service should cease, etc. When the fee is consideration, then professional activity bifurcates into *pro bono* and *pro lucro* practice. This dual motive has the practical effect of introducing uncertainty into the relation. Is an individual a client before the fee has been paid? Do clients cease to be such if they fall into arrears? May the professional ethically "dump" a client in order to maximize fees? These questions are but a few that arise under the contract model. The reasonable client would want them answered before entrusting life or liberty to the professional. Yet the contract model offers no answers and is unable to do so. By its own logic, it is split over which principle – the good or the fee – actually controls the relation.

In addition to minimizing uncertainty, treating the fee as gratuity increases client trust by somewhat equalizing the risk run by both parties. The client is a vulnerable being. By definition, clients are in need of help they cannot adequately provide for themselves. Already vulnerable, they become more so when they seek assistance from a party who is likely to be a total stranger. They cannot rely upon a known, shared history to provide evidence of the trustee's good will. Patients must trust a strange doctor in order to appear naked before him. Having stripped, they must further trust that he will honor the distinction between palpatations and caresses. By placing their own fees at risk, professionals signal that they comprehend and honor the risk their clients have assumed in trusting them. Under the contract model, by contrast, clients retain little power with which to offset their vulnerability. They cannot withhold the fee. The fee is a precondition of service to be collected upfront (I had a dentist collect for a root canal before performing the procedure) or sued for should the client fail to pay. Given that such contractual fees compound clients' already considerable vulnerability, it is small wonder that they resent them so much.

These reflections do not preclude the use of fee schedules for professional service, but they do suggest that any method of client payment, including a national health service, will not be perceived as legitimate unless it is combined with prohibitions on client dumping. Moreover, if clients are going to be deprived of the ultimate power of withholding payment, then the method of payment should provide clients with some alternative practicable way of protesting about incompetent, or even vicious, service by the professional. By ignoring the need for such prohibitions and procedures, the contractualist ironically tends to decrease client power in the name of empowering the client.

The fifth problem: contract undermines practical training

The final problem arises because the contract theory fails to distinguish between allowing a client to decide between alternatives the professional has deemed appropriate; and permitting a client to establish an agenda drawn from an infinite array of options the client finds attractive for one reason or another. The contract theorist opts for the second approach, requiring that "the professional shall consent to any special, unusual agendas and goals of the lay person in the relationship."[36] Such mandated flexibility tends to undermine professional competence. Professionals can be trained to help their clients only if they define the limits of and give a single focus to the service they offer. Without such a limit, training and service to the client is impossible because all training involves instruction in doing one particular type of thing. Dancers perform exercises designed by instructors to enable them to produce and control movements of the sort choreographers ask them to perform. Although they jump high, it does not follow that a dancer can compete either well or safely in the high jump. Her instructor aims at training dancers, not athletes. This end, this limitation on the activity to be undertaken, is precisely what makes perfecting the activity possible. If instructors had to teach dancers how to perform all movements of which the human body is conceivably capable, they would never produce good dancers.

Similar reasoning applies to the professions. Mentors and teachers can hope to teach people how to be doctors and lawyers as long as each profession takes a particular kind of activity as its core practice. The contract theorist dashes this hope by making fulfillment of client desire the principle ordering the relationship and underlying all contract negotiations. The irrationality of this requirement is apparent: no professional can be *trained* to perform an unusual agenda which is unknowable in advance of the client stating his or her request. And if professionals have no special training or education, formal or informal, which makes them particularly able to help the client, there is no reason why the thinking client should seek their assistance in the first place.

SECOND DEFENSE OF AUTHORITY UNSUCCESSFUL

In conclusion, the argument contractual ethicists offer for grounding professional authority is no more tenable than the position advanced by experts. The contract theorist's argument, like the expert's, actually weakens authority by diminishing or destroying the trust the client must repose in the professional in order for assistance to be rendered. If neither expertise nor a contract grounds professional authority, what then does? To this question we must now turn.

Chapter 4

The public pledge as the ground of professional authority

Although the expert and contract models fail to legitimate professional action on behalf of the client, the failures nevertheless are enlightening as to the conditions any successful grounding of professional ethics must meet. Using the discoveries of Chapters 2 and 3, we can now say that for professionals to have moral authority they must be trustworthy. Moreover, we can specify conditions they must meet if they are to be so. For example, to be trustworthy, professionals must have the client's interest at heart. This requirement derives from the nature of trust. Trust is simply the trustor's expectation that the trusted will act to benefit the trustor. Since in this relation the professional is the trusted party and the client the trustor, it follows that the professional must aim at the client's good to be worthy of the client's trust (condition 1).

Good will alone is not sufficient to merit trust, since the client is looking for help to be rendered. The best evidence that the professional does in fact aim at the client's good is *action* on the client's behalf. The lawyer who promises to help a party but who never gets around to making an appointment to talk with that would-be client will not appear trustworthy in the client's eyes. Exhibited willingness to act is thus also necessary for trust in this relation (condition 2). In addition, this willingness must be open-ended. To be helped the client may have to be seen or assisted on many occasions. The willingness must be sustained since the client expects the professional's good will to be forthcoming not just for the next minute or hour but for as long as it takes either for help to be rendered or for a determination to be made that nothing can be done to help the client (condition 3).

Even a sustained willingness to help will not make a professional trustworthy unless the professional is actually able to competently determine the client's condition and to then do what will in fact tend to help that client. Doctors need not be able to heal all brain tumors but they must be able to perform well procedures the profession thinks helpful or that they themselves, given their knowledge of health and their past experience, judge likely to heal the patient. Together the profession's and individual practitioner's judgment constitute a standard of practice defining what it means to act for the benefit of the client. To be trustworthy, the professional must conform to this standard or offer compelling reasons for deviating from it in the case at hand. In short, professionals must be competent to be trustworthy (condition 4). Furthermore, since it takes two to make help possible, the professional must also be able to demand from the client the degree of accountability and discipline necessary for treatment to proceed or a legal case to be developed (condition 5). The doctor cannot be truly trustworthy if the patient refuses to divulge information necessary to make a competent diagnosis.

We must add as well that a legitimating ethic will allow the professional room to exercise discretion. We have seen that trusting another always entails permitting the entrusted to use her own judgment within limits to do what is best for the trustor under the circumstances at hand. To the degree that the professional's clientele has an organic dimension, the trustworthy professional must have the freedom to serve each individual client's good with discretion, revising prior commitments and previous allocations of time and energy if such revisions will result in better service for the clientele as a whole (condition 6). A legitimating ethic cannot therefore be a mechanical one which specifies in detail exactly what the professional should do, but rather must be one which suggests some general guidelines for, and limits upon, professional behavior.

Finally, we must not forget that, while most clients can work with the professional to address their need, not all are capable of doing so. Professionals are sometimes asked to act on behalf of vulnerable and often very young, very old, or reason-impaired clients who cannot monitor, much less assent to, every action the professional undertakes on their behalf. In order to be trustworthy not just in the eyes of clients but also in those of the guardians and representatives appointed to look after the infirm, the professional must have a highly internalized sense of responsibility. No one can watch over professionals all of the time, so the professional must be bound to monitor her own behavior (condition 7).

While I have no proof that these conditions for trustworthiness are formally exhaustive, they seem to be the key conditions for establishing and maintaining client trust in professionals. Other important professional traits taken up in subsequent chapters (e.g. professionals as preservers of client confidences) are variants of one or more of the above traits. Grounding professional authority thus becomes a matter of showing either that professional practice is already structured to meet the above requirements or that it can be altered to do so. In this chapter and the ones that follow, I shall argue that the practice of professions is already essentially morally sound. I do not mean that professionals can or should rest on their ethical laurels and do nothing to improve their relations with clients. I mean rather that, in discerning what professionals are, one simultaneously sees that they are trust-worthy as long as their behavior accords with what it is to be a professional. Of course, this is merely to assert what now must be shown – that professionals are in essence beings whose speech and action merit our trust.

PROFESSIONALS AS PLEDGORS WITH A MORAL COMMITMENT

While the criteria for who qualifies as a professional vary widely, five traits are frequently cited. Professionals: (1) are licensed by the state to perform a certain act; (2) belong to an organization of similarly enfranchised agents who promulgate standards and/ or ideals of behavior and who discipline one another for breaching these standards; (3) possess so-called "esoteric" knowledge or skills not shared by other members of the community; (4) exercise autonomy over their work, work which is not well understood by the larger community; and (5) publicly pledge themselves to render assistance to those in need and as a consequence have special responsibilities or duties not incumbent upon others who have not made this pledge. While the last criterion is perhaps the most controversial, it is also the one which is the most defensible. The other traits are neither necessary nor sufficient to define a professional.

Although professionals such as ministers and doctors have been licensed by the state to act as they do, a license alone does not make one a professional. The state licenses people to drive cars; but not all drivers are professionals. Nor is a license necessary to be professional. The clergy are widely recognized as such, but the US Constitution's Sixth Amendment rules out state licensing of ministers. Nor is membership of a practice-regulating organization a necessary condition for professional status. It is true that some lawyers, doctors, and ministers do belong to groups which promulgate ethics codes and in some cases discipline members for offenses against the codes. However, it is equally true that many doctors do not belong to the American Medical Association (AMA). While some officials of the AMA might consider these doctors unprofessional renegades, many consider these doctors' renunciation of membership a sign of professionalism, particularly when the doctors resign, for example, to protest against AMA policies which they think restrict health care access. Those who stress group membership as a criterion for professionalism would do well to remember that it has not been that long since America was served by itinerant country doctors, lawyers, and ministers who had minimal interaction with colleagues. For these reasons, group membership does not seem necessary for professionalism and it obviously is not sufficient. If it were sufficient, Ku Klux Klan members would all be professionals.

Chapter 1 showed that having esoteric knowledge and applying it autonomously cannot be a distinguishing trait of professionals. When such expert knowledge is applied in interactions with clients, the application proves self-undermining because it weakens the client trust necessary for the voluntary interactions in which the knowledge is applied. This problem with the definition can be avoided by restricting the class of professionals to researchers who never act on behalf of clients. But this definitional maneuver is somewhat suspect. The persons most consistently and universally recognized as professionals are the so-called learned professionals who *do* serve clients. We either refuse to call academics who do only research "professionals" or we give them the dubious name of "scholarly professionals."[1] I term such usage dubious because if esoteric knowledge and autonomy over work were sufficient for professionalism, then a coven of Satanic witches would qualify as professionals. Yet we do not consider Satanists professionals precisely because we do not see clients trusting them and seeking their help in obtaining a good.

This last observation brings us to the fifth trait of professionals, their "atypical moral commitment."[2] Making and honoring a publicly stated commitment to aid clients does seem a prerequisite for professionalism. No one considers slaves, sharecroppers, or family farmers professional because these groups neither proclaim nor exhibit fidelity to clients. We agree with fine artists' and craftsmen's rejection of the label on the ground that they create for themselves, not for a clientele because we, too, think a commitment to clients defines the profession. *The Oxford English Dictionary* captures our sense of professionals as client-centered when it takes professionals and clients to be correlatives, defining a client as "one who receives professional services."[3]

A professional then is a person who provides service to a client. We must be careful at this juncture to clarify what precisely is comprehended in this definition. While professionals do aid clients, this initial definition does not entitle us to conclude that clients are no more than recipients of professional attention. Individuals clearly do not seek assistance because they are clients. Instead, persons become clients because they seek some good they lack and are unable to provide for themselves. The unhealthy, injured/accused, and sinful soul all want help in obtaining or recovering something they think desirable – health, a fair share, or spiritual wholeness respectively.

These three types of "wanting" individuals existed before professionals came on the scene. Moreover, they would continue to exist even if doctors, lawyers, and clerics were to disappear from the face of the earth. These desiring persons give professionals their being. Trusting that the minister, doctor, and lawyer will act on their behalf, the spiritually unfulfilled, the sick, and the accused/injured enter into relations with unfamiliar professionals. By virtue of this relation, they become, *in addition to what they already are*, the minister's "congregant," the doctor's "patient," and the lawyer's "advisee" or "client." While acting to address the want which brings the client into the professional's presence is not sufficient for professional intervention to be trustworthy and legitimate (the want itself could be immoral), it is necessary. The trustor's expectation that the trustee will exhibit good will toward him constitutes trust. And it is trust, not the perceived power of the professional to manipulate things or people, that bestows moral legitimacy. This legitimacy is always at risk[4] and in need of being grounded precisely because persons can refuse to extend trust and to become clients. And where there are no clients, there ultimately are no professionals.

It is equally important to see that the professional is more than the correlative of the client. Desiring legal representation when one is accused does not bring a lawyer into existence. Nor does it seem that persons have a duty to become lawyers, doctors, or ministers. Although some assert that people have a right to health care, no one in the free world takes this "right" as creating an enforceable obligation for persons to become physicians.

We must therefore refine our initial definition of a professional. A professional is an agent who freely makes a public promise to serve persons (e.g. the sick) who are distinguished by a specific desire for a particular good (e.g. health) and who have come into the presence of the professional with or on the expectation that the professional will promote that particular good.[5] In other words, agents become professional by virtue of what they profess or publicly proclaim before persons lacking particular goods. The history of the term "profession" confirms the importance of the public statement to the ability of professionals to practice within the community. The word "profess" comes from the Greek verb *prophaino* meaning "to declare publicly."[6] The Greek *prophaino* became the Latin *professio*, a term applied to the public statement made by persons who sought to occupy a position of public trust.[7] As early as the first century AD, the physician Scribonius spoke of physicians "professing" and compared them to soldiers bound by a public oath to render service.[8] During the Middle Ages, priests desiring to learn and then share church teachings had first to profess themselves dedicated to this mission.[9] Centuries later the great jurist William Blackstone called attention to the public statement of lawyers, describing them as agents who have sworn to do their duty.[10]

In all of these cases, the profession or statement binds the speaker, but not the listener, to act to help those needing a particular form of assistance.[11] The agent's profession differs from a contract, which requires performance from both parties in order to be valid. Furthermore, unlike a contract which must be explicitly accepted by both parties in order to be binding, the profession binds the speaker upon utterance. A profession no one ever spoke would not be a profession at all. Speakers make these pledges or professions in order to encourage others to trust them.[12] For example, God's covenant with Noah never again to destroy the earth is a pledge intended to fortify His people. With this unilateral and unconditional vow, God gives mankind reason to turn to Him again and again. Men and women have cause to believe that even in times of pestilence or war, God will not abandon them.[13] In a parallel fashion, professionals unilaterally pledge to serve those who desire aid in obtaining a particular specified good. The pledge is not made before any particular person but rather before all who may find themselves afflicted or injured.

As I noted above, medicine, law, and the clergy each use a pledge to bind would-be helpers to assist parties.[14] Like God's covenant, these pledges are relatively unconditional. They bind their utterers to serve those who qualify as clients irrespective of clients' ability to pay, their personal traits, or the personal liking the professional may feel toward them. In the Hippocratic Oath (sworn by doctors until recently),[15] the doctor pledges to act for the "benefit of the sick."[16] The sick are to be helped because they are sick. Note, too, that the profession is open to anyone who is willing to publicly dedicate themselves to preserving or restoring people's health. As the philosopher and physician Leon Kass has noted, nothing in the oath makes medicine into a closed shop.[17]

The lawyer pledges to uphold the law when he becomes a practicing member of the profession.[18] As a lawyer, he is bound by the ABA *Model Rules of Professional Conduct*. The very first of these rules, which have the force of law, requires that a "lawyer shall provide competent representation to a client."[19] Although this wording might be interpreted to mean that the client is simply whomever the lawyer chooses to represent, the *Rules* go out of their way to deny this construction and to make the relation between the two covenantal. While "most of the duties flowing from the client–lawyer relationship attach only after the client has requested the lawyer to render legal services and the lawyer has agreed to do so," there are other duties such as preservation of client confidentiality which may apply whenever a person in need of help seeks assistance from counsel.[20] In other words, the client cannot be reduced to a person upon whom the lawyer decides to bestow service. Rather the client is the person seeking legal justice who has come to the lawyer because of the lawyer's public promise to promote legal justice, which is the good the client desires.[21]

It goes almost without saying that Judeo-Christian theology revolves around pledges. Judaism conceives of the rabbi as *promising* to teach others the Torah and to observe the terms of God's covenant with His chosen people in his own life.[22] Honoring this promise or pledge in turn entails assisting others because they are God's creatures. The person's race, sex or socio-economic background does not lessen the rabbi's responsibility to love the person. A rabbinic pledge or promise of service is widely understood as implicit in the practices of orthodox Judaism. Within the orthodox Judaic tradition, a congregation can ask anybody they want to act as their rabbi. However, as a matter of practice, having confidence in a candidate means believing the individual competent and willing to teach and abide by the Torah. Congregations place a high priority on learning, asking prospective candidates about who their own rabbis have been. No rabbi takes on students who are not publicly committed to Judaic (as opposed to Christian, Mormon, etc.) beliefs, including Judaism's understanding of the rabbinic role. Within the American Reform movement, the rabbinic promise is formally proclaimed. The President of Hebrew Union College asks each graduate whether he or she is prepared to serve as "rabbi of Israel."[23] Christian priests and ministers take ordination vows committing them to support certain dogmas and to assume a pastoral role in which they minister to all in need, especially those at the margin of society. Furthermore, a "profession of faith" is required of a cleric when circumstances make it important to re-establish the cleric's dedication to service. Thus, whenever the cleric assumes a role to which people will look for spiritual help and guidance (e.g. the cleric is promoted to a new office within the church), he must profess anew.

THE TRUSTWORTHINESS OF THE PROFESSION

If then professionals become such by virtue of a largely unconditional public pledge to promote a specific end desired by a particular group of needy people, does the pledge suffice to make professionals trustworthy in the eyes of the clients who provide the professions with their *raison d'être*? That is, does the pledge meet the requirements for trust listed at the beginning of this chapter?

The pledge quite obviously meets the first criterion. The

pledges of the learned professions all commit the pledgors to promote the good of the client.[24] If clients qualify as such, they deserve service. Just as God's covenant means He will always be present for anyone who calls to Him in need, so the professional's pledge has the effect of placing its adherents continually "on call."[25] While professionals take time off to attend to personal matters, they protect their clients by arranging with colleagues to substitute at the hospital, in the pulpit, or in court. Such devotion to the client's welfare is vital because clients in crisis often must expend a great deal of time and money just to see the professional. In the western United States, people may drive several hundred miles to consult a lawyer or doctor. Thinking persons do not undertake such treks without some assurance that the professional will take an interest in their condition. The pledge provides them with this assurance. Moreover, since in extreme cases the client's life is at stake,[26] the vulnerable client must believe the professional will continue to be interested in him as long as the crisis continues.[27] The primacy of the client's welfare under the pledge provides this assurance.

Of course, no single lawyer, minister, or doctor can help everyone in need of legal justice, salvation, or medical assistance. Although the pledge is open-ended and invites any and all who qualify as clients into the professional's presence, no single professional can help all clients. Since a promise cannot bind an agent to do the impossible, the pledge must be taken as binding swearers to make a good-faith effort to personally aid those who come into their presence and to assist others whom they cannot help to obtain aid elsewhere. For example, a doctor could discharge this obligation by working with legislators to create incentives for graduates of medical schools to locate in rural or other under-served areas of the country. In other words, the pledge obliges professionals to work for ever-increasing client access to help, not to treat every client personally or to intervene in every case of client neglect. Only when the client is actually in the professional's presence and in dire straits, does the responsibility to serve begin to approach an absolute obligation to help *that* client. If the professional does not render assistance in this situation, help will probably not be forthcoming in any situation and the professional's pledge rings hollow.

Subject to these caveats, the pledge meets the first requirement of binding professionals to make the client's welfare their primary focus. The pledge meets the second requirement for trust as well by binding professionals to *act* to promote the client's welfare. A doctor or lawyer cannot lessen this obligation to act by saying, "My colleagues may be bound by this pledge, but I personally never swore an oath to act for the benefit of the sick (or accused, etc.)." Professional pledges engender public expectations and have been intended to do so since they first began to be used in the first century AD.[28] These pledge-generated expectations regarding what an agent will think, do, or say constitute a role. Swearing the pledge and occupying a role are therefore for all practical purposes one and the same in the case of the professions. Like the various roles in a play which are identified by a name (e.g. King Lear), these public roles also go by names (e.g. doctor or minister). These named roles are in the public domain and belong to all who share in the expectations that have been created by agents' professions. Just as one is not free to unilaterally rewrite the script of Shakespeare's *King Lear* and then to represent oneself as staging that play, so individual professionals are not at liberty to treat their pledge-based roles as private property with scripts to be rewritten at whim.

Cavalier treatment by professionals of these role responsibilities is particularly egregious because no one else occupies these roles. The professional either honors the pledge and provides clients with the help they have been led to expect or clients do not get served. There are no understudies in our society waiting to step in should professionals fail to fulfill their role. Professionals are their own understudies, and they recognize as much. When the city of Knoxville, Tennessee needed more lawyers to serve as public defenders, the local judge (who is also an attorney) cited the attorney's professional obligation to serve the accused and ordered all lawyers in town, including the mayor, to do a stint as public defender. The attorneys grumbled but ultimately they complied because they knew their pledge/role obliged them to act on behalf of clients.[29]

Professionals have no ground for complaint about such demands. They have voluntarily assumed a role largely defined by the public statements of those in the role. The responsibilities are self-imposed. Furthermore, these role-related obligations are not unknown. The pledges are public; the pledge-based responsibilities are thus readily discernible by anyone who bothers to consider what role he or she is assuming. A would-be professional may choose to remain ignorant of such responsibilities. But just as ignorance of publicly decreed law does not mitigate responsibility for unlawful actions, so ignorance of publicly known responsibilities attendant upon a role voluntarily assumed does not diminish their binding character.

We can say, therefore, that the pledge grounds client trust by providing clients with a reason to expect and demand service from those occupying the roles of doctor, lawyer, or cleric. The client may reasonably expect not merely action (trust condition 2) but also consistent, ongoing help (trust condition 3). The client is entitled to think of the profession as permanently binding because the pledge cannot be renounced at the professional's pleasure. Once made, the pledge belongs to the public. The public's continued willingness to allow professions to exist constitutes its acceptance of the professional's pledge-defined role. Once a pledge is accepted by the public whose expectations have been shaped by the pledge, those who make the vow explicitly or who make it implicitly by occupying the pledge-defined role have forfeited any claim to repudiate the pledge at will.

The ministry has been particularly clear on this point. Solemn professions of the religious are forever binding. The other professions also behave as though the vows defining their roles are permanently binding. As the sociologist Everett Hughes has observed, "[a] man who leaves a profession, once he is fully trained, licensed and initiated, is something of a renegade in the eyes of his fellows."[30] Hughes might have added, "in the eyes of laymen as well." For example, the public always referred to the businessman Dr Armand Hammer by his medical title even though he stopped practicing medicine early in his life. Having once been a doctor, he always remained such in the public's eye.[31] In the event of a medical emergency aboard an airplane, passengers no doubt would have looked to Dr Hammer for help. One suspects he would have felt obliged to provide it.

Unlike the service contract recommended by contractualists, the pledge does not oblige the professional to fulfill any and all special agendas of clients. Instead, it orients professionals toward a single end, thereby making their education possible. Lawyers benefit persons not by healing them but by representing them in court. This single end of assisting the client to have his or her day in court (or in settlement proceedings which may lead on to the courtroom) informs legal education and serves to define a standard of practice, a standard which is necessary if the education system is to produce trustworthy lawyers. In this fashion, the pledge makes for competence (condition 4).

The pledge also empowers the professional to hold clients accountable for doing what must be done if they are to be aided (trust condition 5). Although more needs to be said about client accountability, it is clear that the pledge does allow disengagement from the client if and when help of the sort promised cannot be rendered. The doctor vows to try to heal the sick but those who are non-compliant cease to qualify as patients since the doctor cannot restore their health. The doctor can no longer act for the benefit of the sick in such cases and may withdraw from "treatment."

When and whether certain clients' behavior or condition is such that they cannot be helped must be determined by professionals exercising their judgment and discretion. Professionals do retain the discretion necessary for trust under the pledge (trust condition 6). The sphere of professional activity is limited, as we shall see in the next chapter. But, within that sphere, the pledge grants professionals scope to use their best judgment to decide the tactics of service. If triage procedures maximize the healing power of physicians, then they have the flexibility under the pledge to adopt such procedures. Professionals need not obtain the clients' approval for every tactic adopted. An attorney may call witnesses in the order she judges most favorable to her client without clearing this order with the client. The client will generally know far less than the attorney about the effect of various tactics upon the jurors' reasoning processes and perceptions. In addition, the client may be distraught and unable to think clearly about the tactics of the case. As long as the decision is tactical and does not affect the client's ability to arrange his life in light of his priorities, the pledge leaves the professional with the trust-eliciting power to develop and initiate appropriate strategies for promoting the client's end.

Finally, the professional pledge respects clients' vulnerability (trust condition 7) by letting those whom professionals help be clients in the original meaning of the term. Clients are seen as human beings who are doubly vulnerable. They are at risk not only because their life is threatened but also because they are dependent upon the assistance of a benefactor. Unlike the contractual service provider, who requires that clients argue for why they deserve to be helped[32] and who is free to turn away those whose actions are considered by the service provider to be immoral,[33] the pledging professional helps persons simply because they need the particular good she has promised to promote. She acknowledges that clients are dependent precisely because they are lacking in the means to lead a self-sufficient life. Consequently, she does not expect them to act or argue like healthy, self-reliant, upper middle-class philosophy professors before she will extend them help.

Granted, some parties, particularly corporate clients of attorneys, are not marginal members of society, teetering on the brink of death or in danger of losing their freedom. Nevertheless, corporate representatives sometimes do find themselves braving intimidating foes.[34] For example, the Internal Revenue Service and UK Inland Revenue have immense power and have been known to abuse it. The court has rebuked the IRS for what it has perceived as a kind of high-handed harassment on the part of government agents.[35] Confronted with such an antagonist, representatives of the corporation are grateful to have a tax attorney on their side. Even if the corporation does not start out vulnerable, it and its employees certainly become more so as a consequence of conveying highly confidential material to hired counsel. Competitors would dearly love to know such things as the corporation's strategic plans, the status of pending patent applications, and earnings forecasts. Furthermore, when we speak of a "corporate" client, we do well to remember that the corporation is only a legal fiction. The lawyer deals with individuals who are often stressed and are afraid of losing their jobs or their liberty as a result of litigation. It is not farfetched to think of the lives of corporations and the livelihood of those within corporations as dependent upon the assistance of a professional benefactor.

The pledge model recognizes client vulnerability by identifying the client with the life-impairing need responsible for bringing the client into the professional's presence in the first place. The defendant is a person in need of justice, not simply a party the lawyer happens to want to help. In addition, the pledge sensitizes professionals still further to this vulnerability by reminding them of their own vulnerability. Commenting upon the Hippocratic physician's pledge to share the life of his teacher, to meet this mentor's needs, and to teach his teacher's sons free of charge, Kass observes that:

Such a physician will understand that he is not a self-made man or self-sufficient man, and that a belief in his own autonomy and independence is mistaken. He will appreciate that he owes both his life and his work to those who came before, that the art of medicine, like the rest of civilization, is a monument to the ancestors. By remembering his teacher and looking to his students, he will be kept aware of his own mortality.[36]

The pledge makes clear that a professional has a profession and a livelihood only because those who have gone before took care to pass on the medical practice to students. Professional, student, and client are all part of this fragile network we call community. Like his patients, the doctor is mortal and dependent upon the good will of past and present members of the community. In fact, the very practice of the profession leaves the doctor susceptible to harm. The truly professional physician may find himself in need of funds at the end of life precisely because he has both served patients and taught future professionals regardless of their ability to pay. The oath's requirement that doctors aid their own mentors can be read as a reflection of medicine's understanding that it is a practice of helping needy patients who ultimately may not be so different from the doctor himself.

This mutual vulnerability is recognized by the clergy, who are bound to pray regularly for forgiveness, acknowledging that they, like the laity, are sinners who can and do hurt their fellow man. Legal practice shows the least explicit awareness of human fragility, neediness, and interdependence. From the perspective of the needy client, this lack of awareness is a defect. It is not surprising that the public appears highly ambivalent about attorneys' trustworthiness. The large number of jokes made at attorneys' expense may be an attempt to puncture their illusion of invulnerability.[37] Or, viewing this behavior more sympathetically, one might argue that lawyers tell these jokes on themselves as part of an attempt to show the public that attorneys know they share their clients' frailties.

CONCLUSION

Summarizing the previous discussion, we may say that professionals' unilateral, unqualified pledge to serve a specific end of a particular group of vulnerable human beings grounds professionals' authority, legitimating their power of initiating and performing or authoring life-altering actions on the client's behalf. The pledge functions as a ground because, and to the extent that, it meets the objective requirements for a trusting relation between the professional and the client. It binds only the pledgors; and it legitimates only the authority of those making the vow, not all human authority. It can thus properly be said to be a ground of professional authority. In addition, the pledge can be said to be the ground of professional authority because, like all grounds, it reveals in whose eyes professionals have authority: those making the pledge have authority to do what they have promised to do both in their own eyes and in those of their clients, actual or potential.

Although I have used the past history, practices, and statements of the profession to show how the problem of professional legitimacy can be solved, the analysis is nevertheless essentialist rather than historical. Adherence to the pledge meets the requirements for client trust; the pledge itself can be thought of as a structure embodying these requirements. It is irrelevant to trust whether this structure came into being yesterday or two thousand years ago. The origin of the structure in period and place does not affect its ability to serve as a legitimating foundation for professional practice.

What does matter to professional practice is the recurrent need to demonstrate its legitimacy. The psychiatrist Harry Stack Sullivan is right to suggest that the question of legitimacy arises in every interaction with every client because in order to continue to merit a client's trust the professional must repeatedly show that he is in fact acting for the benefit of that client.[38] In other words, professionals must have some way of establishing that they are worthy of the clients' continuing trust. Adherence to the professional pledge in each and every interaction with the client constitutes a solution to this problem. It may not be the only one. But anyone who proposes an alternative understanding of professions must show how exactly this other model solves the legitimacy problem. The dismal failure of the expert and contractual service provider models to address and resolve the problem suggests that the task is not an easy one.

Chapter 5

The legitimacy of the professions' ends

Grounding professionals' authority in their public pledge to render clients a particular good seems then to meet the conditions for trustworthy service. In this sense, our covenantal model is more authoritative, more grounded than the other models we have considered. Nevertheless, objections may be raised against this account as well. Three objections are particularly worrying.

First, the relation between the professional and client is not morally legitimate just because it is trusting. "Made" members of the Mafia swear an oath of loyal service. Members rely upon the good will of one another in order to protect their turf and loved ones from competing families. Nonetheless, we do not view this pledge-defined role with its attendant responsibilities as a good one deserving of our praise. Furthermore, while we concede that the Mafia has power, we do not grant it authority. As was suggested in Chapter 1, the content of the pledge or promise must be acceptable to and accepted by persons affected by the pledge if the pledge is to legitimate authority. Thus, the role of Mafiosi is not worthy of trust because its end of preserving its status and revenue streams at all costs is not an end desirable in its own right and consequently acceptable to all agents affected by the gangsters' actions. Most members of the community have no desire to become mobsters. Mafia members themselves often desire to cut ties with the mob but remain connected after being made an offer they dare not refuse. For professionals to have authority, the end to which they dedicate their lives must be desirable in its own right. While I have repeatedly alluded to the client's good, it remains to be shown that the respective ends promoted by medicine, law, and the ministry are goods of this sort.

Second, as we saw in Chapter 3, the trustor grants the trustee power to affect the trustor's life but expects the trustee to exercise this discretion *within limits*. Once again, although the argument has established that the pledge provides for ample professional discretion, the argument has not shown whether and how the pledge limits what the professional may do on behalf of the client. These limits must be investigated more thoroughly.

Third, if the pledge really is the legitimating ground of professional authority, then any individual who makes and adheres to a pledge of the sort described in the previous chapter will qualify as an ethically good professional. Membership of a professional organization, informal ties with other practitioners, and state licensure will be irrelevant to an assessment of an individual's trustworthiness. Yet clearly more must be said on this score: can professions really exist in the absence of an organizational framework? Trust would seem to presuppose accountability. Can it exist if clients lack institutional mechanisms (e.g. professional disciplinary and state licensure boards) to hold professionals accountable for their behavior? This chapter and the next are devoted to addressing these objections in the order raised.

THE GOODNESS OF THE ENDS SERVED BY PROFESSIONALS

Few would disagree about the stated aims of the learned professions. We readily grant that doctors aim at restoring and maintaining health; lawyers at securing legal justice for the person they are advising or representing in court; and the clergy at enabling their listeners to gain spiritual salvation.[1] The problem arises when one tries to state a comprehensive definition of health, justice, or salvation. Long treatises have been written by philosophers attempting to define even one of these notions. Investigating all three is clearly beyond the scope of this book's argument.

Nor is it clear that a final definition can be given. Every profession struggles to state its end. Doctors wonder: does mental health exist or is the term "health" merely used analogically when applied to the mind? Does a life have a natural term and allotment of health or can healthy individuals potentially live for ever? The meaning of justice is similarly elusive. We usually apply the notions of "just" and "unjust" only to persons and to their voluntary actions. But this says little, since philosophers disagree over who is a person and what is to count as an action, much less as a voluntary action.

Theologians face perhaps the most daunting challenge of all. Trying to define who is a Jew or a Christian is taxing; articulating what each religion means by "salvation" seems a task fit for Hercules. The history of these religions largely consists of believers breaking away from established sects because no agreement could be reached regarding the salvific role of grace, faith, the law, penance, and human works. New faiths have arisen as believers have emphasized some previously overlooked or underemphasized strand or nuance of their inheritance. Offering a comprehensive account of salvation may be the most difficult problem the theologian faces.

If this inquiry into the source of professional legitimacy required a full-blown definition of the ends of the various learned professions, we would have to stop here. However, the inquiry imposes no such onus. The question at hand is simply: are health, legal justice, and salvation genuine human goods? In the following sections, I will argue that there is, in fact, at least one major component of all three professions' ends which is an end desired for its own sake; and that professionals lose their authority when and to the extent that their practice does not promote the good so understood.

Health as a good

Some have argued that health is no more than a word.[2] On this view, any attempt to state a core meaning or component of health is doomed to fail because some changeable societal or interest group value underlies and colors every conception of health. Proponents of this view point to our changing ideas of such things as alcoholism and midwifery. Alcoholism, now considered a disease, was thought of as a vice at an earlier date.[3] Physicians who wanted to force midwives out of medical practice tried to turn pregnancy into a disease treatable only by licensed physicians. Pregnancy was transformed from a normal condition of women into a "tumor of the belly" to be cured by obstetricians. Or to take a more current example: present-day cosmetic surgeons refer to small breasts as deformities and "really a disease" in need of a surgical cure.[4]

Our conception of disease unquestionably has varied as values have changed. But it does not follow from this observation that every era conceives of disease or health equally well. Furthermore, some conditions always and universally have been viewed as unhealthy: "A broken arm is still a broken arm" regardless of how anyone defines health.[5] Other things being equal, no one wishes to have poorly functioning limbs. If this is true, there seems to be some condition or norm of healthiness that everyone desires. What might this be?

The example of the broken arm gives us a clue. In this case, we focus on the fact that the broken arm is not *whole*.[6] Healing the arm means returning it to a state of wholeness. Indeed, the Indo-European root of the word "health" is *kailo-*, which means whole.[7] Only that which can be made whole qualifies as an object for the doctor's attention. No physician in any culture has ever tried to heal a rock or a star, because inorganic things are neither potentially nor actually wholes. Inorganic objects are accretions or accumulations of matter. They have no well-defined parts. One can add to or subtract from their "stuff" without destroying what they are.

Animate organisms, by contrast, can be healed or returned to wholeness because they possess wholeness intrinsically. Organisms manifest their wholeness in a variety of ways. Rather than just growing through addition, they exhibit a special kind of growth – they *develop*, differentiating themselves as they grow from seeds or zygotes into mature beings. Moreover, they maintain their differentiation by replacing aging cells with those of the same type and by preserving a boundary between the inside and outside of the organism. They seem to know what is a part belonging to the whole and what is not. When the body is healthy, its immune system recognizes and rejects alien cells.

Organisms have some limited power for restoring themselves to wholeness if a part or organ is damaged. Animals will scar, replacing damaged skin tissue with new skin tissue. Some organs regenerate. Plants will regrow missing roots. A sponge forced through a sieve will even reconstitute itself into an organized living animal. Being healthy seems to mean maintaining the whole.[8] The unhealthy organism is one which has lost the ability to differentiate and maintain the whole with all of its parts.

This notion of health is fine as far as it goes. But it tends to understate the dynamic character of health. The body's ability to keep individual parts functioning and fulfilling their specific tasks within a complex of such parts depends upon the kind of activity in which the whole organism engages. Organic powers are a function of what the organism actually does. Muscles atrophy if they are not used. Experiments on monkeys have shown that if the eyes are not allowed to focus on different objects during the first few weeks of life, the organism permanently loses the ability to see.[9] My body can metabolize today only because my past nutritional habits have been such as to permit continued bodily functioning. Men and women who repeatedly substitute non-food (e.g. cocaine) for food wind up dead.

This interdependence of organic structure and appropriate habits is captured in *euexia*, the Greek word for health. *Euexia* may be translated as "well-habitedness." The term implies that health consists in possessing and developing habits which promote and maintain the structural soundness of the whole organism, not just in the structural soundness itself. We are loath to call the habitual drug user healthy because his way of life is not such as to maintain the body's wholeness. Nor would we call a man who slept all of the time healthy. In the long run, his health would fail because the body needs exercise to keep functioning.

But even if his body stayed in good working order, we would still hesitate to call him healthy. For to the extent that health consists in "well-habitedness," the concept presupposes a being who is actively engaged in the host of human activities through which we acquire and exhibit our habits. Such engagement necessarily involves choice because not all of our activities are mutually compatible. Choice results in habits. The eternally sleeping man makes no choices and develops no habits. We do not know what type of man he is or might become. Since we cannot judge whether he is "well-habited," we withhold judgment about his health or lack thereof.

Acquiring habits or ways of acting constitutes character and affects the course of the life we lead. This "course" or individual "career" (understood as a history, not as the practice of some trade, art, or profession) is equally a whole with a beginning, middle, and end. Our notion of health has deep ties to the fact that we live a life that comes to an end. Health applies only to beings with careers. Yahweh and Allah are neither healthy nor unhealthy because they lack organic bodies to be affected by their history and to force career choices upon them. The wholeness of the organic body and the purposefulness that gives life meaning and unity are bound together. It is precisely our awareness of our mortality that forces upon us the need to order our priorities and to decide who and what we are. The actions we undertake in light of these priorities, in turn, necessarily open some options and close others. Unlike the gods, we do not have an eternity in which to make up our minds about what to do. We must choose in the here and now. We even have to decide how much time we will spend on the care of our bodies versus other purposes and then live with the consequences of the resulting habits for our future purposes and choices.

This reflection highlights a key dimension of health. Health always involves a balance, "an equilibrium established between inborn or acquired diseases or limitations and the use of our bodies for transbodily purposes – to advance persons' interests, plans, or aspirations."[10] As we carve out a course for ourselves, we always work with some limitations to our power to meet desired objectives. We begin life with limits. For example, very young children at play are often frustrated by their lack of muscular control. They simply have to do the best they can with the control they do possess. No doubt everyone wishes at some time or another for better eyesight, a stronger back, a more discriminating ear. Nevertheless, each of us makes a life using the constitution with which we were born, which we develop through our better (or worse) habits, and which we acquire through accidents and the operation of forces beyond our control.

Some activities improve our powers. Others limit our abilities to do as we wish. While people do not wish for mangled limbs or the infirmities of old age, they do adjust and find a new equilibrium when confronted with such impediments. We see people making these adjustments and often comment that someone is "healthy for his age" or "healthy, given the circumstances." When persons have achieved a balance between their body and transbodily purposes, they are healthy. Disease destroys health precisely because it introduces an impediment to our accustomed functioning. It impairs our easy activity, making it a matter of "dis-ease." Restoring health means achieving a new balance that enables our body and mind to work together, rather than at cross-purposes.

Doctors work with patients to help them redefine purposes so that a new unity of living becomes possible. Although her physicians could not cure the multiple sclerosis that ended Jacqueline du Pré's career as a world-class cellist, they did urge her to develop a new life teaching the instrument. It is not strange that Ms du Pré felt indebted to them *as doctors* for this assistance.[11] Healing consists in providing such equilibrating help.

If we take health then to be at least in part the balanced functioning of a well-habited whole, we can readily see why it is good in the eyes of both the individual client and the community at large. Individuals desire health because they love life. To be alive is to be striving to realize purposes. We seem to desire to be purposive, striving beings apart from any consideration of specific purposes. Given a choice between being a beautiful diamond or a lower life form such as a mouse, we would choose life as a mouse. Why? Because the mouse is alive, busily trying to realize or fulfill its "mouse capacities." Health, like life, is good in itself because health is the *balanced* striving (i.e. living) of an organism with a career. Where there is no health, living is attenuated. A person who is chronically depressed, sits days without moving, and makes no choices is rather like our eternally sleeping man – not healthy and leading an attenuated life at best.

To say that health and life are loved as good in themselves does not entail that individuals will never forgo them for the sake of some other good. We know, for example, of people who have endured martyrdom for causes in which they believe. Nevertheless, that healthy living is highly esteemed for its own sake seems beyond question. As long as people have some sense of internal balance and can place their body at the service of some desired good, they tend to hold onto life. From the outside, the so-called "quality of life" of a person may look low. But it is the inside view that matters to each of us. We ought not to assume too quickly that an individual's life has become undesirable. As the philosopher Phillipa Foot reminds us, suicides in concentration camps were virtually unknown: "The more that life became desperate, the more a prisoner seemed determined to hold onto it."[12] Nor should we be too quick to conclude that the prisoners were leading unhealthy lives just because they experienced pain or suffering. Being healthy is not inconsistent with either.[13]

As individuals, we value health because it is part and parcel of the balanced striving that constitutes life for human beings.

However, health is also good in a second, instrumental sense. Many of our projects require the help of others in a community. Health is good for life insofar as it makes communal life possible. A nation of unhealthy citizens could not defend itself; educating masses of sick persons would be difficult if not impossible. Public works projects would grind to a halt if no one were well enough to staff them. Therefore, nations quite properly concern themselves with "public health." Yet we must be careful to specify what we mean by this term. Just as "the rights of the majority" refers to the rights of individuals comprising the majority, so "public health" means the health of the individuals who live in a given community. Each individual's health logically must count in an assessment of the public health. Insofar as public health is a precondition of public life, we can say that the individual's health, which is part of the public health, is a public good. However, health is first and foremost the individual's good, desirable for its own sake. It does not cease to be a good when a human being leaves or is exiled from the community. Hermits love their health as much as London residents do.

The goodness of health explains our willingness to accord doctors authority. If health is something all desire as a good in itself and as something of instrumental benefit to all of us as members of a community, then the physician's use of power to further health is also good. It follows in turn that their therapeutic actions are evidence in the patient's eyes of good will. The patient will trust such a physician. Thus, to the extent that physicians abide by their pledge to restore and maintain the balanced striving of an organism with a career,[14] they have authority. Authority disappears if and when patients become convinced that physicians are not committed to helping the patient achieve a balanced striving but rather to some other end, such as maximizing wealth through the performance of non-therapeutic and possibly even life-threatening procedures (e.g. inserting silicon breast implants) or manipulating the patient to achieve fame or sexual gratification.

The goodness of justice

What should we say about lawyers? Is their practice also good in the eyes of both the client and community? Lawyers' practice of advising and representing clients aims at securing justice for the client. But what are we to say about justice? What is it, and do all value it? Plato's Socrates contends that there is justice even among thieves;[15] St Augustine implies the opposite when he argues that "states without justice are no more than robber-bands enlarged."[16] Is justice only a word? Once again, I think that justice has a core meaning and that these two seeming conflicting claims about justice are, in fact, reconcilable. But before sorting out these claims, I must make a few preliminary remarks about justice.

As the legal philosopher H. L. A. Hart has noted, the ideas of justice and of morality or goodness are not co-extensive.[17] A few examples suffice to show the limited applicability of the idea of justice. While we would term a man who slashed a museum painting or who went out of his way to squash bugs and to mow down flowers "evil," "wicked," or just plain "cruel," we would not call him "unjust." Similarly, we might term a particularly offensive work of art "bad" or "corrupting" but we would not label it "unjust." Finally, although animals may behave badly when they refuse to obey their owners' commands, animals are never just or unjust. We reserve the terms "just" and "unjust" for praising and blaming actions by one person which affect another.[18]

What precisely are we assessing when we use the notion of justice? In general, justice and fairness mean roughly the same thing. We apply the notion when burdens and benefits are being distributed among persons. Punishment becomes just or unjust, depending upon whether the burden it imposes is distributed equally or not. If two people committed exactly the same crime,[19] but only one is punished, the justice of the punishment is called into question because the burden has not been fairly shared or distributed in proportion: equal crimes have not received equal treatment.

At the heart of justice is the notion that "individuals are entitled in respect of each other to a certain relative position of equality or inequality. . . . Justice is traditionally thought of as maintaining or restoring a balance or proportion and its leading precept is often formulated 'treat like cases alike' ".[20] Which differences and resemblances matter in the balancing act varies among regimes. The way in which people are thought of as equals clearly depends on the morality of the people doing the balancing. As Judge Dorothy Nelson observes, "Law plus X equals justice and X is morality."[21] We know, for example, of nations (e.g. South Africa; United States) which have, in the past, given whites the vote while denying the franchise to blacks. The whites, like the robbers to whom Plato refers, treat one another as equals in order to gain the co-operation they need to maintain the apparatus that keeps them in power. Among whites there is justice; like cases are treated equally. This state becomes unjust only if we accept an argument to the effect that individuals of all races are persons and that, in the case of distributing the franchise, personhood, rather than the color of the skin, is the relevant determinant of who shall have the franchise.

Should we accept this argument from personhood? At this juncture, St Augustine's suggestion that only certain distributions of benefits and burdens are just becomes relevant. We can well imagine a powerful tyrant who tortures all subjects equally.[22] In this case, like cases are treated alike yet we do not call the regime just. Note that the regime does not fail in justice because the tyrant, who is really like the subject, has erred in exempting himself from the treatment. The regime would not become just if the tyrant began to torture himself as well. The problem here is that justice requires not equal treatment but rather treating each individual as equal in personhood and dignity. The torturer fails to see his victim as a person and therein lies the injustice of this tyrannical regime. A similar failing plagued the pre-1994 South African apartheid regime: the blacks were little more than tools of those in power and were not respected as persons equal in dignity to the whites.

Stating what is meant by this notion of "respecting others as persons equal in dignity" is not easy. Often respect for personhood is equated with treating others as ends-in-themselves, not as means.[23] That is, we respect others when we permit or enable them to achieve their purposes.[24] Yet this formulation, too, needs further elaboration. A kidnap victim may desire that her parents pay ransom. The kidnapper may, in turn, permit and even encourage the victim in the realization of this desire by allowing the victim to call her parents, and so on. Although the kidnapper promotes the fulfillment of the victim's desire, the victim's person has not been respected. The situation created by the kidnapper in which the victim and parents are acting is itself coercive. Neither the victim nor the persons from whom money is being extorted have chosen the roles in which the kidnapper has cast them. Similar reasoning clearly applies to our tyrant-torturer. He does not respect the victim's person by stopping the torture, thereby fulfilling the victim's wish for the torture to cease. As long as the victim–torturer relation remains intact, the victim's person is not respected. The victim has no freedom to alter the situation so that her desires will be more adequately expressed, nor does she have any access to friends, family members, and fellow citizens who could help her understand herself and her purposes and make these purposes more fully her own.[25]

In general, we treat others justly, respecting them as persons, if our actions create and maintain a system in which all persons are equal insofar as all have the freedom to originate actions and to structure their environment, lives, and relations so as to satisfy their desires. While additional restrictions may have to be placed on the formation of the purposes on which the agent acts (e.g. they cannot be the consequence of subliminal manipulation), enough has been said to establish justice and its subspecies of legal justice as a good desirable in its own right. All people desire justice in the sense that all want a share of the freedom to originate action and to exercise control over the environment in which they lead their lives. Injustice does not consist in wanting no share of this freedom but in wanting too great a share for oneself.[26] All want a share because justice, like health, is constitutive of life. Those who lack justice, like the sleeping or catatonic man, lead at best an impoverished life. After all, what kind of active life can one "lead" if one is, for example, locked in a closet for years? It is not surprising that upon hearing of cases of children so confined we exclaim: "That is no sort of life to have!"

A legal system and the lawyer's role in it are just because they permit people, on the one hand, to originate actions against those who, they believe, have harmed them (i.e. denied them their share of a free and active life) and, on the other hand, to devise and present a defense against such accusations. The verdict eventually rendered by such a legal system may not be well reasoned. A litigant may really have been harmed, but the jury or judge may choose out of prejudice to believe a liar. Or certain facts may either not come to light or be presented so poorly that their significance is lost. But such problems will plague any legal system which attempts to render justice. We do not conclude that no legal system is just. Instead, we treat a given legal system as just if it struggles to ensure that every person obtains a hearing of his or her case. I include within this "we" both plaintiffs and defendants, as well as the other court participants and the community at large. In this connection, it is worth remembering the famous Gilmore case from the 1970s. While the murderer Gary Gilmore did not want to be apprehended, once caught he most certainly did want to suffer the death penalty for his crime. Furthermore, he wanted his voice to be the one the court listened to in deciding his fate, not the pleadings of his mother or the arguments of the American Civil Liberties Union.[27] Litigants who have their day in court receive the fair share a human system is able to provide.

While it may be impossible to spell out in advance all that is entailed in "having one's day in court," we can identify practices or procedures which preclude having one's case heard. Litigants are not given their fair share if lawyers prejudge their case and consequently fail to argue it well in court. The case is represented as the client's while in reality the client is given no voice. Preventing litigants from discharging attorneys would similarly restrict litigants' ability to act upon their purposes. Denying parties opportunity to speak with their counsel or giving attorneys little or no time to prepare the client's case may also be added to the list of unjust practices.

I do not want to give the impression that I am arguing for a merely formal view of legal justice. Legal justice as I have described it is very much a substantive matter, since justice, understood as obtaining one's share in the form of getting to state and then act upon one's purposes in court, is itself an intrinsically desirable part of an active life. Legal justice is thus a good in itself. But, like health, justice has an instrumental dimension as well. If persons' voices are not heard in the forum in which penalties are imposed and benefits granted, then the community will have difficulty initiating and sustaining communal endeavors. As Plato argued, the thief who does not get his share of the loot is likely to turn against his accomplices to stop them from enjoying their gain. Or if you abuse me in conversation, I can always walk away, leaving you unable to achieve whatever you hoped to gain from talking with me. Since we both benefit from joint activity, we desire the justice, including the legal justice, that makes communal life possible.

Nevertheless, although justice has an instrumental dimension, it is best understood as a human good desired for its own sake.

As long as attorneys advise clients on whether they have been injured and as to what kind of redress they can expect; and represent them in court so that their claims for redress or for a redistribution of benefits and burdens are heard, attorneys maintain authority. The authority becomes problematic when the lawyer pursues justice for his client in such a manner as to deny others access to the court or the ability to present their cases in court; the lawyer substitutes his own purposes for those of the client; or the lawyer in some other manner fails to act in a manner consistent with potential, as well as actual, clients obtaining a hearing of their case in court. The diminution of authority in these cases is not surprising. The injurious pursuit of justice by definition cannot be just. Lawyers who fail to respect the personhood of others divorce themselves from the good – justice – that grounds their authority. As a result, they fail to warrant client confidence and lose their ability to initiate and execute actions on the client's behalf.

The goodness of salvation

Both Judaism and Christianity think of salvation as something individuals desire for themselves. Unlike Buddhism, which recommends the dissolution of the ego and therefore, strictly speaking, cannot offer anything an individual would desire, these two religions presuppose persons with histories and purposes who desire spiritual salvation. Though they resemble one another in this important respect, the two religions differ sufficiently to warrant separate treatment.

Judaism

How does Judaism understand salvation? This religion promises that those who, through birth or acquired belief, acknowledge and keep the covenant God made with Abraham and his seed will reap peace on earth. Human beings do not merit the covenant.[28] Nevertheless, those who observe the commandments of the law, performing the loving, just actions God desires, will be rewarded. What is this reward? Peace.[29]

Why does fidelity bring spiritual peace and quietude, and what is intrinsically good about this peace? The righteous person has faith in God's covenant. This covenant assures each of us dignity and nobility. Each person is created in the image of God and shares in God's divine, noble grandeur. However, no one may claim nobility for herself without also according it to her neighbor. For God created all men and women in His image:

> Though [my neighbor is other], God's covenant with me is simultaneously his covenant with him and therefore links him to me. There is no "man" without "fellow man" and there can be no faith in myself without faith in him.[30]

All life is one, bearing the mark of our creator. Reverence for one's own life demands respect for all life. Recognizing the unity and kinship of all life allows one to take the initiative and to trust enough to at least attempt to establish community with others:

> Have we not all one father? Has not one God created us? Why then are we faithless to one another, profaning the covenant of our fathers?[31]

Those who observe the covenant benefit by gaining eternal confidence in the possibility of a just world. Jews bind themselves to act as though all persons, including strangers who may not know of the covenant, are beloved of God and have a place in the human community. To refuse help to those on the edge of communal life (the poor, the sick, the despised transgressor) or to enslave a person is to fail to have a God: "When you are not My witnesses, I am not God."[32] God and His covenant are what they are when humans treat one another well. When men and women freely embrace this duty to love one another, they create and then live peacefully in a just world in which each person's dignity is respected.

In Judaic thought, no person can be treated as a means to an end, not even for the sake of some apparently good cause. To love a person is to respect that person or, equivalently, to treat him justly. As we saw in the previous section, justice does not simply mean not interfering with people's attempts to realize their own purposes.[33] Acting justly also requires taking positive steps to ensure that the environment is such that people's own will can be active.[34] Providing attorneys who are bound to present the client's case is one such positive step. The pious Jew is similarly bound to perform actions which help people to act upon their own purposes. For example, the pious are obliged to say prayers for the dead. Like the community's insistence upon redress for murder victims, this practice grants the dead a victory over the oblivion of death. Equally importantly, it functions to ensure that all persons for all time receive a share of respect. In this way, the practices of the pious bring into being an inheritably just world. These acts also comfort the pious by giving them a reason to hope for eternal peace for the past and present inhabitants of the world they are participating in creating.

There is a third way in which the pious person's righteousness benefits her by bestowing an enduring confidence. People do not totally control what they undergo or suffer. But humans can strive for justice. Those who do so need never fear that they will lose their place on earth. God's chosen people are partners working with God to realize His vision of a world peopled by just men and women. By living a life in accordance with divine revelation, the individual Jew benefits himself by creating a world in which all peoples have a place. The pious person believes that God wills such a world.[35] This faith invites and challenges the Jew to fight for the ideal. Actions undertaken on its behalf deepen the faith, turning the believer back to God again and again. This returning – the *teshuvah* – is the renewal of spirit God promised to all those who act as children of God. Invigorated, the believer turns back to the world, struggling to live the good life and to realize God's just vision.

Since private and public goods are interwoven in Judaism, the rabbi who adheres to her promise to teach and interpret the Torah benefits the individual and community alike through this teaching. By teaching the Torah to God's chosen people, the rabbi makes it possible for God to illustrate what God wants from all men and women through the example of the Jews. By perpetuating the inherited revelation, the rabbi also makes it possible for God to bestow His blessing of a just world in which all persons are respected. In Judaism, life as the chosen people is not the means to some other good; it is the good God covenanted to bestow upon anyone who believes in His word.

Living in accordance with God's will is good in itself on two scores. First, the righteous, peaceful life is a just life and, as we saw in the prior section, justice is desirable in its own right. Second, since life too is desirable for its own sake, the Jewish life must be judged intrinsically good because it is the source of

future life. The rabbi Leo Baeck expresses this second dimension
of Jewish salvation simply and beautifully:

> No people is heir to such a revelation as the Jews possess; no
> people has had such a weight of divine commandment laid
> upon it; and for this reason no people has been so exposed to
> difficult and exacting times. This inheritance has not always
> been realized, but it is one that will endure, awaiting its hour.
> Judah ha-Levi, who saw into the soul of the Jewish people and
> the Jewish religion as few men have, meant just this when he
> said that the prophecy is alive in this people and that for this
> reason this people will live.[36]

As long as the rabbi honors the revelation to which the Jews
are heir, he serves a genuine human good and maintains legitimacy in the eyes of others. He forfeits authority if he deviates
from his inheritance, advocating racial assaults, murder, or other
unjust actions. A hate-mongering rabbi might very well attract a
following and possess the power to manipulate their opinions. But
he would not have legitimate, professional authority. In Biblical
language, the rabbi would be a "false prophet." The fact that this
category both exists and is employed by Jews to dismiss the
teachings of persons who have trampled upon the inheritance
tends to prove the point: salvation does have a core meaning or
an essence and honoring this essence is the source of authority.
Only actions in the service of salvation properly understood are
deemed trustworthy by potential and actual clients.

Christianity

Like Judaism, Christianity promises triumph over death. What
do Christians mean by "death"? The definition offered by theologian Paul Tillich may be the best: Death is "the loss of the
inner *telos* of one's being."[37] Tillich's description leaves open what
human beings' end or *telos* is. This openness is entirely appropriate since the Christian church itself has interpreted salvation in
various ways over the years:

> [F]or the early Greek church death and error were the things
> from which one needed and wanted to be saved. In the Roman
> Catholic church salvation is from guilt and its consequences in
> this and the next life. . . . In Classical Protestantism salvation

is from the law, its anxiety-producing and its condemning power. In pietism and revivalism salvation is the conquest of special sins and progress towards moral perfection.[38]

Different as these interpretations have been, one still discerns a common thread running through them. As Tillich notes, all of these views hold out some hope for a restoration of purpose and the achievement of some sort of new wholeness and balance "between God and man, man and his world, and man and himself."[39] This return of purpose constitutes a triumph over death. Belief in God restores to man the ability to function even in the face of worldly forces which work against a person's purposes.

Finding this spiritual equilibrium is akin to the sick woman's discovering of a new bodily equilibrium. While the distinction should not be pressed too far, one might say that Judaism promises a just order, Christianity a healing order. In fact, the word "salvation" comes from the Latin word "salvus" meaning "to heal."[40] Anyone who would be healed must, like Jesus, be willing to rethink the whole of life and the world: "We understand life and death only through Jesus Christ. Outside Jesus Christ we do not know what life is, nor death, nor God, nor ourselves."[41] Comprehending life and death through Jesus means acknowledging the radical contingency of one's own existence and confronting the despair that accompanies this realization. To restore the world's foundation one would need the power to make things as one willed. But earthly power is itself an illusion. The high are brought low. To feel sheltered and secure is to be far from salvation. In Jesus' words, "[I]t is easier for a camel to go through the eye of a needle than for a rich man to enter the kingdom of God."[42]

Those who lack power are closest to being healed, for they know the contingency of the world. To be powerless is to be subject to great suffering at the hands of others. The powerless can hardly hope to hope. Yet it is for persons such as these that Jesus' life has meaning. "Those who are well have no need of a physician, but those who are sick."[43] Through suffering salvation is somehow possible. But how? Human beings cannot save themselves. They may try to do so through suicide. While suicide ends temporal suffering, it does not solve the problem of despair, the loss of purpose that is death. For suicide gives no ground for hope.

Nor can one hasten the arrival of God's kingdom on earth through martyrdom. Jesus did not advocate martyrdom for the sake of the world. Instead, he lived his life without regard for the consequences for the world. One should watch for signs of heaven but the kingdom will come only when God wills it.[44] Suffering does not redeem the world. Still less can humans hope to save themselves through self-abnegation. The death of the self Buddhism holds out does not give meaning to suffering. Instead, it denies the reality of suffering and of the self.

So how does the believer find her life through losing it? Jesus' death on the cross reveals the possibility of transcending death through "the silent, all-embracing genius of consent."[45] The death on the cross reveals the ultimate contingency of the world. Facing a painful death alone and feeling lost, Jesus has no power to reverse his fate. God could help. Yet God seems far away. Though Jesus cries out, "My God, my God, why hast thou forsaken me?" God remains silent.[46] Jesus then too falls mute. Like the psalmist who spoke these words before him, Jesus has no power to compel God to speak. However, like the singer of the psalm, he can freely place absolute trust in God's will: "Yet thou art holy.... In thee our fathers trusted."[47] Everything he has experienced up to, and including, this death in some way serves God's purpose: "[Nevertheless] not my will, but thine, be done."[48] From this act of trusting belief comes a quietude, a peace, and the reclamation of one's *telos*. Jesus dies trusting in the ultimate rightness of his death on the cross: "Father, into thy hands I commit my spirit!"[49] Although man does not control whether he suffers, he can choose what to believe.[50] Believing in God means seeing oneself as a being who stands in relation to a Being beyond finitude and contingency. This Being, not the world, is the ultimate judge of the goodness of our actions, including how we choose to die. So we should not let the world tell us what our death means. Dietrich Bonhoeffer's writings capture something of the spirit of this saving belief: "It is we ourselves, and not outward circumstances, who make death what it can be, a death freely and voluntarily accepted."[51]

The saved person is free to write her own history, even when dying at the hands of others. This blessing quite obviously cannot be merely an instrumental good in the eyes of the individual. Applying as it does to the moment of death, it is not desirable because of some benefit it brings one later in life. Nor is salvation good because it serves some national or public purpose. The reclamation of one's life and death as one's own, like health and legal justice and Judaic salvation, is a good desired in its own right. Everyone has purposes. Life is, recall, striving to realize one's purposes. Christianity promotes the good of human beings because it allows them to act upon their own purposes, especially when external forces are trying to co-opt or supplant these purposes and when the opportunities for voluntary action are at a minimum. One does not need to embrace the Christian ethic as a complete theory of good or right action in order to see that it, like Stoicism, does have the merit of making ethical action possible in those cases of extreme distress more or less neglected by other ethics.[52]

As interpreters of the recorded life of Jesus, Christian clerics promote the reclamation of purpose by exhibiting its desirability in their own life. Martyrdom need not be sought after because every moment of life is an opportunity to be a witness or martyr (the Greek word for witness is *martus* from which we derive the word "martyr"[53]) to the contingency of the world and the glad news of salvation. By word and action, the cleric strives to show persons that they may either seek after worldly power or embrace the way of the cross, choosing to freely accept one's suffering in a world in which one has little power. As long as the clergy stay within this role, their authority is legitimated by the goodness of the salvation toward which they help their listeners.

It might be objected that the role of witness falls to anyone who believes in the way of the cross. Christianity acknowledges the truth of this rejoinder. The Christian church has at various times pushed for understanding all members of the church as "clergy."[54] Clergy and laity exist along a continuum, possessing different degrees of knowledge of the church's written inheritance (in Greek, *klerikos*) but standing in the same sinful relation to God, others, and themselves. It would be a mistake to see the professed cleric's activity as radically different from the actions of the laity. Having decided to devote his entire life to understanding the meaning of Jesus' life, the cleric is more versed than his audience in the words of Scripture and in the possible ways in which that message applies to the human situation. But he has no privileged access to esoteric knowledge necessary for salvation. To suggest as much is perhaps the surest way for the Christian cleric to lose professional authority in the eyes of congregants.[55]

Conclusion

Professionals exercise authority if (and as long as) their actions promote a particular human good desired for its own sake by persons before and on behalf of whom the professional has promised to serve this particular good. The pledge would not ground authority if the promised good were actually an evil. However, the goods of the learned professions are legitimating because they are genuine goods. Furthermore, health, justice, and salvation are goods in themselves. People need not desire some more ultimate good in order to want to be healed, to find spiritual peace or to receive their fair share.

A cautionary note, though, is in order. The claim that these goods are desirable in themselves might be read as meaning that their pursuit is justified under all circumstances. Interpreted in this way, what is *a* good in itself becomes *the* good. The physician, for example, appears justified in concluding that, since disease is bad and since the patient who has come before her obviously wishes to be rid of this evil, she may legitimately do whatever conduces to the patient's health. Yet this inference is unsound. One can easily imagine a sick attorney who is unwilling to consider any therapy which involved a hospital stay and thus interfered with this patient's ability to represent a client in an important civil rights lawsuit. Since justice, like health, has been shown to be a client good desirable for its own sake, we cannot conclude that the patient's desire is unreasonable or ill-formed. Clients will have good reason for objecting if professionals override the client's desires on the ground that the professional knows what action is best under the circumstances.

This caveat brings us to the second and third objections raised at the very beginning of this chapter: does the professional's pledge itself in some way limit the helper's discretion, preventing the professional from elevating the good pursued into *the* good? Or must we posit a "meta-ethic" which regulates the manner in which professionals promote the particular good of their professions? Furthermore, what role, if any, does an institutional framework play in establishing or maintaining limited professional authority? To answer these questions we must consider the professional's pledge-based ethic in greater detail.

Chapter 6

The limits of professional discretion

We have discovered that health, legal justice, and salvation are ends desired for their own sake rather than as means to some other end. We have learned as well that, although the attainment of these ends does promote the welfare of the community as a whole, the ends are primarily goods of the individual. As long as professionals serve these genuine goods of the individual client, they are worthy of client trust. Moreover, they merit the trust of the larger human community because the ends they serve are intrinsically desirable. That is to say, these goods are not desired simply by actual clients but potentially by any human being. However, care must be taken at this point to specify to what extent a client such as a penitent has authorized his minister to exercise discretion in furthering the client's salvation. Trusting someone does not entail giving this party *carte blanche* to do just anything on the trustor's behalf. To take an example from Annette Baier's analysis of trust: when I hire a babysitter, I expect the babysitter to feed, bathe, and clothe my child. I do not expect, however, that the babysitter will repaint the child's bedroom yellow, even if yellow has been shown by studies to lift children's spirits.[1] Trust imposes limits the trustee must respect if trust is to continue to exist.

These limits are what make betrayal of trust possible. A dog may rely upon its master to feed it and walk it. But the dog does not and cannot trust its master because the dog has not imposed any limits on what it expects the master to do on its behalf. Similarly, a newborn infant does not trust its mother, although it is dependent upon her for nourishment. Children begin to trust their parents at the point at which they can establish some limits the parents should respect, limits born of the child's developing sense of himself as a self-directed being with his own attachments and ends. If parents were to get rid of a dog they had given to their week-old infant, they would not harm the infant nor would they betray its trust. But if the puppy were a gift to a ten-year-old who had longed for it, the act would be a betrayal of trust because the child's well-functioning as an organism capable of directing his own life is bound up with the pet he chose for himself. The child implicitly grants the parent access to the dog with the understanding that the parent's actions with respect to the animal will honor the child's love for it and the part the animal plays in the child's unfolding history. If the parent disposes of the dog with no regard for the child's feelings and unfolding history, or worse yet, with the intention of undermining the child's self-development, then trust is violated.

Trust, then, requires the trusted party to care for the trustor's end in a manner consistent with viewing the trusted as an active agent with at least some rudimentary ability to discover and organize his own way of life. If we are to ground professional ethics successfully, we must consider whether the grounding pledge imposes any limits on what the professional may do on behalf of the client and whether these limits are such as to instill trust. That is, does a pledge ethic itself impose limits which respect clients as active, self-directed, self-realizing agents; or must professional ethics appeal to some outside ethic, such as a Kantian ethic of respect for persons, in order to establish the limits human trust presupposes? And, if the pledge does impose limits, what role if any is played by institutional mechanisms for enforcing the limits (e.g. disciplinary boards)?

PART ONE: LIMITS TO PROFESSIONAL PROMOTION OF THE CLIENT'S END

The first question regarding the source and presence of limits on what the professional may do on the client's behalf is both an easy and a hard one to answer. Insofar as the professional pledges to promote a *particular* good, the pledge obviously restricts what the professional is entitled to do on the client's behalf. To say the good is particular is merely to say the good is only one among many desirable ends human beings choose to pursue. Although health, justice, and salvation are desirable in themselves, professionals are bound, like the rest of us, to recognize that under various circumstances we choose one over the other. Heroes and human rights activists have sacrificed their lives and health in the quest for justice and salvation. Some believers make it a tenet of their faith to forgo legal justice in the spirit of saving mercy. The sense of competing goods is common to all of us. While I would not claim that choice presupposes competing alternatives, I would insist that to speak of *particular* goods is to tacitly acknowledge the existence of at least one other good that reasonable people may choose in preference to another good.

To put the point slightly differently: assessing the relative desirability of competing goods goes on throughout life. It certainly does not stop the moment a client crosses the threshold of a professional's office. The professional has technical knowledge and clearly brings this knowledge to the relation. Thus, a physician legitimately may infer that the sick man who has come to her desires that she use her technical knowledge to promote health. Health is, after all, the particular good the doctor has both promised and been educated to serve. What the physician cannot justifiably conclude is that the patient desires above all else to be cured. This conclusion is not warranted because the client, too, has knowledge:

> The client [has] superiority in "knowledge" concerning the comparative value and disvalue, to him at least, of certain crucial elements in the problematic situation, e.g., how much risk or disability it is worth to eliminate the present pain or the threat of death, or when the side effects of specific treatments cancel the value of the relief possibly to be gained through that treatment.[2]

If the surgery the doctor recommends turns out to entail that the patient postpone his fight for civil rights, the patient may very well choose not to be healed on those terms. Professional doctors honor the patient's refusal of treatment because their pledge to serve the particular good of health only entitles them to work to return the sick to a well-functioning, organic state, not to decide that the sick should cease to struggle for civil rights.

In other words, professionals have authority because they do not presume to know better than clients which goods matter most to the particular client at hand. This view can be usefully contrasted with that of professional authority advanced by philosopher Alasdair MacIntyre. MacIntyre argues that for professions to flourish, community members must attain a shared vision of the relative importance of various goods.[3] I am arguing that the professions possess authority precisely because they do not presuppose community-wide consensus on some absolute ranking of the goodness of bodily health as opposed to legal justice. I doubt any such consensus has ever existed, and I have no reason to think such a ranking is possible. Nevertheless, professionals *do* have authority and have flourished. They have been trusted because they have not drawn the unwarranted inference that, because a patient desires health, she desires health above any and all other goods.

So, from the particularity of their covenanted good, professionals derive one regulative principle or limit: their practice should never elevate the limited good they serve into the final human good. This principle applies to every profession with its particular end and acts as a limit on professional discretion. Since the limit acknowledges clients as action-originating human beings trying to order competing goods in such a way as to realize an organized or whole way of life for themselves, the limit is of the sort trust requires and therefore serves to legitimate professional practice.

I call this answer to the question of limits the "easy" one because it is relatively uncontroversial. All of the learned professions grant clients the ultimate privilege of refusing help. Congregants need not take communion, participate in certain rituals, or even remain a member of the minister's church.[4] Clients may fire their attorneys; patients are entitled to refuse treatment. The more difficult issue regarding limits turns on the question of what professions may positively do on the client's behalf while still preserving legitimacy. Here we need a different sort of limit, one which sets bounds on what professionals may do in an ongoing relation with clients. If the pledge provides a limit of this sort, it does so not by virtue of the singleness of its end but because of the character or content of the end pursued. To determine whether the content of the ends regulates professional discretion, we must reconsider in some detail what these ends are.

Health

Given the nature of health, the doctor cannot bestow health upon clients but must work with them to maintain or restore their health. Considered structurally, health is a wholeness of organism maintained by that organism through differentiation and self-healing. The physician assists the patient's innate organic tendencies towards self-healing but he does not cause a person to act organically. When the physician is most interventionist (e.g. when doing surgery), he still relies heavily upon the self-organizing body to make good use of what he has done. The doctor can amputate a person's leg in an effort to save the patient's life. But the amputation will not help someone whose blood will not clot or whose body will not produce scar tissue.

Intervention proves similarly fruitless if the patient lacks appropriate habits. Wiring a patient's mouth shut may cause a short-term weight loss. But if poor eating habits are not changed, in the long run these habits will result in impaired functioning. True, the doctor can help inform the patient's appetites. Indeed, the word "doctor" comes from the Latin word for "teacher."[5] But no teacher grants learning or habits to another. Conceiving of health as a "well-habitedness" of the individual, we are driven to see physicians as beings who assist patients to help themselves, not as givers of health.

Finally, if we think of health as an achieved equilibrium between bodily limitations and human purposes, healing must involve the patient's will and desires because the balance aimed at is inherently subjective. I may not wish to have my back pain relieved if treating the pain leaves me perpetually drowsy and unable to teach or write. The doctor may help me find a way to manage the pain, but the purposes that my hurting body constrains are *my* chosen purposes, nobody else's. Therefore, no equilibrium can be achieved without involving me in the discussion of pain management. More generally, when the recommended treatment affects the patient's ability to establish priorities among the goods in his or her life and to realize the preferred and chosen course of action, then the therapeutic decision is not merely tactical but is one in which the client must be involved.

In fact, doctor and patient must consult with each other because for the most part health cannot be promoted unless the doctor learns about health by interacting with the patient. A person with a severed spinal cord must discover what will be possible in his new life as a paraplegic. The doctor treating such an individual must discover through therapy what she wants for that patient with that condition. If all the doctor wants is to see the patient walk again, then the physician's own balance becomes doubtful. The physician who cannot see beyond her own inability to return the patient to full mobility will fail to comprehend what she can do for the patient. The paraplegic who wants to be as healthy as he can be and to get out of the hospital soon certainly would have little reason to expect help from a non-consultative physician.

When seen in light of its three core components, health clearly requires that the physician's thinking take its principles in part from patient priorities uncovered as part of therapy. The professing physician does not reason: "My patient Mr Jones wants to be cured above all other things. He suffers from gangrene in his leg. When the disease has advanced to this stage, the best way to stop its spread and to prevent further harm to Jones is to amputate the limb. Therefore, I will operate on Mr Jones." While some have asserted that this technical reasoning (i.e. "given this end, this means to the end is justified, and you, the patient, must follow my orders") characterizes the "traditional" physician, such a view (assuming it ever existed as a dominant one, which I doubt[6]) is not consistent with the nature of healing.

However, it does not follow that, just because professing doctors work with the sick and take care not to substitute their will for the client's during therapy, they are therefore obliged to honor every client whim. Trust is a two-way street in the professional–client interaction. As we saw in Chapter 4, professionals are also present in the relation as vulnerable beings who are trying to realize and pass on a way of life. As helpers, they trust the client to co-operate in a way which will further the end they have devoted their lives to promoting. The professional therefore need only will what the client wills *as client*. This tension inherent in trust can be clearly seen if one considers what, if anything, the doctor is bound to tell patients about their condition and their chances of recovery. On the one hand, the pledge binds the physician to err on the side of telling the patient too much. When the individual does not understand his own body because the physician has either refused to interpret the body's responses or has lied to the patient about his condition, healing will not occur. Pledging physicians truthfully share information with their patients not because the sick have a "right to know" certain things about their body or a "right to be autonomous," but because healing is difficult, if not impossible, without such sharing.[7] And where no healing is possible, the doctor cannot claim to benefit the sick.

On the other hand, speaking the truth may cause suffering. For the patient, learning that his condition is worsening, incurable, or fatal may prove terribly upsetting. Nevertheless, since the physician does not know precisely how the individual understands pain, suffering, or death, any assumption that the news *will* upset the patient is unjustified. Moreover, we all live under a death sentence. Being healthy does not mean avoiding death; it means living well. A decision not to share medical information because revelation of human finitude upsets the patient casts the physician in the role of rubber-stamping patients' illusions. Health care providers are not bound to waste their time performing non-therapeutic procedures. Psychiatrists know that sometimes the patient needs to be confronted with his or her illusions in order to become healthy. Nurses insist that they cannot effectively help a patient with rehabilitation if the patient does not understand what is wrong with him. Given that communicating the diagnosis and prognosis is a functional requirement for healing to occur, medicine need recognize no patient "right to know nothing."[8] Instead of respecting patients, physician lying or hiding of unpleasant news makes it impossible for patients to achieve the balance which motivated them to seek the doctor's help in the first place.[9]

Note that willing what the client wills as a client is consistent with allowing a patient to choose death. A mother giving birth may be faced with the unenviable prospect of having to choose between her own life and the child's. We think the choice heart-rending but do not view the mother who sacrifices her own life as a moral deviant. We simply say the mother has opted to conduct her life with a view to bringing new life into the world despite the heavy cost to herself. Her action in this case conforms to a way of life we recognize as motherhood, a role which often requires sacrifices for the sake of the child. The physician who works with the mother to maximize the chances for the child's survival serves the mother's health, construed as her self-initiated active unfolding of her whole career or way of life. Such mediating activity accords perfectly with the medical pledge. It also seems consistent with our moral intuitions in the matter: if we would condemn anything in such a case, it would probably be a decision by the obstetrician to overrule the woman's expressed choice and to sacrifice the child in order to save the woman's life.[10]

There are, of course, cases in which the patient cannot collaborate with the physician to restore health. How does the professional will what the client wills as client in such cases? We must distinguish two kinds of situation. In the first, the doctor must make a treatment decision for a patient who cannot retrieve control over his life. The patient is never going to achieve an equilibrium because there is no longer an organizing self aiming at finding a new balance in life. In such cases, there is no health to serve. Under the pledge ethic, the doctor withdraws. He refuses to revive drowning victims who have been submerged for long periods of time and who, experience shows, will not recover the ability to lead a self-directed life; to provide antibiotics to those who are in the last stages of death; or to operate on babies born without a brain.[11]

In the second situation, the patient may be temporarily unable to communicate her wishes but with the physician's help will probably be able to articulate and act upon her own purposes. For example, a suicide victim may be comatose but may be restored to life with the doctor's help. Is such intervention warranted? Let us begin by noting that even those ethicists who oppose "paternalistic" intervention end up advocating it in a case such as this. For example, the philosopher Alan Goldman rails against physicians willing the good of their patients but he begrudgingly allows emergency room physicians to try to revive patients.[12] The philosopher Gerald Dworkin also wants to insist that an act by one party on behalf of another is legitimate only if the affected party has consented in an informed manner to receiving the help in question; yet Dworkin, too, allows for the possibility of emergency assistance.[13] The intervention cannot be warranted on the ground that the patient has given informed consent to receiving the help. The patient is assumed to be incapacitated. As such, he is unable to speak or write or to hear and interpret information. Nor can we assume, as Dworkin does, that the person necessarily desires the benefit in question – restored health.[14] A would-be suicide victim may really want to destroy her health. To cope with such a case the autonomy-defending theorist is forced in the direction of arguing that self-destructive desires are unreal. This argument, though, makes these theorists difficult to distinguish from the paternalist they attack for assuming to know better than the client what the client's "real" desires are.

The pledge-based ethic can handle the emergency case far more cleanly. The case resolves itself along the following lines: the incapacitated yet healable patient is before the doctor. The patient has come into the physician's presence on the strength of the pledge to act for the benefit of the sick. If the ambulance attendant or family members had not assumed such a pledge, the victim would be in a courtroom, restaurant or some place other than the hospital. The patient's presence thus invokes the covenant. Furthermore, the end the covenant binds the physician to serve is a genuine human good, although not the best of all human goods. The physician should act therefore to fulfill the terms of the invoked pledge, while taking care when promoting health not to foreclose the patient's options to order his own life.

Taking such care normally requires consulting with the patient. In this case, however, the physician cannot so consult. Nor can he assume that the patient wants to be healed. The patient may very well really have wanted to succeed at committing suicide. On the other hand, the healer does not know that the patient does not want to be healed. The "suicide" victim may be the victim of a relative's botched murder attempt or of a house intruder's assault. What the physician does know is that, since health is a genuine human good, promoting health when the covenant has been invoked (as it has in this case) is an action consistent with public trust. If it should turn out that the patient does want to die, the option of killing himself has not been foreclosed. The patient can still do so after he is discharged, trying harder this time to succeed at suicide.

We conclude, therefore, that while covenanting physicians do not roam the streets in search of incompetent persons to heal or would-be suicide victims to revive, they are bound to try to heal those critically ill, inarticulate persons who are in their presence and whose health seems restorable. Not to do so would be a violation of the physician's public pledge to try to benefit the sick and would undermine medical authority.

Justice

As we saw in the preceding chapter, the concept of justice entails treating persons as equal in personhood. While justice has a formal dimension, captured in the precept "Treat equals as equals," justice is not merely formal. Only when we think of justice as the recognition of the claim all people have *as self-directed organisms* to have their own story told and heard in the public forum, where benefits and burdens are meted out, do we get close to what makes justice good in our eyes. While we could have treated all persons equally by denying everyone access to the courts, we would not consider this arrangement just because people would not have the opportunity to initiate their own actions and to recount their own stories. Legal justice consists in providing this opportunity.

Though legal justice so conceived is intrinsically desirable, I must once again emphasize that a decision not to use the courts to initiate an action against another, like an agent's desire to refuse life-saving therapy, cannot be overridden on the ground that it is irrational. For example, I might not prosecute a friend for theft out of the belief that doing so would tie up my energies. My suit would effectively allow my former friend, who has already taken my property, also to usurp my freedom to order my day as I see fit. My decision not to avail myself of legal justice but simply to break off the friendship would not be the act of a madwoman but of a human being who is fully aware of herself as a free, self-directed being who has chosen the goodness of, say, writing a book over the good of legal justice. This kind of reasoned choice between competing goods is not unreasonable but is part and parcel of what it means to act deliberately.

The legal pledge ethic respects these personal deliberations. Nothing in the legal pledge entitles attorneys to press fellow citizens to sue one another and to function indirectly as instigators of actions at law. Cases coming before the court should originate with the plaintiff. If the client has not originated the action, the court has good reason to suspect that the case is not the client's own; and the client has cause to worry that the attorney just wants to make some money litigating. It is worth remembering in this context that the Bar arose in England as part of an effort to rein in those attorneys who were frequenting local fairs and creating discord by urging people to lodge legal complaints against one another.

I stress this point because it bears so directly and mightily upon the question of limits upon attorney discretion. On this point, the pledge-based legal ethic accords perfectly with the Anglo-

American tradition of requiring that a litigant's case be that party's case. The tradition does not permit an attorney to initiate a case on behalf of the litigant because to do so calls into question whose case is being pursued. Class action suits constitute an exception to this rule and are worrying as a consequence. We now see interest group attorneys pursuing lawsuits on behalf of sane, reasonable people who do not even know they are party to a lawsuit and who might not want to be such.[15] Under such conditions, it is ludicrous to pretend that the litigant has empowered the attorney to be his or her advocate in court or that the attorney's action respects the person of the non-consenting litigant. A pledge ethic would frown upon attorney involvement in class action lawsuits unless the attorney can show that the parties to the suit have been given ample opportunity to arrive at a reasoned decision as to whether to opt out of the case.[16]

The court tries to guard against attorneys substituting their will for that of clients by permitting only lawyers with so-called "standing" to appear before it.[17] In both the US and UK, counsel has standing if and only if it appears in the person of the client. For the case to be the client's, the client's person must be in the courtroom. In fact,

> [o]riginally, all litigants were required to appear in court personally (*in propria persona*) – no lawyers. . . . A survival of the old *no right to counsel* is the practice in small claims courts, where lawyers are banned; and unlike the usual rule requiring corporations to appear by attorney, even corporations must represent themselves.[18]

In criminal trials, where the very ability of the client to act as a free agent is always at stake, the court both permits and encourages the client to appear in the person of an educated lawyer. When the stakes are lower (as they are in small claims court), the client must appear in his own person because this arrangement best ensures that it is the client's case, and no one else's, being presented in court.

The professional ethic of attorneys derives and should derive from these underlying notions of legal justice and standing. For example, even if the attorney thinks the client should not alter a plea, plea bargains offered by the prosecution ought to be passed on by defense counsel to clients.[19] My defense attorney should not say to me, "You told me you were innocent and innocent you must plead." As a client, I remain free to tell my story as I see fit, changing it or remaining silent if I so choose. People's perception of their own guilt or innocence does change.[20] Furthermore, people's judgment of which risks are worth running alters as they get more information about their situation. One can easily imagine, for example, that an innocent black or Hispanic individual accused of resisting police arrest might desire upon reflection to change his plea after learning that an all-white middle-class suburban jury has been selected to hear his case. Plea bargaining for a reduced prison term might very well be the best option for this person in such circumstances.

Similarly, although attorneys may negotiate settlements on behalf of their clients, the pledge ethic authorizes them to do so only when the client in question has approved the settlement or when there are very strong, documentable grounds for inferring the client's consent to the terms of the arrangement arrived at by the attorney.[21] The client initiated the action out of some sense of being wronged. It remains up to the client to decide when and whether to give up the chance to present his story to the court. The larger public may favor or oppose settlement. The attorney, too, may have an opinion as to the wisdom of settling. As long as the case has legal merit, these other parties' opinions are irrelevant and ought not to enter into the attorney's deliberations concerning how best to obtain legal justice for the client.

In all of these cases, the lawyer serves as an adviser. In fact, the term "counsel" originally meant, and continues to mean, "adviser." When the court provides a defendant with "stand-by counsel," it hearkens back to the early usage of the term.[22] A litigant has a right to counsel insofar as the government cannot prevent him from seeking the advice of a lawyer of his choice.[23] The right is also understood as including the privilege of dismissing counsel. The existence of this privilege is the client's insurance that his lawyer will not develop a case that does not coincide with the litigant's view of events.

This principle of appearing in the person of the client commits the pledging attorney to a good faith effort to represent the client's position. Denying an attorney the opportunity to consult with the client before presenting a case may violate the client's right to counsel.[24] If counsel behaves as though the client is guilty, despite having entered a plea of not guilty, the defendant may have grounds for a mistrial.[25] And when counsel advises a client in the writing of a will, the wishes or "will" expressed in that will must be the client's. Under the pledge ethic, the court rightly looks with suspicion upon a will drawn up by a lawyer who stands to gain by its terms.[26]

Listening to and respecting the will of the client is not some second-order good that needs to be grafted onto the lawyer's professional ethic. Respecting the client's will is built right into the procedures, structures, and laws of the entire legal system. As long as the lawyer adheres to her pledge to serve the particular good (legal justice) of the client, she will of necessity show great sensitivity to the plight and wishes of the client she represents. The client's will may sometimes seem unreasonable. For example, the lawyer may think it imprudent for a client to leave all of his worldly goods to a charity and nothing to his own children. Counsel may express some doubts as to the wisdom of this course of action. But he will let it stand. Respect for the client as action-originating agent – the principle underlying the administration of justice – means letting the client act upon his own understanding of the world. These purposes may seem strange but the client probably knows his own family better than the lawyer does. Perhaps the children have verbally assented to the arrangement. Or maybe the father correctly assesses that his children will be better off in the long run if they are cut out of the will and forced to make their way in the world using their own wits. Even if the client's will seems misguided, respecting his person means, in part, letting him make his own mistakes and live with the consequences of doing so.[27] No doubt lawyers have misgivings about many wills, but, then again, attorneys will also sometimes wonder about the wisdom of pleading someone innocent when the facts of the case seem to shout the person's guilt. Under such circumstances, the client may get a tougher penalty by pleading not guilty and then being convicted than if he had just pleaded guilty from the beginning. Yet we let the client run this risk. Not to do so would be to deny him legal justice.

Honoring the client's will does not mean that counsel is passive in the relation. Like the pledging physician, the professing lawyer comes into the relation with training which enables her to tell the client certain things. Most clients do not know what to expect in a courtroom. Learned counsel informs the client's expectations of how he will be treated, what risks he will run, and the nature of the legal justice he should expect to receive from the court. However, like professional physicians, professional attorneys discover what they want for their clients through talking with the client. A divorce attorney might desire to see a protracted, bitter fight over assets. Yet his married client, desiring an amicable divorce, may be perfectly willing to split the property in half. It is up to the attorney to imaginatively enter into the spirit of amiable negotiation and to see that the client receives half of the property. If counsel is unable to present the wishes of the client convincingly but insists upon substituting his preferences or pursuing his own pet cause, he has no business being an attorney in the first place.[28] He does not understand the end of legal justice, the end which gives him standing in the eyes of the court and legitimacy in the eyes of the client.

Having ascertained the client's will, the attorney aggressively develops the best case for his client. If the client does not want to take the stand, counsel does not give the opposing side the opportunity to cross-examine by forcing the client to testify. Nor need counsel help the other side build its opposing case by handing over notes, interview results, or other work product.[29] As a general rule, each side must develop its own case and cannot require opposing counsel to do its legwork for it.[30] This responsibility flows directly from the lawyer's pledge to serve legal justice. It simply is the lawyer's responsibility to see that the client's case gets heard in court or in out-of-court settlement proceedings. An attorney who sits back and expects counsel for the other side to produce a strong case for her client has neglected her profession.

The attorney is not bound, however, to do any and all things which the client may want. In general, the legal pledge obliges an attorney to act in a fashion which gives clients access to the court, where access is understood as getting one's own case presented with a view to having the law applied to this case and a verdict rendered. Thus, attorneys must disclose adverse precedents because such disclosure helps ensure that the court will apply what is in fact the law to the case at hand. Since both sides are trying to obtain legal justice for their client, counsel's actions must be consistent with providing access for both sides' clients. To couch the point slightly differently: having one's day in court means have one's position represented in a forum which allows all parties to a dispute to have their positions heard before an authority which applies the law relevant to the dispute. Thus the pledge ethic will proscribe steps such as undertaking legal actions aimed solely at harassment or delay; advancing a claim not supportable by any good faith argument; engaging in illegal or fraudulent conduct; failing to disclose an adverse precedent when opposing counsel neglects to do so; inflicting needless harm; degrading a witness by posing irrelevant questions; or threatening criminal action in order to obtain an advantage in a civil matter.[31]

All of these actions are prohibited not because they happen to be illegal but because, if performed, they would undermine legal justice by diminishing or restricting parties' access to the court. Access may be inhibited by preventing an opponent's arguments from receiving a hearing (e.g. lawyer employs delaying or harassing tactics; lawyer intimidates or overwhelms the opposing side's witnesses with irrelevant questions). Pressing frivolous claims wastes valuable court time, thereby delaying the hearings other claims deserve; while threatening lawsuits simply to gain advantage implies that the court system functions not as a mechanism for adjudicating between competing claims but as a means for coercing people into abandoning their claims. Lying or manufacturing evidence (or switching or altering it) violates the legal ethic because inventing a new case is no different from confusing two cases and presenting evidence from the prosecution of IBM when one is supposed to be prosecuting Xerox. In both cases, the attorney acts unjustly by presenting a story which is not the client's as though it were such. No doubt many litigants will find misrepresentation attractive because it will permit them to avoid the consequences of their actions or enable them to manipulate the legal system into incarcerating an innocent party. But the fact remains that what is presented is not the client's case but a case the attorney invented. Here, as in all the other examples, the forbidden act is prohibited because the act in some way impedes clients' ability to come before the court and to present their story with a view to having the law applied to their case. The professional attorney is not obliged by the legal pledge to perform any such unjust acts, irrespective of whether the client happens to desire the attorney to do so.

As in the case of medicine, the lawyer acts upon the client's will but only insofar as that will represents a desire for legal justice. And as with medicine, the lawyer's life is complicated when the client cannot or will not converse reasonably with the lawyer. These sorts of case are difficult, but one of the merits of the pledge-based ethic is that, unlike the contract-based ethic, it does provide the lawyer with a guiding end. For example, if the client is insane, the lawyer can try to get the client medical help with the hope that the client will one day be able to make his case and have his day in court. The attorney's intervention respects the person of the client because it aims at seeing legal justice done in the long run. In the short run, it does not deprive the client of any options he should have as a client. The client may be confined to a hospital, thereby losing the option of roaming the streets. But, having been declared unfit for trial, the client need admit neither guilt nor innocence. The client's ability to tell his or her story is not hampered.

If the client is not obviously incompetent but simply refuses to speak with the lawyer or to take up his own defense before the court, then the lawyer can tell the court as much. Having described the situation, counsel should not say more. The court can and should test the claim by asking the defendant what he pleads. If the client still will not speak, or talks incoherently, then the lawyer has no standing because he cannot represent the will (i.e. person) of the client. Continuing silence on the lawyer's part is entirely appropriate. For justice to be done, the judge must rule on how the client's silence or rantings should be interpreted and on whether the lawyer has any further role to play in the courtroom. This silence might seem unjust or unresponsive. In reality, it simply highlights the legal profession's ethically proper dependence upon the expression of the client's will. Presuming to speak for the client, not keeping silence, would make the professional untrustworthy.

Salvation

The clergy are our final case. I will use the example of Catholicism to show how the concept of salvation, like the notions of health and legal justice, has respect for the individual built into the idea itself. Although an examination of the Judaic and various Protestant understandings of salvation would yield, I would argue, the same conclusion, my intention in this work is not to evaluate every nuance of every profession but to demonstrate that the pledge ethic for which I am here arguing is sufficiently general to ground professions as such. Establishing the applicability of the analysis to the practice of Catholic clerics, whom many view as the clerics most inclined to enforce church dogma at the

expense of respect for the individual, will go a long way toward
showing the generality and defensibility of pledge-based professional ethics.[32]

In Catholicism, the priest assists the parishioner towards salvation, the free reclamation of purpose in life. Confession can be
seen as the process in which the priest forces penitents to reveal
what is in their hearts and then tells them what to do to atone
for their sin. If this is, in fact, what professing priests are entitled
to do, then the pledge ethic would be in deep difficulty indeed.
In the first place, on this view, the priests are empowered to
ignore what clients think. This power is difficult to reconcile with
our earlier argument that clients have superior knowledge of the
relative value of certain actions for the sort of life they are trying
to realize.

Second, if priests require people to confess any and all sins to
them, then their profession does not appear to honor the limits
to discretion which, I have been arguing, the trustor imposes in
any act of trust. The penitent trusts the priest to provide help
in reclaiming her purposes; she does not authorize the priest to
remake her entire life. Preserving trust would seem to require
therefore that confessees retain discretion over which portions of
their lives they make public. Not to retain such discretion would
tend to destroy the very trust that grounds the priest–penitent
relation. To see why, consider the case of friendship. Friends often
share confidences they expect us to keep. Acting in a trustworthy
fashion will be difficult for parishioners if their own salvation
requires relating these secrets to a priest in order to be saved.
Such a confession may jeopardize the friendships so vital to our
ability to come to an understanding of what we want in life. It
would be more than a little ironic if the priestly pledge designed
to elicit and maintain trust of clients wound up making these
same clients into untrustworthy beings who, by implication, could
not be depended upon to work with the priest toward the reclamation of purpose in life.

The problem of priestly authority here raised is genuine; its
solution is rather complex. I begin by noting that the penitent
does not need a priest to know he has sinned. The healing skills
of the priest come into play only after the penitent has already
acknowledged to himself his alienation from God and has confessed to sinning. Second, who controls what must be confessed
depends on how the sacrament of confession is understood. Some

Catholic theologians understand every sin as a transgression against the church as well as against God's order.[33] On this view, since penance is a necessary part of reconciliation; and since the church is one of the parties to be reconciled through the penance, the church must hear the confession of the sin. This requirement, though, could be met through a general confession of sin. And, in fact, the Catholic church has not always made penance contingent upon private confession to a priest. The early Christians used public confession to disclose serious sins. Penance for these sins was public as well.[34] Debate continues today among Catholic theologians over the merits of a general confession which need not enumerate specific sins versus a specific confession made to the church's representative. A general confession would by its very nature permit the penitent to retain control over disclosure of his or her private affairs. When this latter arrangement is employed, the issue of respect for persons does not arise.

I would also add that the issue of secrecy and forced confession may be something of a red herring in the debate over whether Catholicism respects personhood. The requirement to confess specific sins did not develop because priests wanted to violate the privacy of parishioners. It arose as a solution to the problem of imposing some disciplining check on people's free will. We know through training and observation of the corruption of human nature and its tendency to hide its sinful being from itself. To give people the unbridled power to judge in their own case grants them earthly power. History shows that such power is itself corrupting. Confession to a priest aims at lessening the temptation to sin by providing a means for a heartfelt re-examination of one's life:

> [T]he specific accusation of sin is also for our own good. Being men, the sincerity, depth of contrition, and purpose of amendment that we bring to the sacramental event can be intensified greatly through its externalization in accusation.[35]

The above understanding of confession restores the confessee to a position of power in the relation. To the extent that a desire for sincerity underpins the requirement to confess, disclosure cannot be anything but an intrinsically personal matter controlled by the confessee. Irrespective of whether the parishioner enumerates his specific sins to God alone or to a priest, what matters is the integrity of the confession. Only the person confessing can know what lurks in the recesses of his heart. Like a psychiatrist, the priest may probe for information bearing upon the cause of the parishioner's dissatisfaction with his own conduct: is the confession merely a hasty mechanical run-through of a catalogue of "standard" sins or does it reveal an awareness of the manner and extent of suffering one's actions have caused others? The priest certainly is not duty-bound to make the penitent feel good about the performance of evil acts. Nor need the professional relieve client anxiety by saying in effect, "Yes, God forgives you for this wicked act; think no more about it." The priest's willingness to probe, to lovingly rebuke, and to insist upon responsible action makes confession meaningful.

Still, the priest is at most a mediator between God and the sinner. He mediates the sinner's experience by revealing the connection between the individual's confessed sins and particular expiatory acts of penance that God sees this sin as requiring. The priest helps the penitent whose confusion, guilt, or shame may be obscuring this connection. But the connection only matters to the confessee whose heart is already repentant. Whether shame is sincerely felt depends upon individual conscience. As mediator, the priest has no authority to press for a full or sincere confession. The full confession might in theory benefit the penitent. But given that all of us are prone to acts of bad faith or poor judgment in which we misrepresent to ourselves the extent of our guilt, the priest has no way of knowing when all sins have been confessed.

In addition, there is Biblical warrant for thinking that the penitent may not comprehend the extent of his sin and cannot therefore be forced into revealing "all" of his sins. One could argue that Peter's denial of Jesus on the night of the crucifixion is the paradigm for Christian sin. Although Peter proclaims himself immune to the temptation to betray Jesus, Jesus can foretell Peter's denial because he sees the illusory character of all that humans set apart as above corruption. Peter portrays himself as incorruptible, thereby revealing that he does not understand the illusion to which Jesus points. In a sense, Peter has already committed the sin of betrayal when he proclaims himself willing *always* to stand by Jesus' side. Peter never confesses this sin of betrayal because he does not comprehend it. If he understood the underlying illusion, he would have felt shame in Jesus' presence when he first denied he would ever be capable of betraying Jesus. But he felt no such shame, despite the structural identity of these two denials. The pious see that they, too, could be like Peter. The extent of their sinning may exceed their comprehension. If so, the Bible itself denies the possibility of finding some standard for measuring or assessing the fullness of the confession. Consequently, any attempt to force a confession is futile at best and pernicious at worst. Pressing the sinner to confess sins is likely to alienate the penitent both from the priest and from his own choice to trust this priest. Since the penitent as penitent wills the reclamation of his own purposes, the priest cannot be furthering the client's end by insisting upon a full confession and has no authority to do so.

Just as the professional attorney withdraws when the client refuses to speak or becomes unable to do so, so does the professional priest leave off probing when the penitent falls silent or in some other way indicates an unwillingness or an inability to disclose more. Although I have been focusing on the dynamics within the confessional, the pledge ethic would also prohibit the administration of last rites if the party is already dead; or if the party is alive and capable of genuinely consenting to the performance of such rites but has not been consulted. In the second case, the priest has no authority to make a person submit to the sacrament since the parishioner is still able to order her life's activities but the priest has made no effort to consult with the parishioner. In the first case, the priest also has no authority to minister the sacrament because the priest cannot be inferred to be promoting the client's good without foreclosing the client's future options. The priest is not like the emergency room doctor who revives the comatose suicide victim because, assuming that the person is already dead (or will definitely be so shortly), the priest cannot legitimately claim to be acting in such a way as to restore another's ability to act upon his or her own will.

To summarize: the pledges of all three of the learned professions authorize those who profess these pledges to recommend actions they believe best suited to meet the specific need of their clients. However, the pledge gives the professional no authority to force compliance with the recommendation or to assume that the end being promoted is the only good the client seeks to realize in his or her life. What one can say is that, if the client voluntarily remains in the relation with the professional, the professional may legitimately exercise discretion to actively promote what the client wills as client.

In fact, the professional is bound by the nature of health, justice, and salvation to try helping the client to better comprehend what he or she is desiring as a patient, litigant, or penitent. But again, client desires have a claim upon the professional only because, and insofar as, they are part of the professional–client relation brought into being by the pledge – i.e. insofar as their fulfillment is willed by the client in the capacity of client. The professional may legitimately refuse to help the client if the client insists that the professional fulfill some wish the professional has neither the obligation nor the authority to fulfill (e.g. a desire for castration; a desire to have evidence manufactured).[36] When the client is not present as a client, the professional has no ethical basis on which to serve that client and therefore withdraws.

PART TWO: THE ROLE OF ENFORCEMENT MECHANISMS IN A PLEDGE-BASED ETHIC

So far our focus has been on how professionals should behave. But how do we get them to behave as they should? And what do we do if they violate the limits to their activity by, for example, forcing medical treatment on a patient or exorcism on a parishioner?[37] While we can blame, sue, or simply ostracize professionals for perceived misconduct, historically we have relied upon professionals to review the conduct of their peers. Professional disciplinary boards generally make a determination of misconduct; the professional's license to practice may then be suspended or revoked, sometimes by the professional society, sometimes by a public authority (often on the recommendation of the disciplinary board). These boards typically are justified on the ground that they help ensure that professional behavior is in the public's interest and thereby maintain public trust. However, it is far from obvious that these boards are either necessary for public trust or that they do in fact serve the public's interest. I will take up each of these points separately.

Boards unnecessary for public trust

It is worth noting that none of the oaths or vows traditionally sworn provides for the establishment of such boards or disciplinary penalties. The American Bar Association's *Model Rules* do not discuss disbarment. The Hippocratic physician holds himself

accountable before the gods, not the American Medical Association. If a third-party disciplining mechanism is necessary for
trust, it is rather remarkable that these pledges have never
bothered to provide for such an arrangement. It is more plausible
that trustworthiness does not require accountability to some outside human third party. As grown children we trust our parents
not to lie about our parentage and to try to make some provision
for their old age. Our trust in this case does not depend upon
the existence of a parental disciplinary council. Nor is there some
substantial penalty we can impose upon our parents if they betray
our trust. (I am assuming the child is an adult and that we are
not talking about betrayals amounting to prosecutable child
abuse.) In fact, if persons are not free to betray us or if they suffer
some substantial penalty upon betrayal, then our relationship with
them is no longer a trusting one or is at least far less so. In Guy
Oakes' words, trust is the trustor's "means of coming to terms
with the freedom of the [trustor] and the risks this freedom
entails" for the trustee.[38] Trust does not require the elimination
of all risk in order to exist.

Still, trustors must *expect* trusted persons to exhibit good will
towards them. Used in the context of professional ethics, the
parental case is misleading because adult children usually have a
lifetime of experience of the parent's actions to draw upon in
forming expectations as to whether the parent will behave appropriately or not. Clients usually do not have an extensive history
of the professional's acts on which to similarly base an expectation of genuine assistance. The profession therefore needs some
mechanism for engendering trust.

Such a mechanism does exist: professional self-monitoring. But
this phrase is ambiguous. It may refer to individual professionals
holding themselves accountable to the terms of their pledge, or
it may mean professionals judging one another's performance.
Self-accountability is clearly necessary. As we have seen, agents
qualify as trustworthy and professional only when they understand and discharge the responsibilities of the pledge-defined role
they assume the moment they call themselves by that role's name.
This professionalism does not require a supporting institutional
apparatus. The profession exists whenever a single individual
freely utters the grounding pledge or assumes the role and abides
by its terms. A doctor marooned with a crew on a desert island

qualifies as a professional healer as long as she acts for the benefit of any sick crew member.

Indeed, professionalism must be achievable by a single person who has identified conditions necessary for trustworthy service and who is willing to make a pledge designed to meet these conditions because such pledges do exist and a multi-party origin seems unlikely. There are no historical data to suggest that a group of persons banded together, simultaneously conceived and uttered a profession-grounding pledge, and agreed to monitor one another's adherence to that pledge. On the contrary, the Hippocratic Oath derives its name from a single agent, Hippocrates, which suggests that professionalism is a matter of individual professing and self-accountability. Christianity as well as the Lutheran, Calvinist, Amish, and Hutterite sects all get their names from the particular individuals in whom the laity reposed its trust.

In this connection, the historian Robert Bonner is quite right to think of the ancient Greek *logographoi* or speechwriters who composed and presented speeches on behalf of persons appearing in court as the first lawyers. These individuals qualify as such not because they belonged to a Bar or a rule-enforcing guild but because individual practitioners evolved for themselves rules designed to ensure that the client's case was fully and well presented in court. For example, after Demosthenes aroused public ire by allegedly writing speeches for both sides of a case, the lawyers/speechwriters came to see that they would not be trusted if they served both parties to a dispute. Such employment would inevitably arouse suspicions that the speechwriter was using information obtained from one party to help the other party win the case.[39]

Furthermore, while it seems a bit fanciful to speak of marooned professionals, the modern world has witnessed plenty of situations in which individuals have acted professionally (i.e. ethically) without being part of a formal organization. Those few priests who performed underground masses in Eastern Europe did not cease to be trustworthy priests just because they were disowned by fellow clerics who had allied themselves with the ruling repressive regime. Nor did they cease to be priests when the state revoked their license to practice or when the local church hierarchy repudiated them. Professionals sometimes must go it alone or even act against the recommendations of colleagues. The test of the rightness of their actions is adherence to their grounding pledge, not conformity to professional board recommendations.

The problem with third-party accountability is that any judgment rendered by a professional organization or some arm thereof must itself ultimately be evaluated in light of the trust-engendering and trust-maintaining pledge. Holding professionals accountable to a standard of practice which does not elicit trust obviously will not make for trustworthy professionals. This fact alone makes the pledge, not institutional approval, the ground of professional authority. The crucial disciplinary issue thus becomes whether a given board will enforce the pledge ethic.

Disciplinary boards may not serve the public interest

Whether professional norms will be enforced depends on board members' self-perception and character. If the board is composed exclusively of professionals who see themselves as experts, it is likely to impose few sanctions. Many disputes among these experts will be arcane ones centered simply on technique.[40] Furthermore, since experts' ends are, as we saw in Chapter 2, intrinsically private, the most a board of experts can do is to oppose their private likes and dislikes against those of the person to be disciplined. Within the framework of expertise, these oppositions must assume the form of mere differences in taste; and differences in taste are notoriously amoral. One must also consider the history of those on the board. Some evidence suggests that psychiatrists who sexually abuse their patients pass these clients on to colleagues who also abuse patients.[41] If corruption becomes widespread in a group of professionals, the result will be an unprofessional board passing judgment on the professionalism of colleagues with whom the board is in cahoots.

There are two additional reasons for questioning the ethical value of disciplinary boards. First, even if the board is composed of persons who scrupulously adhere to the terms of a grounding pledge and hold others accountable to it as well, any action they take is after the fact. Since clients must trust professionals before they seek their help, an *ex post facto* disciplinary hearing will do little to bolster clients' willingness to risk consulting doctors, ministers, and lawyers. Second, while a fellow practitioner probably will be better able than the client to ascertain whether a peer has made a technical error, the professional will not be better equipped than a layperson to discern moral lapses. Citizens write the laws which express our collective sense of what is right, good, and just, and they sit on the juries which apply this law in particular cases. Having the professional appear before a professional ethics board on a murder or theft charge would be suspect and delegitimating because there is no reason to reserve judgment to peers in such a case.

The case for peer review is strongest when an act is not criminal or tortious but nonetheless is thought to violate the professional ethic. If, as I have been arguing, there is indeed a distinctive professional ethic that has evolved from a long history of intelligent people reflecting upon the conditions for delivering trustworthy service to needy, vulnerable beings, then it is right that those with the experience of thinking about such matters should hold their colleagues accountable for conduct violating these conditions. Insofar as professional organizations provide opportunities for regular informal contact with colleagues, the organizations can further self-accountability by creating and perpetuating a kind of collective memory on which individual agents may draw when trying to think through how they should behave. The question is whether these organizations' disciplinary boards provide additional value above and beyond what informal contact supplies; and what penalty if any, should be imposed upon those who have been judged by their colleagues to have violated the profession's ethic.

These questions are perplexing. One wants the offender to act in accordance with the profession's distinctive moral commitment. Yet no one can give an agent a moral commitment that must be freely assumed. Should then the offender be denied a state license or the privilege of administering sacraments? Removal of the institutional seal of approval may not do much good. Although it is sometimes asserted that such disciplining will preserve or increase trust in the profession as a whole, this claim seems dubious. Those making it must show that clients trust a "whole profession" rather than its individual members. Human beings have a remarkable capacity for looking beyond stereotypes to the behavior of the particular person with whom they are interacting. As long as their own doctor or minister abides by the pledge ethic, clients will probably continue to trust these persons. Peer disciplining is better defended on the ground that defrocking or disbarring keeps those expelled from the profession away from other clients whom they might harm. If peer disciplining actually can prevent the disciplined person from working with clients, then a few potential clients might be kept from harm. Yet even this benefit seems dubious given the fact that disciplined members can simply lie about their credentials and resume practice; that disciplinary hearings may last for years before any action is taken;[42] and that conflicts between various disciplinary boards' jurisdiction often allow a disciplined member simply to set up shop across the state line. Sometimes disciplined members may just change practice slightly to conform to the letter of the sanction and go right on practicing. When one local society of dentists removed a colleague's periodontal specialization certification, the dentist simply extended his practice beyond the periodontal specialty and increased his practice even more.[43]

Moreover, the whole practice of disciplining is not without its dark side. Boards must not be too quick to excommunicate a fellow practitioner, lest they slip into hubris. As we have seen, the history of the professions includes debates over what constitutes professionalism. Although the expert and contractual service models are flawed, they have grown out of legitimate concerns of both professionals and clients. Similarly, the maverick professional may have something to say which the profession should consider.

Perhaps then we should conclude the following concerning the role of institutionally enforced accountability: disciplinary boards are not required for professions and their members to be trust-worthy. Nevertheless, when professionals interact, they should hold one another accountable to the pledge, arguing for its binding character and asking those whose speech or actions do not appear to conform to either (1) demonstrate conformity or (2) argue for an alternative standard of practice. (I here assume that the profession will have some channel or office for receiving client or peer complaints about individual practitioners.) Challenged professionals should appear to defend their behavior before a group including laypersons as well as peers. Clients, as well as professionals, think about service and trust and should be part of the process for reflecting on professional practice because they are the party most affected by professional incompetence. Furthermore, their insights and support can afford some protection to courageous "maverick" professionals who may be unjustly attacked for having raised a problem with their peers' performance.

If a challenged party refuses to make any public statement or profession in defense of his or her actions or speech; or if the statement given seems an inadequate defense, then the listening group should publicly declare this party unprofessional in a statement listing supporting reasons. Such a public statement would serve as a vehicle for members of the profession to reflect further upon its essence and also to assess the professionalism of those serving on the board. This "follow-on" profession would also provide potential and actual clients with an opportunity for educating themselves as to what service they may reasonably expect when they consult a member of the profession. A penalty of this sort would certainly not render the profession any less trustworthy. It might make the profession more so by clarifying the profession's commitment to the client's good. At a minimum, such an arrangement would seem preferable to the current one in which disciplinary boards neither make their judgments public nor state the reasons for the disciplinary action. Since their private judgments may or may not be professional, this type of disciplining adds little, if anything, to professional legitimacy.

Conclusion

The pledge-based ethic does set limits upon what the professional may legitimately do in the name of helping a client. The ends the professional pledges to promote entail respecting the person of the client. There is no need to appeal to a second-order ethic in order to establish such limits. Nor do we need formal disciplinary boards. They are neither a necessary nor a sufficient condition for ethical conduct by professionals. Nonetheless, some sort of public listening group could perhaps be usefully employed to occasion further reflection by professional and client alike as to the character of trustworthy behavior. This might result in professionals becoming better able to comprehend and thereby abide by the requirements for legitimacy and in clients becoming better able to identify and then protest about apparent violations of this ethic.

This chapter and the preceding ones have explored how actions in accordance with the professional's pledge benefit the client. What remains unclear is how the professional benefits from voluntarily assuming the responsibility of making and adhering to the pledge to help. We saw in Chapter 1 that medieval professionals saw their profession as perfecting their lives. Such language implies that professionals, as well as clients, reap some good from their service. How, if at all, does the professional gain from the relation with the client? And is the professional's good consistent with establishing and maintaining client trust? These questions are the focus of our next chapter.

Chapter 7

The professional's good

We have seen that the pledges grounding the ethics of the various professions bind these agents to act for the benefit of the client. Our inquiry into the basis of professional legitimacy must now consider professionals' motivations in making these pledges and in assuming the often onerous responsibilities these pledges entail. Since the necessity for such an inquiry is not obvious, I will begin by stating why the issue of professional motivation is relevant.

On the one hand, it could be argued that the client is perfectly indifferent to an individual professional's motivation for helping that client. Indeed, as I myself have been contending, what is crucial is that the client trust the professional. To trust a professional, clients need only believe that the professional is both committed and able to provide genuine help to them. On this line of argument, why the professional chooses to provide this assistance is irrelevant. On the other hand, this reasoning is problematic to the extent that it ignores the dynamic of belief formation. Client beliefs regarding whether professionals are likely to be truly of aid take into account (1) whether the professional has competing incentives which may weaken the professional's commitment to client good;[1] and (2) whether the professional's motives are such as to impair the professional's ability to further the client's welfare.

The entire debate over professional conflicts of interest attests to the importance of the first consideration. The debate reflects the legitimate concern of reasonable clients that some commitments or actions of some professionals are such that promoting the welfare of the client has ceased to be (or will cease to be) the professional's primary motivation. If my doctor is selling renal tissue or organs, I have good reason to wonder whether his decision to remove one of my kidneys truly aims at promoting my health or at maximizing the doctor's income, perhaps at the expense of my health. Nor can a client's concern with the effect of a professional's motivation upon that professional's ability to be of genuine assistance be lightly dismissed. For as the ethicist Warner Wick has observed, it is likely that a professional's performance will improve, "perhaps even to the extent of making contributions to 'the state of the art',"[2] only if the professional finds some intrinsic satisfaction in her work.

These two concerns alone suffice to give us reason to explore whether certain extrinsic motivations sometimes alleged to motivate particular professionals – e.g. the desire for large sums of money or for fame;[3] a general love of mankind and desire to give joy to others – are consistent with professional legitimacy; and, if not, whether there is any professional motivation as such that is consistent with legitimacy. The first two desires, for example, arguably tend to undermine a long-term commitment to one's clients good. Fame and wealth are not a sure bet in law, medicine, or the ministry. The clergy are notoriously poorly paid. The government can alter Medicare reimbursement schedules, thereby drastically reducing a doctor's income. Contingent fees of lawyers by definition depend upon the outcome of a case, a result not totally within counsel's control. And, given that legal and medical fees are usually not collected in advance of service, the lawyer or doctor sometimes must settle for providing service and not being paid.[4] As for fame – she has always been a fickle mistress. Many professionals never get the recognition they deserve. Ungrateful clients slander the professional; others are embarrassed to admit they have needed another's help. This uncertainty of reward in turn affects the trustworthiness of any agent suspected of acting for the sake of money or fame. Such people must be expected to wax hot or cold depending upon whether fortune smiles upon them.

Nor can we save professional trustworthiness by positing an altruistic or philanthropic motivation. As we saw in Chapter 1, altruism will not ground the trust of clients. Moreover, philanthropy bears no obvious relation to professionalism. The sick do not come to the doctors to be loved. They come to be healed.[5] I am not here denying that doctors or ministers often experience a joy in giving to others. Freely giving of oneself may be a mark of virtue as well as a source of pleasure.[6] It may also be a fitting way for professionals to return to the community some of the benefit they have unquestionably reaped from it (e.g. from community funding of their medical or legal training; from community financing of the institutional framework of hospitals and court systems in which they conduct their practice). Nevertheless, whether the client trusts the professional clearly depends upon what is being given. While sexual intercourse is often a form of joyful giving, it is not fitting in all situations or for all parties. The appropriateness of sexual giving is determined by the character, age and circumstances of the parties involved. For example, sex with children or relatives is ethically problematic in part because it tends to destroy trust. Caught by surprise, family members may have no chance to think about the act, much less voluntarily assent to it. Fearing reprisal from those on whom they depend or who have the greater power to inflict physical harm, vulnerable individuals are often forced to lead a dual life in which they pretend to the outer world that everything is normal while simultaneously engaging in acts of which they want no part. Trust can be said to have been destroyed in these cases because there is no longer a single person who can form and entertain an expectation of good will; and because the act does not honor both parties' values but instead substitutes the will of one party for that of the other. Similarly, clients who have come before the professional seeking one kind of help may find themselves surprised by a doctor's or lawyer's sexual overtures. If no one else seems likely to aid them, they may, like the victims of incest or child abuse, submit to such acts out of desperation but they can hardly be said to have been helped. For their part, professionals may pretend that this sexual manipulation constitutes "help." Nevertheless, such pretense does not alter the fact that to the extent that the professional's actions do not aim to achieve the particular genuine good the client seeks *qua* client, the actions violate the first condition of professional trustworthiness. Consequently, we must be wary of accepting a professional's desire to be "giving" as a legitimate professional motivation.

Neither a desire for fame or money nor a wish to give of themselves provides professionals with a reason for acting which is simultaneously a reason for clients to trust them. Our motivational dilemma would be solved if professional service could be shown not only to benefit the client but also necessarily and

intrinsically to satisfy the professional. Indeed, we are driven to
entertain the possibility of intrinsically satisfying service the
moment we consider the practical consequence of denying its
existence – namely, that if professionals do not obtain satisfaction
from the practice itself, then practice threatens always to become
nothing but a means to an end. And this returns us to the second
client concern mentioned above, the close connection between
professionals' motivation and their ability to develop skills for
helping clients.[7]

When practice is instrumentalized, it tends toward the mechanical or sloppy. The prevailing attitude becomes "a job's a job."
In addition, extrinsic motivations seem to lead toward the objectifying of the client and loss of the client's stature as a person. It
is more than a little curious that as motivations have become
increasingly extrinsic to practice and as professions have come to
be seen as no more than job monopolies, the learned professions
have become the "service professions."[8] When the client is at the
fore, *as he or she always is in pledge-based practice*, this terminology is redundant. To be a professional just is to serve a client
good. Growing references to servicing the client signal an alarm-
ing shift toward objectifying the client. "Servicing" occurs when
the tasks being performed are defined prior to, rather than
through, an interaction with either a thing or another human
being. Thus, robots can "service" automobiles, stallions mares,
and weapons targets, because the things acted upon are identical
in the relevant respects and need not be individually evaluated.
A client, though, must be consulted, not adjusted like an auto-
mobile or struck like a target. Instrumentalizing of practice dimin-
ishes clients' status as persons who are helped to assist themselves
and turns them into objects acted upon. When professional motivations are extrinsic to the activity being performed, professional
legitimacy becomes problematic just as it does when the professional is reduced to an expert or contractual service provider.

The case must not be overstated. It is not inconceivable that a
money-loving or fame-seeking professional may be of genuine
assistance to a client. The attorney who wishes to become a
partner in a law firm may provide scrupulous care to clients in
order to keep advancing toward the big payoff of partnership.
But it is equally likely that any help the client does receive from
the "servicer" will be slapdash, incompetent and/or objectifying.
When the practice only matters as a means to something outside

the practice, the practitioner is not focusing on the particular, inherently individualistic client good which makes medicine, law, or the ministry the distinctive practice it is. Paying attention to what conduces to the good is necessary to make the practitioner better at helping the individual gain health, justice, or salvation. But the attention of the professional jobber is elsewhere engaged. The overriding concern of the money- or fame-loving professional is: what must I do for my fee or reputation? If the fee is almost certain to be paid (e.g. by an insurance company), or if the reputation is secure, there is little motivation for such an agent to struggle to perfect practice. In fact, the desire to make money or gain fame may result in the agent doing as little as possible for each client in order to maximize the number of clients seen and fees and reputation gained during a given period. The prospect of quick, thoughtless treatment by an incompetent will hardly entice the would-be client into the professional's office. So once again we seem driven to hypothesize that professional practice must be inherently fulfilling if clients are to have reason to expect their good to be promoted.

In the remainder of this chapter, I will explore the ways in which professional practice might be intrinsically satisfying. It could be intrinsically satisfying in one of two ways. The benefit to the practitioner might be generically professional, enjoyable by all professionals as such. Or the good might be specific to the particular profession. For example, the doctor's pursuing health, as opposed to legal justice, might result in satisfaction unique to the quest for health. Both possibilities deserve consideration. I will begin with the latter, exploring what good, if any, the doctor gets from serving health, the lawyer legal justice and the clergy salvation. Then I will explore whether the fact that the learned professions as a group are pledge-based makes for a generic professional satisfaction.

SATISFACTION SPECIFIC TO THE PROFESSION

The physician's share of health

The physician attempts to heal the patient. Doctor and patient alike consider what sort of equilibrium the patient can realistically hope to attain, given what are often new and permanent impediments to the patient's customary functioning (e.g. irretrievable loss of sensation or motor control). One is tempted to see the doctor simply as a conduit of information who tells the client what to expect as side effects of different medications or as the disease progresses, while the doctor strives to cure the sick patient. Such a view, though, misrepresents the character of the physician's involvement. In the first place, it makes it seem as though the patient is sick, while the doctor is totally free of what ails the patient. Yet, as Dr Harry Stack Sullivan observes, good psychiatrists know that the distance separating them from their "sick" patients is not that great.[9] Similar insight underlies Dr Bernie Siegel's argument that healing ultimately requires that physicians learn to cope with their own limitations as well as those of the patient:

> in the training of the medical profession, the focus is on curing disease. You could spend ten years studying to cure it. Then when you get into the real world, you realize, "I can't cure everything!" What that does is make you feel like a failure . . . I know how painful it is not to be able to cure people. It's lousy, and that's why doctors are all tied up in knots: they just don't know what to do with all the pain and the feelings. They withdraw, they don't show emotion, they don't deal with their patients appropriately.[10]

Healing, like any other activity, brings with it limits. No physician can bestow immortality upon a patient. Indeed, some recent evidence suggests we have reached an upper limit on how far the human life span can be extended.[11] Given this limitation and others like it, we may rightly call physicians *impaired* if they do not struggle to come to a balanced view of what they, as well as their patients, can reasonably accomplish. In other words, physicians must heal themselves while trying to heal others.

I intend my use of the term "heal" quite literally. We have seen that the inherently subjective character of health precludes the physician from granting it to or bestowing it upon a patient. In addition, given that death seems a certainty, the issue for the patient is: "How do I best live the life I now have?" The physician who would help answer this question confronts the same problem of finding a balance between his bodily and his transbodily purposes: "Do I, the doctor, want to live life as a frustrated being, physically stressed by the inability to prevent patients' deaths? Or would it not be far better that I, an embodied, earthbound creature, undertake that at which I can succeed, assisting the patient in aiming for and achieving an appropriate balance between the patient's body such as it is and that individual's purposes?"[12]

The physician who is trying to heal rather than immortalize the patient examines her own, as well as the patient's, experience in light of this concept of health. This self-examination, in turn, makes her particularly worthy of patient trust. In achieving her own balance between her bodily limitations and transbodily purposes, the doctor actually obeys that age-old command of skeptical, mistrustful patients everywhere: "Physician, heal thyself!"[13] The covenanting physician gains a share of health while healing the patient.[14] Since health is an inherently individualistic good desired for its own sake, medical practice, when professional, provides for its own intrinsic satisfaction. And since this good is obtained through and insofar as the physician's furthering client health, no conflict arises between the professional's and the client's good.

The Hippocratic Oath represents medicine's attempt to preserve this identity of interest. The doctor–patient relation is subject to all sorts of pressures. Some doctors, like members of other professions, are obsessed with controlling and manipulating their environment.[15] It is equally fair to say that some patients share in this obsession. The Hippocratic Oath would not forbid the giving of deadly drugs and abortifacients upon demand if it did not foresee that people would pressure physicians to assist them in committing suicide or aborting a fetus. The oath prohibits these two activities in particular because these practices have a great potential for luring the doctor away from healing.

Note that the oath does not require that physicians be in favor of criminalizing suicide or abortion; it merely insists that the physician not be involved in providing patients with these apparent goods. The prohibition keeps doctors focused on health by refusing to involve them in actions which may or may not be good. To the extent that health is constitutive of life, it is an unproblematic good. We do not think life is an evil. About the goodness of abortion and suicide, actions which end life, we are not sure. (One need only think, for example, of the growing number of abortions of female fetuses performed because the parents prefer a boy.[16]) The oath serves the cause of health by keeping physicians' energies free to promote life. Life is short.

The physician's available time is limited. The self-healing physician understands the need to set priorities. The pledge establishes
priorities, favoring the known good of health over more dubious
"goods."

In addition, the oath furthers health by forbidding physician
involvement with two activities which in their essence are
opposed to the inner meaning of health. Consider first the act of
suicide. Young children are not suicidal. People become suicidal
as a result of some perceived change in their situation. The would-
be suicide reasons: "If I cannot live as I did before, then I do
not desire to go on living." The woman seeking an abortion
similarly demands a return to the state of affairs prevailing before
she acted to become pregnant. Instead of bearing the child and
then finding a new equilibrium in her life (e.g. asking others to
rear the child; or raising the child herself), the woman asserts a
right to return to life as it was before she became pregnant.[17]
While this reasoning might in some cases be warranted (e.g. if
the woman has been raped) and might justify committing suicide
or having an abortion, the reasoning involved is not that of a
patient or a doctor. To see why, we need only hark back to what
health is.

Recall that healing consists in both parties attempting to discover a new balance within limits resulting either from external
forces (e.g. an accident; viruses), from prior choices made by the
patient (e.g. bad eating habits), from the natural process of aging
(e.g. deteriorating hearing), or from the constitution of the human
body (e.g. the rate of healing). Medical procedures can remove
some limitations. Broken arms can be set; knife wounds stitched.
There are no guarantees, however, that these procedures will be
entirely successful. The person may never recover full use of the
arm; the stitched wound may become infected. Moreover, many
limits are permanent and simply must be accepted. Finally, some
conditions which in theory could be rectified are ultimately
accepted by patients who are not willing to live with the trade-
offs a given medical procedure involves. The key point here is
that there is always some impairment or disease which the patient
would like to eliminate but which medicine cannot eradicate. This
is why medicine aims at "helping us to accept, and learn to cope
with, our illnesses and disabilities."[18] Suicide and abortion on
demand are intrinsically opposed to healing because healing
becomes impossible when the patient is committed to the view

that, unless events can be exactly as the patient desires, life in the future will be miserable.[19]

Such reasoning is akin to that of Siegel's impaired, manipulative doctor who will settle for nothing less than the total cure he desires to provide. It is just this sort of reasoning the professional physician shuns. Having dedicated his life to medicine, he avoids making medicine into the handmaiden of reasoning hostile to healing. By adhering strictly to the medical pledge, the physician obtains a share of the genuine good of health through the practice itself. Adherence to the pledge fulfills physicians because they must draw upon all of their teaching, counseling and technical skills to help people (including themselves) identify and then cope with their limitations. Having spent years acquiring such skills, they get to use them as healers, reaping healing's unique satisfaction of assisting people to find new life despite and even through bodily illness. Performing the prohibited acts, by contrast, does not give physicians a share of health and does not provide much in the way of a stimulating challenge. It takes few skills and almost no practice to inject someone with a fatal dose of drugs or to perform an abortion. Six weeks' training will produce a competent abortionist.[20]

In addition, by refusing to become agents of death, physicians hold open the possibility of learning from the client in the future. Unlike the ethicist Goldman's physician who honors no pledge but only the right of autonomy and who presumes to know that retarded infants do not have a life worth living and can therefore be killed by the physician,[21] the pledging physician makes no such presumption. She tries instead to help the patient, adult or infant, achieve whatever sort of balance is possible for each, withdrawing only when it becomes apparent that the ability of the organism to achieve balance is gone. The Hippocratic doctor never forecloses the possibility that even at the moment of death the patient may reveal some hitherto unknown and unsuspected way for humans to balance their bodily and spiritual purposes. One can take Jesus' final moments on the cross as illustrating this kind of healing revelation, which no doubt explains why neither doctors nor patients view the dying Jesus as unhealthy or sick. The physician contributes to her own health by being open to learning from others' suffering while at the same time keeping concern for the client's health at the fore of the interaction.

The lawyer's share of justice

In law, unlike medicine, the identity of client and lawyer interest is quite explicit. By law, counsel acts in the person of the client. The lawyer and client are, as it were, one person. Yet it is not clear why counsel should want to take on the persona of the client. The problem of motivation is especially acute here since the lawyer may very well entertain doubts about the case at hand, suspecting that the client for whom she has entered a "not guilty" plea actually did commit the crime in question. One is reminded of Boswell's question to Samuel Johnson: "[D]oes not . . . appearing to be clearly of one opinion when you are in reality of another opinion . . . impair one's honesty? Is there not some danger that a lawyer may put on the same mask, in common life, in the intercourse with his friends?"[22] If practice requires dissimulation, and if deceit potentially alienates persons from their friends and family as well as their clients, what intrinsic satisfaction can justify adopting such a practice?

There are two possible answers. The attorney who zealously represents a client might be thought to gain an indirect share in justice. No one can claim with certainty never to be in need of an attorney. Should the lawyer find himself being accused of a criminal act or the victim of one he may discover in his attorney his only advocate. By conscientiously helping clients to get their day in court, the attorney preserves the legitimacy of the court system and the role of attorney. He defends all the accused or injured to ensure that someone will be there to defend him should he find himself in court.

While I do not doubt the sincerity of attorneys who offer this argument, the reasoning seems something of a stretch. This good is not one most lawyers will ever reap since few become litigants, much less criminal defendants. Consequently, this good does not seem sufficient to entice the would-be attorney to take on the persona of client. There is, though, a deeper sense in which attorneys gain a share of justice for themselves, a share intrinsic to the activity of representing a client. By struggling to ensure that the case appearing before and decided by the court is in fact the client's case, the attorney enables the client's voice to be heard. By voice, I do not mean a projected pattern of sound but rather an expression of thoughts and feelings that may never before have been expressed. The advocate attempts to explain the client's possibly unique concerns and reasoning as these appear to the client. This tale may appear improbable but "it is always probable that something improbable will happen."[23] Although the attorney's client may lose the court battle, the client's voice becomes part of the public record. As law professor Edward Levi has shown, a losing cause may carry the day in the long run as subsequent court decisions revive arguments from this earlier case and apply them in new ways in new contexts.[24] In this fashion the client's voice affects the law and becomes part of what law professor Sir Frederick Pollock describes as the "living temple of justice."[25] Attorneys, like the rest of us, live by this law, a structure the attorney in the person of the client has helped to build. Therein lies the attorney's professional satisfaction: "The least of [attorneys] is happy who hereafter may point to so much as one stone [of the temple of justice], and say, The work of my hands is there."[26]

The attorney's life does not then consist of conniving to let criminals get away with crimes or to see plaintiffs triumph in malicious suits. Rather it is itself a just practice which is intrinsically satisfying and which can become more so over time. By listening carefully to clients and trying to represent their view in court, lawyers develop their ability to understand and argue for clients. Recall that the publicness of the pledge binds the attorney to accept clients as they come. Genuinely professional attorneys do not screen for a particular type of client. This commitment, known in England as the "cab-rank rule," results in the attorney representing a variety of clients over time. Rather than prejudging where truth lies, counsel uses available truth to develop the strongest possible case for each person advised or represented.[27] Since successive clients may be on opposite sides of a given issue, the professing lawyer comes to know the strengths and weaknesses of opposing cases from the inside out. Just as the best judge of Jewish law becomes fit to render decisions by learning to give 59 reasons for and 59 reasons against a specific creature being declared non-kosher,[28] so the lawyer who is committed to getting each client's case the best hearing possible (within the constraints the pledge imposes) develops his critical abilities. Such an attorney is far less likely to judge cases in light of pre-existent stereotypes. The individual client becomes more fully present in the person of the attorney. The attorney, in turn, may be more confident that the law she is helping to write and by which she lives upholds each person's share. The resulting community governed by a law so written functions as a genuine and just whole of separate, distinct individuals, each of whom receives his or her share.

This share of justice is not obtained at the client's expense. On the contrary, potential clients who will necessarily fall on opposite sides of issues benefit when lawyers throughout the profession are able to think clearly about both sides. Unlike those "moral right" ethics which bind lawyers to take on only apparently "moral" clients, the pledge ethic provides all with access to counsel and legal justice.[29] Actual clients benefit because they need not worry that their lawyer secretly resents them because their cause is not "morally correct" or will suddenly abandon them if they say something "wrong." Nor need they fear that counsel is using them to surreptitiously advance some favorite political or pet moral cause the lawyer has chosen to pursue through the legal system.[30]

I might add that the legal pledge ethic also offers counsel the freedom to move on to new cases, a form of liberty crucial to professional development. The pledge ethic binds lawyers to develop the strongest case they can for the client, using available truth and employing all of the passion, ingenuity, and skill they can muster. Having so developed and defended a given client's case, counsel is at liberty to move on to other cases and to develop professionally. Legal justice requires the client get a day, not a lifetime, in court. The pledge ethic thus accords with court rulings holding that a given case does not need multiple hearings nor need it be totally without defect for the litigant to have received justice.[31] The ethic is also consistent with the doctrine of *res judicata* which states that matters heard once are not heard again.[32] Some cases will get a second hearing, but every case is to be argued as though it will receive attention only once. Although a "morally right" lawyer ought not to rest satisfied until the court upholds his own "right-thinking,"[33] the pledging lawyer accepts the court's doctrine. If he has tried to use every favorable bit of evidence and law in presenting the client's case in court, the attorney has seen justice done. The client may not like the outcome. But the attorney can sleep easy without fearing he has been unjust and can move on in the morning to help other clients.

The clergy's share of salvation

In the Judeo-Christian tradition, the professional's and client's good have always been conceived as similar in kind and interdependent. For many Christians, salvation is through the church.[34] By furthering the church's mission and strengthening the institutional church, clerics secure their own salvation. The rabbi who professes Judaism is bound like all Jews to act for the good of mankind. A more just mankind, in turn, kindles hope that all Jews will receive justice. The rabbi's fortunes rise and fall with those of his people: "In himself the Jew is nothing; in his people he is everything."[35]

This formal identification of congregant and cleric, while easy to proclaim, is not unproblematic. Every religion defines itself around some core tenets. Even in religions in which salvation is more a matter of orthopraxy than orthodoxy, believers still hold some central beliefs, if only the belief that right practice rather than right thinking is salvific. Given the inherently individual character of salvation, the question arises: how can it possibly be in the cleric's interest to act as a spokesperson for the religion if doing so requires him to forfeit intellectual freedom? As the philosopher Immanuel Kant observes in his discussion of religious orthodoxy, it seems absurd that an age may "bind itself and ordain to put the succeeding one into such a condition that it cannot extend its (at best very occasional) knowledge, purify itself of errors, and progress in general enlightenment."[36] If a particular religion is identical with a set of beliefs that remains unchanged over time, then we must show how, if at all, thinking rabbis, ministers, and priests obtain their own good through seeking others' salvation in accordance with the tenets of their religion.

Judaism

The rabbi aims at teaching Judaism. Since the believing Jew is one who observes certain practices, the teaching of Judaism aims at encouraging conformity to mandated practices by stating what is to be done and why. But in what does right practice consist? The Jew learns what should be done by putting his or her desires to the test of God's revealed word. Each desire must be examined to see whether it accords with what Jewish texts, traditions, and past commentaries have revealed as God's will. The discipline

of so testing proposed courses of action is the rabbinic discipline. The rabbi is just another Jew who differs from others in
being habituated to this discipline[37] and who encourages congregants to similarly habituate themselves to testing their lives using
the revealed word of God. In other words, the rabbi aims at the
"rabbinization of all Jews."[38] The Jewish rabbi who is nothing
apart from his people achieves his own salvation at that moment
when every Jew becomes a rabbi and every Jew is saved.

But why is the discipline good? What values underlie the discipline itself and how do they benefit the rabbi? The Talmudic,
rabbinic discipline has been described as follows:

> [The Jews] chose to form the most vivid and intense of all
> groups, to sustain what is, after all, one of the most particular
> of all literary traditions, the Talmud itself. Yet they did so in
> full knowledge that their group was not coextensive with
> society, and that their Talmudic tradition did not contain every-
> thing worth knowing about the right way of living life. So the
> Talmud imparted the lesson that men may face a relativity of
> values, but in the end, must choose life in some specific place,
> among some particular group of people. In the end you do
> put your napkin on the cushion – or the table.[39]

We all make choices. And we all stand somewhere in particular
when making these choices. For the disciplined, professing rabbi
the religious issue is not one of transcending all frames of reference but of making the best possible choices one can within a
frame of reference which permits genuine debate.

Rabbinic Judaism aims at improving life on earth by helping
people make better choices. At the core of Judaism lies the
unchanging belief that choice is improved by legitimating dissent
while simultaneously containing it enough for the community to
avoid paralyzing discord. No Jew is free to suddenly decide that
Platonic dialogues or the New Testament, rather than the Torah,
should form the basis of Judaism. Interpretations of the Torah are
binding upon the lives of observant Jews. However, beneath this
"sacred canopy"[40] of Torah-regulated life, men and women are
at liberty to disagree over interpretations of the word of God.
The core belief of Judaism does not enslave believers to any
particular interpretation but frees them to explore other interpretations. There is no restriction on the types of objection which
may be raised. One may, for example, raise an objection suggested

by a Platonic dialogue. Disagreeing with a conclusion or an interpretation does not rob the interlocutor of his or her Jewishness.
In fact, God Himself has legitimated this contained conflict and
speaks through it. In interpreting sacred texts, minority as well
as majority opinions are recorded. Dissent is never nullified but
"remains an eternal part of . . . Torah heritage, and 'these and
those words are the words of the living God'."[41] Just as the
attorney's (and client's) losing arguments become part of the
common law tradition and continue to be influential in that tradition, so the dissenting rabbi's voice becomes an honored and
influential part of the Jewish heritage and law.

By insisting upon the incomplete character of God's revelation
and the need for Jews to involve themselves in the mode of
disciplined human dialogue through which God speaks, the rabbi
serves his own good in two ways. First, rabbinic teaching extends
the "sacred canopy" over an ever-widening community of Jews.
The framework in which the rabbi has led his life thereby
becomes more secure. The rabbi gains confidence that the faith
of his fathers will still be strong, guiding his future choices as
well as those of his children. His children and those of his friends
will inherit what he was bequeathed. Second, the discipline
ensures that practical matters do get resolved so that life can go
on. This closure is no small blessing. People do not want to live
a life forever frozen in indecision. The napkin must be put on
the cushion or the table; discipline decides which.

For the rabbi, action is not mere reflex but a consequence
of deliberate choice informed by the best available arguments
pertaining to the practical problem at hand. Because the rabbinic
life shows evidence of having been so chosen, rabbis become
worthy of wielding practical authority in the eyes of their fellow
Jews. No thinking person trusts maniacs or fools who give no
thought to their actions. Rabbinic discipline justifies the congregants' trust in the rabbi's pledge to assist them while at the same
time helping the rabbi lead a just life. The good of the congregant
and the rabbi merge into one.

Protestantism and Catholicism

The question of whether the clergy derive any good from ministerial practice and whether this good complements that of their
congregants becomes critical in Protestantism and Catholicism.

Unlike the rabbi who holds no office within a church, ministers and priests do hold such an office. One of the duties of office consists of teaching the orthodox positions of the church. Although a sect may grant the clergy a large degree of freedom for challenging these positions, they still must adhere to some core tenets to qualify as a member of the church. In fact, these faiths' commitment to proselytizing requires a degree of orthodoxy since some core dogma must exist to take to the masses. Given such orthodoxy, it must be explained how adhering to a particular position can be good for a reasoning being who cannot consistently assent to forgoing the use of reason (Kant's point) and whose own salvation depends upon possessing the freedom to challenge earthly powers who can become demonic and whose influence threatens one with the "loss of *telos*" or spiritual death.

Kant suggests a resolution along the following lines. The dogma the priest or minister is asked by church officials to defend may very well be true. Moreover, no one forces the Catholic or Protestant to profess as they do. If there were not something in the tenets of the faith which seemed plausible and worthy of defense, the minister or priest should not have taken office in the first place. To take office when one cannot in good conscience assent to its responsibilities is deceitful. On Kant's view, endorsing orthodoxy does not harm the clergy. They need assent to nothing which is obviously false while remaining free to discuss the merits of a particular position in forums (e.g. academic journals) appropriate for such a debate.

To some extent this solution has been adopted by Christianity. Protestant churches have long tolerated radical theologians in their midst. The Pope has upheld the importance of independent Catholic universities in which professors explore the meaning and defeasibility of what is currently orthodox.[42] The Kantian response, though, fails to show whether or how the practice of embracing orthodoxy is good for the church official. It only establishes that the cleric will not be harmed by discharging the duties of office. The argument hardly constitutes a ringing endorsement of ministerial practice. One is left wondering why the thinking man would ever want to become a minister in preference to, say, a university philosophy professor. This defect is particularly serious, given the evangelical character of normative Christianity. If adherence to a particular position is not good for the leader, how can orthodoxy possibly be represented as good for the would-be convert?

Pope Pius XII's resistance to ecumenism suggests an alternative way to defend the minister's decision to abide by the church's mandate to uphold the current doctrine. Pius XII warned that ecumenism should not be bought at the price of renouncing or minimizing doctrinal differences.[43] Catholics should hold onto their particularity not because it is good to be stubborn but because there are reasons for the doctrine. These reasons only obtain a thorough testing when they are argued for by people who know them from the inside out. In order to see one's own position for what it is, one needs debates with other thinkers who believe they have equally good reasons for rejecting the position one is defending and are capable of presenting these arguments well. Individuals and faiths are different and discover their uniqueness through debates about living positions. While papering over disagreements may engender a nice warm feeling of brotherhood and sisterhood, such a strategy does not advance the understanding of another's point of view. Nor does it help one become clear about one's own beliefs.

Clergy who profess a particular doctrine are not, on this second view, enslaving themselves to some static, unchanging church credo. As theologians have noted, Christian dogma has always evolved as a consequence of encounters with peoples of other religions and culture.[44] If salvation is through the church, it is through a church which is constantly affected by what goes on outside it. Every defense of a position in response to a challenge conforms to the particular objection at hand and thus changes prior responses. Revision of salvific doctrine is therefore a given. Being committed to defend the specific tenets of a particular faith is what enables the endless process of revision to be thoughtful. To put the same point slightly differently: doctrinal revision does not signify a failure of Christian apologetics but rather represents its success. Some such understanding of this dynamic seems to underlie Tillich's striking claim that Christian evangelism does not use apologetics but *is* apologetics.[45] Positions most likely to persuade an audience are those which respect the individual intelligence of the listener. A dynamic rooted in particularity depends upon encouraging the individuality of all participants. When their apologetics honors these differences, evangelists and listeners alike are permitted to retain their integrity while they seek for unity underlying their differences. Persuasion occurs not in spite of, but because of, one's limited view.[46]

Understanding the teaching and defense of orthodox positions in this manner enables one to see how clergy and congregations alike benefit from the role of church apologist. Both parties not only preserve their intellectual integrity but also obtain freedom of the sort reasonable people desire. No one wants to be free to be a fool. Instead, the thinking being desires to be free to articulate positions which can and will be tested by others who are trained in such debate. Only after so defending his beliefs will the cleric be able to trust his positions and the life purposes he roots in these positions. The cleric's purposes become more his own. His evangelism saves him, enabling him to avoid that loss of the self's purpose, which is, we recall, "death" on the Christian view.

The congregation equally benefits from this evangelism. The church does not ask members to waste their time considering obviously silly or incoherent positions; only tested dogma is presented. Arguments for and against any particular dogma form part of the church's *klerikos* or inheritance. The cleric functions as a repository of this inheritance, drawing upon it when congregants question the wisdom of certain tenets. The congregation can access this inheritance because the clergy's evangelism has taught them the inheritance. Of course, a given cleric may prove inept at enunciating the reasons for the dogma. But such individual incompetence does not vitiate the overall goodness of an approach which saves cleric and congregant alike.

GENERIC PROFESSIONAL SATISFACTION

We may view professionals' activity as intrinsically satisfying because and insofar as they individually gain a share of the same particular good they are striving to help the client procure. This benefit, unlike fame or money, is specific and intrinsic to the practice in which the professional engages. The doctor gains health, the lawyer justice, and the cleric salvation. But this benefit is not the only one pledging practitioners realize. In addition to this specific good, they derive a good which is formally identical in all three professions. They reap the good of being held accountable only for actions which they in fact can perform and which they legitimately may be expected to perform given their public pledge. Before discussing this second, generic benefit in detail, I must make a few general observations about accountability and control.

Accountability and control are obviously interrelated notions. We do not expect people to abide by promises beyond any human's ability to fulfill. Reasoning adults do not hold fellow citizens to a promise to change the chemical formula for salt or to fly to Uranus and back in one day. Nor do we expect a mathematics professor to succeed in teaching every student in the university advanced number theory. Some students simply do not have the ability to do the work; others choose not to do the reading and exercises necessary to master the subject. Teaching requires the active co-operation of another party if the desired good (e.g. a liberal education) is to be achieved.

The learned professions clearly resemble teaching on this score. The good is inherently individual and cannot be achieved without the appropriate co-operation of the client. But this dependence means that the professional must have some way of limiting involvement with persons who either are totally passive in the relation or attempt to manipulate the professional into achieving an end foreign, if not actually hostile, to the service the professional originally pledged to render. Without some such mechanism, professionals cannot practice the activity from which they derive their authority and their share of the covenanted good.

Despite the clear need for such control, the two models examined in Chapters 2 and 3 do not provide for it. The expert has no means for coping with either client passivity or client over-reaching. The expert model simply posits an agent who knows how to perform a well-specified task consistently and who puts this skill in the service of an end of his own choosing. The client may more or less abdicate responsibility, looking to the expert to run the show. Alternatively, the client may want the expert to knowledgeably execute a specific task the client specifies (e.g. "Administer a fatal dose of morphine to me, doctor"). The expert is indifferent between these two possibilities. *Qua* expert, he uses his skill as he sees fit on a given day.

Although it emphasizes client control, the contractual service model permits client passivity. The doctrine of informed consent designed to empower the client is predicated paradoxically upon the non-involvement of the client. The client contracts to be told what he believes he should know, but the professional does all of the informing.[47] Within informed consent theory, there is no live sense of the client struggling to learn about healing and taking charge of his own fate. Instead, professionals are to be highly responsive to what may be highly irresponsible client desires. The model provides the professional with no principled way of resisting these desires. While it does permit the professional to refuse to enter into the relation in the first place, it leaves unaddressed the issue of how the professional should respond to wild whims suddenly expressed after the relation has been initiated.[48]

Unlike the expert or contractual service provider, the covenanting professional may legitimately lay claim to the client's co-operation. Client passivity or uncooperativeness need not be tolerated. Physicians sometimes encounter patients who refuse to take prescribed medicine or to follow suggested diet restrictions. If a given regimen is, in the doctor's judgment, the only way to safely restore health, then the patient's non-compliance effectively means the doctor possesses no way to help the patient. Continuing to see the patient might give the doctor a good feeling but doing so is a sham. No healing is occurring and none will occur as long as the patient refuses to do what must be done to foster health.

As the psychiatrist Sullivan repeatedly insists, good physicians know their limits. When a patient's behavior is making treatment impossible, the physician no longer has any reason to initiate or continue "therapy."[49] To do so would be to misrepresent what occurs in the physician–patient interaction. This lie constitutes a great breach of trust because the ill individual came to the physician seeking and expecting to be healed yet no healing is going to occur. Turning away patients who have shown themselves unwilling to help themselves be healed is therefore not merely authorized by the covenant but mandated by it.[50]

The law, for its part, requires the client to make certain choices during the course of the attorney–client relation. The notion of a paternalistic altruistic agent who acts on behalf of the client, the allegedly traditional view of the professional, does not now correspond nor has it ever corresponded to the reality of ethical legal practice. Under UK and US law, the client decides the plea. In civil cases, such as personal injury suits, the lawyer may not under present limited standards of disclosure transfer a client's case to another attorney without the client's consent.[51] This rule holds even if the transfer seems to be in the client's best interest. Nor can the defense accept terms of any settlement without prior consent from the client.[52] Moreover, the law holds clients responsible for acts and omissions of their lawyers.[53] The client remains so accountable even if the client has not been informed of the duty to supervise the lawyer's actions.

All of these legally imposed responsibilities ultimately derive from lawyers' public vow to promote legal justice and are binding because of this pledge. I have already shown how the Anglo-American legal tradition and professional ethics meet in the key concept or rule of "standing," which requires that lawyers appear in the person of the client.[54] One important corollary of this rule and the legal pledge ethic is that it is always the client, not the lawyer, who is on trial. The lawyer is the client's agent. So unless there is evidence of gross incompetence, the court should assume that the lawyer's actions and omissions reflect the client's wishes. It should deem the client responsible for having chosen and having continued to employ a particular attorney.

By and large, the court has enforced this responsibility. Although one might quarrel with certain finer points of how the doctrine has been applied, the doctrine itself seems morally sound.[55] The client *is* the one who is on trial. Furthermore, although particular strategies or arguments may appear unorthodox, the case may call for an unusual approach. The lawyer should have the freedom to develop the best possible case for the client. Such freedom is at the heart of legal justice. Short of forcing the attorney to divulge what was said during meetings with the client in which legal strategy was formulated, the court must assume the lawyer knows what he or she is doing and that the client approves. In addition, since lawsuits always involve contending parties, it would not be fair to overturn cases whenever clients maintain after the fact that their attorney did not act as they wished. There is no reason why the conscientious client who has chosen well should be penalized for the other side's unhappy choice. Having once permitted such reversals, the court would find it difficult to prevent clients from complaining of incompetence whenever the case went against them. Cases which now take years to resolve could take decades if the system were altered to remove all client accountability for choices made during the trial.

Legal justice is the goal of a system aiming not only at getting both sides of a case heard but also at reaching a final decision. The client and professional obtain a share of justice when the case is decided and becomes part of the law by which we all live. We would never have any settled law on which to base court and personal decisions if participants in the process of adjudication did not have to assume responsibility for their actions. The court does not permit jurors to change their mind once their verdict has been announced.[56] If a juror is not convinced by his peers, he must tell his peers he disagrees with them. He cannot shirk this responsibility. So too must clients take an interest in their own case and change lawyers if their lawyer is not, in the client's eyes, developing the best case.

We have seen that doctors are entitled to encourage and expect client co-operation. We may now add that lawyers are equally entitled to look to the client to make certain key decisions and then to live with the consequences of the lawyer's actions undertaken on the client's behalf. Failure to entertain such expectations demonstrates a deep misunderstanding of the character of legal justice and the practice of law. If the lawyer tries but fails to get the needed client involvement, then he must withdraw from the case, which by law cannot go forward and which by right ought not to proceed. To proceed with the case would violate the client's trust and waste the lawyer's time.

Client involvement and accountability figure prominently within the professional ministerial ethic. The central problem of religion is one of sin, guilt, or error. The cleric's role is not simply to reassure people "that whatever seems to bring them happiness is what they ought to do and whatever impediments there are to that aspiration, be they natural duties, moral obligations, control of the passions, or rule of moral behavior have no significantly binding force."[57] While the notion that each person is accepted by God as he or she is expresses "one deep strand"[58] of the Biblical tradition, the Judeo-Christian tradition equally insists upon investigating what type of behavior is required if God's purpose is to be realized in an ordered life.[59]

In Judaism, each of the men and women God has created makes a unique contribution to the creation of the world in which humans live. People are saved by accepting the challenge to act justly and to make the world one in which individuals love their neighbor as themselves and in which God can be God.[60] It falls to each person then to strive to discern how to realize justice in his or her life. To believe one is not so accountable is the root of all sin.[61] The Jewish prophets are distinguished not by their perfection but by their willingness to confront God and to probe into the goodness of what they and their people are suffering.

In Christianity too individual responsibility cannot be avoided. Although there are many Christian themes, we have seen that one recurring motif is the notion that individuals are saved from the wages of sin (death) by becoming less passive and laboring to make their purposes more fully their own. Neither an individual member nor an entire congregation has to heed the cleric's call to repent. But the cleric, for his part, is not bound to work with those who have shown themselves either unable or unwilling to respect their own inheritance. Others may prove more receptive to the word of God. The cleric is not bound to lay the pearls of the tradition before swine.

Getting clients to acknowledge the responsibility they bear in healing, litigating, and being saved is one half of the problem pledging professionals face. We have just seen how the pledge-based professional ethic permits them to insist in a principled fashion upon client responsibility. But what should we say about the remaining half of the problem – the proclivity of clients to reduce the professional to a hired hand? Like passivity, this client tendency impedes professional practice. Since this practice is the source of a professional's satisfaction, the latter's happiness would be utterly at the mercy of client whims if some mode of opposing this hubris did not exist. Fortunately for professionals, the grounding pledge leaves them well positioned to resist client manipulation.

Take the case of the ministry. As one Methodist minister observed in a discussion of the religious covenant, a congregation has the right to question a ministerial candidate's beliefs.[62] After all, the faith's inheritance is public, belonging to the congregation as well as to the church's officers. The Christian apologetic honors the questions of those hearing the message.[63] However, the congregation "has no right to hear the answer it desires."[64] It may want to hear that re-baptism is necessary for salvation[65] or that adults may be bar-mitzvahed. Yet where there are no Biblical or historical warrants for the salvific goodness of such practices, the cleric refuses to accede to them, understanding that to do so is to forfeit legitimacy.

That refusal to comply educates the congregant in the beliefs and practices of the faith. Individuals professing to be Jews or Christians ought to know to what propositions they are assenting. Consequently, it is hard to see how the refusal could be anything but good for cleric and congregant alike. The whole of religious education (e.g. confirmation classes; premarital counseling) is predicated upon such awareness being good. Congregations historically have cherished clerical independence because it leaves the cleric free to confront members with the error of their ways. Early churches refused to pay ministers salaries in order to reduce ministerial dependence upon the generosity of a few rich men in the community who funded the salaries and who might not have the best interests of others at heart.[66] When clerics defend their inheritance and refuse to cave in to congregational demands lacking Biblical or traditional warrant, they both honor their profession and benefit the laity by protecting the principles by which they endeavor to live.

Looking to their professed end of legal justice, lawyers find ample justification for resisting a wide range of inappropriate client demands. Attorneys need not, for example, agree to represent or advise every client who comes before them. The client may very well be pursuing a suit without legal merit. Perhaps there has been no injury under the law. Or maybe the law covering the case is beyond dispute. Courts would be swamped with cases if they allowed clients to define what constituted an injury. Cases could not be litigated in a timely fashion, if at all, and all the authority of all judicial players would be diminished.[67] Attorneys who understand that their authority derives from dedication to the furtherance of legal justice have no qualms about turning away would-be clients whose complaints lack legal merit or, more generally, whose proposed actions would impede the delivery of legal justice.

Nor can the client force the covenanting lawyer into the role of conscience for hire. While the lawyer should aggressively represent the client in court, it is a far different matter to advise the client on how to circumvent the law or even to remain silent while the client plots criminal acts: "It is one thing to represent a sometime murderer, quite another to be on retainer to the Mafia."[68] The Mafia expects its lawyers to state the law and, one presumes, to tell them of possible penalties they face for breaking the law. But it most assuredly does not want a lawyer who tells them what to do. That is the godfather's role. While the role of adviser to the Mafia could comfortably be assumed by experts who apply their knowledge as they see fit, the pledging lawyer will not be so cast. For a lawyer to divest himself of responsibility for upholding the law is tantamount to destroying the system in which attorneys have their role and fulfillment. Legal justice presupposes a set of institutions and a whole host of supporting roles whose interrelations are articulated by law. No lawyer can consistently say "I want a legal system to support the roles of judge, juror, lawyer, witness, etc. so that my clients and I may enjoy certain benefits" and then turn right around and assert "I do not want to uphold the law which establishes the system in which my desires are satisfied." To desire the end is to desire the means in this case.

In addition, public confidence in lawyers largely depends upon their ability to resist and mold client desires:

> If it is clear that a lawyer cannot be held responsible for everything his client does, it is equally clear that he must assume responsibility at some point.... The lawyer has to maintain his reputation for professional competence. The practice of law largely involves persuading people to do things that are very unpleasant; a lawyer who cannot induce his client to do what must [legally] be done is almost certainly incapable of exercising such persuasion on others.[69]

In the language of this book's argument, no client (potential or actual) would have any reason to trust the legal profession if attorneys are not free and willing to oppose clients' attempts to manipulate them. Counsel who is easily manipulated by one client may just as readily turn around and, at another party's behest, connive against the interests of this same client.

We might paraphrase the above passage and apply it to the third and final case of medicine. Since the practice of medicine largely involves persuading people to do things that are unpleasant, if not physically painful, a doctor who lacks the freedom to try to convince a patient to do what must be done for the sake of health will not merit the public's trust. This persuasion must often take the form of trying to show patients that the procedures or drugs they think they want are not good for them. While the covenanting doctor consults with the patient regarding the compromises and risks the latter is willing to endure and then honors patient decisions about such matters, he does not consent to actions which destroy the possibility of the patient achieving *any* equilibrium between the body and the person's purposes. No physician is obliged to prescribe a crash diet to an anorexic or to insert health-impairing silicon breast implants just because a woman wishes to look different. A dead patient obviously is no longer able to achieve a healthy equilibrium.

Nor need the doctor consent to whims that impair the doctor's ability to heal others. It has been argued, for example, that patients are morally entitled to have their doctor conduct additional research which is unlikely to have any therapeutic value if this additional research allays the patient's anxiety.[70] This claim seems dubious, given that doctors have never consented to spend their lives placating neurotics; and given that the hours they spend doing such research is time that could be spent actually healing other people. There is no general duty to do research for others. The duties owed have been incurred as a result of the professional pledge. That pledge is a pledge to heal patients. Consequently, the covenanting doctor may legitimately refuse to do such research without violating the patient's rights.

It is desirable, as well as morally right, that the doctor be positioned to resist client over-reaching. While it is no doubt often tempting to succumb to patient desires, doing so can easily backfire. As the illness progresses, the sick individual may very well heap abuse on the accommodating physician. Under duress, it is easy for the patient to forget that he was the one who had been calling the shots. The physician will probably wind up with an ill and angry patient who may refuse to pay for service, with a diminished reputation for competence, and with none of the satisfaction that comes from healing.

Wealth and fame may not come to all who practice in accordance with what they have professed. But at least pledge-adhering physicians, lawyers, and clerics have the satisfaction of engaging in a practice in which they legitimately exercise enough control to accomplish what they have promised to do. Precisely because these professionals are free to oppose client passivity, recalcitrance, and hubris, the community may properly and reasonably hold them accountable for what they have done or neglected to do. The professional should settle for no less in the way of accountability and can ask for no more.

CONCLUSION

The professional, like the client, must derive some benefit from the interaction in order to find practice desirable. Those professionals who content themselves with serving the limited particular good they have professed to serve reap two benefits. First, the professional shares in the specific good (health, justice, salvation) at which his practice aims. Second, covenantal professionals gain the freedom necessary for practicing in a satisfying manner. They can be held accountable by themselves and others for discharging their responsibilities because their pledge enables them to oppose client attempts to shirk responsibility or to ask too much of the professional. Under this arrangement, the professional and client are equal as agents. Both parties can fulfill themselves by pursuing and obtaining a good which is a genuine good and which is the one they value most in the circumstances in which they find themselves. Far from being paternalistic, these professionals insist upon the responsibility of each party. Within the relation, each party is, in Sir Isaiah Berlin's description, a free person who is "deciding, not being decided for; self-directed and not acted upon by external nature or by other men."[71] Each party can truthfully say, I am "conscious of myself as a thinking, willing, active being, bearing responsibility for my choices and able to explain them by reference to my own ideas and purposes."[72]

If the analysis of this chapter is sound, it explodes the myth that the professional is a passionless, self-denying, disinterested creature. Ethical or true professionals are passionately concerned with and satisfied by the upholding of their public profession. It is largely this passion that supports the institutions, such as hospitals, the courts, churches and synagogues, in which professionals operate. Clients come and go. Professionals provide the core of stability on which institutions depend for their continued survival.

Such passion, though, raises further questions about professional legitimacy. The professional's pledge to serve the good of the client results in a client-centered practice. This practice, when conducted in accordance with the terms of the pledge, benefits both the professional and the client. But where does society at large enter the equation? Is the professional entitled to undertake acts which benefit the client if these same acts harm others in the community? To these questions we now turn.

Chapter 8

The professional and the public good

Many attempts have been made to state what qualifies as a morally legitimate relation between professionals and the larger public in whose midst they practice. Although the attempts vary in their details, they fall roughly into three categories: professionals either (1) are entitled to act as exclusive agents of their clients' welfare and, as a consequence, are governed by norms different from those by which the rest of us are bound; (2) stand in no special moral relation to their clients but are bound by the same moral norms as everyone else in the society; or (3) have moral obligations to clients that are special but that nonetheless have been established in accordance with a given community's moral norms binding on all members of that community. Since the relation I wish to defend has certain affinities with each of these three positions but is different from all of them, I will begin by briefly describing each position and stating what seems to be problematic about it.

THREE MODELS OF THE PROFESSIONAL–PUBLIC RELATION

Relation one: public interest promoted by exclusive and zealous professional loyalty to individual client

On the first view, professionals are the most ethical and the best servants of the public good when they zealously promote the welfare of the individual clients who comprise the public. Philosopher William May, for example, argues that the doctor benefits individual patients and that excessive loyalty to the patient poses no direct problems of injustice to others.[1] Thus, while May concedes that it is trivially true that when a doctor helps one patient he is not helping another, the doctor's assistance to one party does not simultaneously cause harm to another party. In his discussion of attorney responsibilities, attorney Monroe Freedman similarly argues for overriding loyalty to the client. While Freedman knows that the actions of one attorney will affect the other side's case, he contends that the state's power always so far exceeds that of the embattled client of the defense that the latter's rights will be insufficiently protected unless attorneys are left relatively unfettered to do their best for defendants.[2] Doing their best may include allowing a witness to perjure himself or refusing to tell the court the whereabouts of a client who has jumped bail. Freedman's can be seen as a "traditional" legal position which merely extends the jurist Blackstone's view that "the public good is in nothing more essentially interested than the protection of every individual's private rights."[3]

Although Freedman and May differ in the details of their defense of client loyalty (Freedman focuses on threats to individual rights, May to individual health), the two men see no conflict between serving the individual client and promoting the public good. While the public good may consist, in part, of the good of the individuals within it, a view to which I will return shortly, this first portrayal of the relation between professional and public is rather naive. It ignores the professions' own understanding of themselves as having responsibilities to persons other than their current client base. Lawyers historically have seen themselves as "officers of the court," ministers as "servants of the church." These roles are the professionals' way of talking about responsibilities they have to members of the public who are not actual clients but who certainly qualify as potential clients. The professions recognize that their loyalty to an individual client is limited by these other persons' legitimate desire also to obtain a share of the good the professional is promoting. No doctor puts a patient with a highly contagious disease in a double room. The other person in the room also falls within the class of the sick the doctor has vowed to protect. So, although the doctor may not be the attending physician for this other person, the doctor is bound to consider the second party's health as well as the health of her own patient. In the case of law, the other side is not, as Freedman would have one believe, always the all-powerful hostile state. Very often court cases involve corporations and individuals suing one another. Even when the state is prosecuting, care still must be taken to ensure that both sides have had a chance to present their case in court if the resulting verdict is to qualify as just. When lawyers exercise such care to preserve the system in which the good of legal justice is obtained, they are thinking and acting as officers of the court as well as in the person of their client.

For its part, the ministry has never pretended that clerics may ignore the effects of their acts upon persons other than their parishioners. Since the profession of faith is made before all congregants and would-be members of the church, the cleric is always in a moral relation with the whole church, understood to consist of both actual and potential members. To return to our example in Chapter 2: a minister who counsels a teenager to have an abortion would be hard pressed to argue that this act does not betray the trust of the parents of the girl or of the congregation as a whole if their faith prohibits abortions. When ministers refer to themselves as "servants of the church," they are emphasizing the organic dimension of their profession. This dimension rules out an exclusive loyalty which would make the minister a hired hand of the individual parishioner.

This first model of the relation between professions and the public good works best for medicine. And it does not work all that well in this case either. Current events provide numerous counter-examples to May's thesis that service to the individual client does not directly implicate the physician in harmful acts. The family practice physician who treats an HIV-positive patient but who takes no steps to see that the patient's spouse is informed of the diagnosis cannot abdicate all responsibility should the spouse contract AIDS. The physician has sworn to practice preventive, as well as curative medicine, to protect the sick. ("Sick," incidentally, is in the plural form in the original Greek oath, suggesting again an organic dimension to physician practice.[4]) The physician knows the virus is transmitted through sexual intercourse. Moreover, it is reasonable to assume spouses are having, or have had, such intercourse. In such a case, inaction becomes culpable because the doctor's pledge commits him to keeping the spouse healthy, and failure to take steps to protect the spouse will be a contributory cause to the spouse becoming sick. (I assume the spouse is not yet HIV-positive at the time of the husband's initial visit.) Contrary to what May and Freedman argue, exclusive loyalty to the client does sometimes result in direct harm to other members of the community. Such harm cannot be reconciled with the fact that the *public* statement of the professions commits them to promoting the good of all potential clients, the very clients who will be harmed if the professional is exclusively loyal to an actual client.

Relation two: professional morality identical with ordinary, public morality

On the second view, professionals owe no particular loyalty to their clients. In fact, they do not stand in any special moral relation to the client at all. The philosopher Alan Goldman, for example, contends that professional morality, like "ordinary morality," must consist in honoring the rights of all rational autonomous persons. Autonomy is understood roughly as the power to order one's own life priorities as one sees fit as long as this ordering does not unduly infringe upon other persons' autonomy. Thus, since it is a violation of personal autonomy to act in such a way as to endanger another's life without their consent, the professional must not do anything that would pose such a danger. So, if a client confesses to having committed a crime for which an innocent party is serving time, the lawyer must disclose this information to protect this third party.[5] Or, given that we all have as autonomous beings a right to know what we think we need to know in order to plan our lives, a doctor must honor both the patient's moral right to know a prognosis[6] as well as the moral right not to hear an unpleasant diagnosis.[7] In the case of the patient who has tested HIV-positive, Goldman would presumably have the doctor honor the spouse's moral right to know this news since it bears so significantly and directly upon the spouse's ability to lead a satisfying, self-directed life.

Unlike the first position, this position explicitly acknowledges that professionals have responsibilities to members of the public as well as to actual clients. The public good consists in respecting persons' right to autonomy and all the subordinate rights deriving from it. This sensitivity to all parties' good is its strength. However, its weaknesses are many. The universal rights position badly misrepresents the character of what it calls "ordinary morality" when it denies that we have obligations to some persons (e.g. our friends or family members) not owed to others created by or resulting from our past actions, promises, and undertakings with respect to these persons. Under every ordinary morality the West has ever known, such actions and undertakings do cause people to stand in a variety of special moral relations with one another. Parents who contrive to bring children into this world and who promise at birth ceremonies to rear these children have a responsibility to raise them. While it is true, as the rights theorist observes, that parents may place the children in day care centers or with the child-rearers on a kibbutz,[8] parents do not thereby escape their moral obligation to the child. If the day care center or kibbutz goes bankrupt, we look to the biological or adoptive parents to nurture their own children. It is therefore quite plausible that the professions' public commitment to promote the good of persons who qualify as clients similarly places them in a special moral relation to clients, be they actual or potential.

The universal rights theorist also forgets that particular goods such as health, justice, and salvation must be at the moral center of the professions. If the doctor will not or cannot promote health, any talk about patient rights during treatment is simply moot. No real treatment is going on in such a case. The doctor–patient relation does not exist when healing is not the focus, because patients go to the doctor to be healed, not to have their autonomy respected. While the need to listen sensitively to the client and to respect the client's life priorities do matter in ministering, healing, and counseling (see the whole of Chapter 5), they do so as part of the ongoing trustworthy relation in the service of a particular, genuine good. As we have seen, the client's will is binding only insofar as what is willed is consistent with service in accordance with the pledge to promote this good. The patient has no right to know nothing or to be put on a crash diet if either forces the doctor to be a destroyer of the patient's health. The professional is present in the relation as a helper and is under no obligation to become an untrustworthy agent who abuses the client.

This last comment highlights the need for any professional ethic to respect the professional, as well as the client. Most universal rights theorists have been so intent upon establishing the rights of clients that they have forgotten, by their own universalist principle, that the professional, too, has some claims which must be honored. While Goldman asserts that everyone except a fanatic would see that the moral lawyer is bound to instruct clients how to lie in order to circumvent a divorce law Goldman thinks is archaic and unjust,[9] it is hard to see how the attorney can possibly be under such an obligation. Surely one is not a fanatic for believing that litigation exists precisely in order to test the justice of laws. It is not extreme for an attorney to insist upon her clients using the system to get the law changed by, for example, appealing against an unfavorable ruling. While, in rare cases, a lawyer perhaps should help a litigant circumvent the law, the rights theorist is surely bound by his own principles first to show us that creating an environment in which lawyers are effectively licensed to break the law is not more destructive of persons' rights the theorist wishes to protect than the current arrangement in which attorneys, like the rest of us, are bound to obey the law and benefit from doing so.[10] Professional lawyers can certainly be forgiven for wanting to hear more before endorsing Goldman's suggestion that they overlook "the precise bounds of law"[11] and lie to the court on behalf of welfare recipients who defraud the government because they think their payments are too small.[12]

There is an additional problem here. The client is not entitled to use the professional–client relation to manipulate the professional.[13] Manipulation by the client would in many cases undermine the trustworthiness so crucial to professionals' ability to render help. The client who has been "helped" by a lawyer willing to lie to the court has little reason to believe this same attorney's promise to help her have her day in court. This promise too may be a lie. The "moral" obligations Goldman's theory imposes upon professionals will tend to deprive the same professionals of clients if these obligations are discharged. Professional obligation as understood by the universal rights theorist amounts to a duty to professionally self-destruct. No professional can consistently will such an outcome as a professional. Therefore, there is no such duty.

To summarize: the universalist approach is weak because it ignores the special relations persons are in with respect to one another by virtue of past actions and public commitments and because it tends to forget that the professional–client relation is a two-way street morally centered in the promotion of some specific particular good. No one has to become a professional. They are legitimately motivated to do so because they derive some intrinsic satisfaction from the promotion of a good. The universal rights approach errs in binding professionals to perform actions destructive of their trustworthy character and of the very possibility of satisfying practice.

Third relation: professional ethics as an institutionalized expression of prevailing public morality

The third approach, like the first, recognizes the importance of professional loyalty to the client. This view sees professions as the public's chosen, institutionalized way of providing aid to its members who are particularly vulnerable. Like parents who protect and nurture their children, professionals exist to promote their clients' goods. Paul Camenisch, a leading proponent of this third view, argues that professionals are under a special obligation to render aid to those who qualify as clients for two reasons. First, while ordinary citizens have not promised to help the sick, the accused, or the spiritually troubled, the learned professionals have made such promises.[14] Moreover, the public has accepted these promises. Indeed, to say professionals occupy a role is simply to agree that they are subject to the public expectations that have been formed by and coalesced around such promises. Promises are binding under ordinary morality. So, on this view, professional roles are sanctioned by the prevailing morality of the particular community in which professionals exist.

Second, professionals are bound by the morality of gift-giving and gift-receiving to provide aid to potential and actual clients. The public has granted professionals their legal monopoly of practice protected by the mechanism of licensure. In addition, professionals are able to make a living only because the state has provided them with an institutional infrastructure of hospitals, clinics, law schools, etc. in which to serve clients and to learn how to do so. These benefits and professional roles may be understood as a gift of the public to itself. To take Camenisch's example: just as my acceptance of my grandmother's gift of silver commits me to honoring her tacit expectation that I will not use it for chemistry experiments, so accepting and occupying a professional role in society commits the agent to abiding by the public expectations and moral consensus regarding how the role will be discharged.[15] In particular, since these professional gift-roles have been granted with the understanding that clients will be helped irrespective of their ability to pay, their personal idiosyncrasies, or their intellectual ability to negotiate contracts, professionals are bound to render aid to the indigent litigant or defendant and to the distressed child or accident victim even if the professional would prefer not to do so.

Unlike the second view, this one focuses less upon rights and more upon the professional responsibility to promote health, legal justice, and salvation. This focus enables it to keep the particular good of the client at the core of professional ethics where it belongs. The focus also enables the model to address the character and limits of morally legitimate professional authority without having to appeal to such dubious rights of autonomy as the "right" not to hear unpleasant news. Given that we learn what is right and wrong through the praise, blame, and suggestions of friends and family members, it seems doubtful whether there is a moral right to avoid hearing that one is acting in a selfish or sinful manner or that dressing in the way one likes will hurt one's chances of being acquitted by the jury.

Despite these strengths, this position, too, has weaknesses. Camenisch treats gifts and promises as though they are intrinsically moral. They are not. As we have seen, only voluntarily elicited promises which commit agents to good acts and which have been understood and accepted by the parties affected by the promise are moral.[16] Camenisch does not show that what professionals promise to do is in fact good or accepted by all parties. For example, the professional promise to keep confidence may not have been accepted by all parties affected by this promise precisely because the affected parties would in their eyes be harmed by the fulfillment of this promise. Similarly, conforming with the gift-giver's expectations may be immoral. My aunt may give me a hatchet with the expectation that I will use it to smash up saloons. But it does not follow that my destruction of bars legally owned and operated by others is morally justified.

This view can also be faulted on practical grounds. As stated by Camenisch, it does not provide much in the way of practical guidance. Should the lawyer disclose a client's past crimes? Should the doctor tell the wife her husband is a carrier of a deadly virus? The answer apparently depends on whatever happens to be the public's current moral consensus. Camenisch's professionals, who exist because the public authorizes their practice and who are bound by the usual standards of honesty, integrity, and trustworthiness[17] bring no special moral expertise to the relation.[18] Any help they provide must accord with the whole host of principles, maxims, values, norms, and commitments citizens hold as members of the community. When the community is pluralistic, consensus may be hard to obtain and the professional will presumably be stymied.

When consensus does emerge, it reflects whatever values or ideas are common to all or most of the parties who happen to be part of the conversation. If large portions of a given community (e.g. a nation) are wicked and unjust, Camenisch's professionals are in a real bind.[19] They will be bound to perform acts which do not serve a good end, and since their professional legitimacy is rooted in communal consensus, the professional will have no alternative ground on which to stand in opposing the community. There is no reason why, on this third view, a physician, lawyer, or minister in a racist society will not be bound to help only white or non-Jewish patients.[20]

Moreover, if the professions are no more than institutionalized purveyors of prevailing moral consensus, then the professionals face an insoluble problem of legitimacy. Those actual or potential clients who are the victims of communal repression will have no reason to trust the professions because there is no reason to think that the latter will treat them in any manner substantially different from others whom the community permits to oppress them. In addition, the third view is unsatisfying as a theory of professional ethics because it fails to explain how professionals have managed to gain and maintain legitimacy in states which have explicitly disowned them (and which are, on this third view, responsible for institutionalizing the professions) and among community members who have implicitly repudiated these professionals by not opposing what the state has done. The underground priests in East European bloc countries who struck out on their own and who were rejected by the state, by representatives of the official church and by those who supported this state and this church eventually came to possess far more moral legitimacy in the eyes of the parishioners they attracted than the priests who had the society's imprimatur. Understanding professionals as agents of the ruling regime and the community which allows this regime to rule it leaves this fact unexplained.

Yet, despite these difficulties with viewing professions as a communally sanctioned, institutionalized expression of controlling values, we ought not to reject this view too hastily. It is importantly right on several scores. Like the second position, this one insists upon seeing an underlying unity in professional and communal ethics. Clearly there must be some such unity. No ethic evolves without regard for community values. To be persuasive and to be seen as practically useful, the ethic must appeal to some goods, norms, ends, or ideals members of the community either explicitly or implicitly value. If the East European priests stripped of their state licenses had not been committed to offering service which others could see as genuinely helpful, they would not have developed their underground following.

We must also remember that professionals become such as adults. For the years before professionals make their profession, they develop character and principles as members of a public. If a professional ethic is to have any practical effect, it must somehow "hook" into the public ethic. While a professional ethic might extend and develop one dimension of an agent's existing morality, such an ethic will not replace the prior ethic wholesale.

For these reasons, conceiving of professional ethics as a further specification of ordinary morality is attractive. If we can show that there is a professional ethic that affords a ground for sometimes opposing a particular community's moral consensus, while at the same time being an action-guiding extension of genuinely moral public norms or values, then the main problems with this otherwise sound position can largely be avoided. That a pledge-based ethic provides just such a ground I will now attempt to show.

THE DEFENSIBLE RELATION: PLEDGE-BASED ETHICS AS AN INTENSIFICATION OF PUBLIC TRUST

Let us begin by recalling just what is comprehended in the notion of pledge-based professional ethics. Professionals act morally and consequently have authority if and when they abide by the terms of their publicly made pledges. These pledges in turn are to be understood as specifications of the requirements which a professional must meet in order to be worthy of the trust of clients. This trust of which they must prove themselves worthy is not just any trust but rather a moral trust. The pledges require professionals to be not just able to aid clients but consistently willing to do so. They also commit professionals to furthering an end which is genuinely good and to pursuing this good in accordance with well-understood, publicly known limits acceptable to reasonable men and women.

To the extent that professional roles are, as I have been arguing, public expectations originating in and coalescing around professions so construed, occupying a professional role is a moral act binding the occupier to observe the conditions for genuine trustworthiness. Conceived in this manner, professional ethics and roles are clearly extensions of ordinary morality. Professionals have not invented trust nor the conditions under which vulnerable clients will reasonably extend trust.

But to say that professionals have invented neither trust nor client vulnerability is not to claim that they have simply conformed their behavior to societal expectations. Their ethic is properly understood as an intensification of the value of trust in interpersonal relations. It is an intensification of trust in three senses. First, because trust is at such a premium in these relations between strangers and highly vulnerable human beings, trust figures more prominently in professional ethics than it does in other relations which are governed by contracts to which substantial penalties attach in the event these contracts are breached. Second, professionals, more than any other group, have worked out consistently and explicitly the many conditions for trust in general and for trust of clients in particular. The claims of Camenisch notwithstanding, the professions do have a kind of moral expertise. True professionals spend their lives investigating and learning about the conditions for trustworthiness. Their public statements of their ends and values and their debates over these public oaths and codes are the evolving record of their discoveries of binding conditions for trustworthy practice. This statement does not mean that all of the paths taken by professions have been equally good. It does mean that the whole of a profession's activity can and should be judged by the extent to which the practice functions to preserve moral trust. Indeed, my argument has mirrored professional practice insofar as it too has used this public record and the history of practice to explicate the conditions for moral trust and then to judge professions relative to that standard.

Third, the structure of professions makes for the growth or intensification of trust. Trust admits of degrees. The structure of professions enables a trustworthy relation to develop and to grow. Insofar as the client grants the professional access to matters of great value to the client and does so with the expectation of benefiting from the professional's good will, the client must be said to trust the professional. The pledge grounds this initial trust which also has a large element of hope in it. Clients always hope that their expectation of benefit will be confirmed. In this sense, St Thomas Aquinas is right to define trust as "a hope which through strong conviction is itself grown strong."[21] As a professional repeatedly adheres to the terms of the pledge and thereby confirms the client's initial hope,[22] the client's belief in future benefit strengthens. The client's own experience with this particular professional begins to function as a reason to expect future good treatment. In this manner, the trust presupposed by the relation is generated by and within this relation or is "intensified" by it.

As intensifications of moral trust, professions are moral. Still, the suspicion may linger that, although the professional acts trustworthily in the client's eyes and in her own, insufficient attention will be paid to the good of persons who are not part of that professional–client relation. In other words, it seems as though professional legitimacy might be bought at the expense of the public good. I think this worry is largely the result of having failed to adequately specify what one means by the public good. I cannot here offer a complete theory of the public good and the ground of political legitimacy; however, I will try to show how pledge-based professionalism accords with four of the conceptions of public good prominent in the Western liberal democratic tradition. While this approach will not satisfy everyone, it does provide a way of addressing concerns we Westerners are likely to have. Furthermore, the approach will throw into relief the relation between professions and liberal democracy, a relation which deserves close scrutiny because professions have thrived largely in liberal democracies.[23]

FOUR CONCEPTIONS OF THE PUBLIC GOOD

Conception one: public good as the good of individuals

When we speak of the public majority, we refer to the majority of individuals in the public, not to some abstract entity existing apart from the individuals comprising this majority. Similarly, the public good may be thought of as the sum of the good of individuals who are members of the public in question. When the public good is interpreted in this manner, professionals are necessarily "workers for the common weal."[24] Every professional promotes the good of an individual client, a good which is itself, as we saw in Chapter 3, inherently individualistic. Individuals are at the fore of the professional–client relation when and insofar as the professional acts professionally. A doctor or attorney need not be a "meta-agent" of the public good in addition to being a professional in order to further the public good.

In fact, as a public we do not expect our professionals to be general do-gooders. We do not ask doctors to also write wills, hear people's confessions, and marry men and women. The public accepts professionals as ethical and trustworthy if they appropriately care for those things of value to which individual members of the public give them access. Appropriately caring for health does not entail taking on multiple causes in the public interest, but rather meeting the requirements imposed by patient trust – i.e. the physician "acts for the benefit of the sick" by trying to heal the sick individual by listening to the patient and honoring what he wills as a patient while simultaneously realizing her own balance of bodily and psychic purposes. In order to be trustworthy and to possess authority the doctor does not have to crusade for health everywhere. Agitating for better nutrition in Madagascar may be a good cause, but the doctor's time is limited. Realizing the actual good of clients who come into the professional's presence on the strength of the professional's pledge has priority over promoting the many possible goods of human beings around the world.

Of course, to the extent that professions see a direct link between their clients' distress and public policy, it will be appropriate to focus public attention on impediments to human thriving. The American physician who sees patients suffering from diseases probably caused by the presence of breast implants has a good reason to ask the Food and Drug Administration to reconsider its decision to permit such devices upon the market. But, in such cases, the professional's involvement with larger public policy issues – e.g. how new medical technologies should be accessed and regulated – grows out of the engagement with individual clients. This local focus does not diminish the professional's trustworthiness. On the contrary, it seems to increase it. Just as we are prone to assert that "charity begins at home" – i.e. that persons learn to love and to treat others well through interactions with those with whom they live most intimately – so too may we without contradiction view professionals as agents who learn to care for the public good through interactions with the particular clients at hand. This fact explains why physicians who opposed their patients' wishes for breast implants on the ground that these implants would complicate early detection of breast cancer currently enjoy far more credibility than those plastic surgeons who stopped implanting the silicon pouches only after the government declared it was in the public's interest for there to be a moratorium on the procedure. The former group of physicians exhibited and acted with local concern from the beginning, while the latter group seemed to care little for their patients until the implants became a public policy issue receiving government scrutiny.

The professional then does serve the public responsibly and morally through being loyal to the individual client. However, to be moral this loyalty must remain consistent with the pledge which justifies client trust in the professional. If no one is representing prisoners on death row who have filed appeals claims, then attorneys are bound to look beyond their current clientele and to volunteer their services to these inmates. As I argued in Chapter 4, the open-endedness of the pledge binds those professing it not to serve everyone around the world but to make a good faith effort to increase client access to assistance. The local concern of the professional expands to take more clients' needs within its purview. The professional, therefore, cannot consistently claim to abide by the terms of the pledge if she sees only one client or even one type of client. In the words of the poem "On the Eternal Duties of the Physician" inscribed on the temple of Asclepius, the physician will be a savior "equally of slaves, of paupers, of rich men, of princes. . . ."[25]

Furthermore, to be trustworthy the professional must be able to help. Ability consists not just in listening well but also in maintaining a degree of independence from client whims. One can certainly argue, along with Yale law professor Geoffrey Hazard, that service to a varied clientele increases the professional's sensitivity to the nuances of client speech and the professional's freedom to oppose the client.[26] For this reason alone, the real "pro" will voluntarily increase his or her availability to clients as part of becoming more professional. So, while on the first view loyalty is static and owed only to current clients, under the pledge ethic loyalty tends to enlarge beyond the current clientele. The public good is enhanced as an increasing number of individual citizens gain a share of the genuine goods the professions promote.

Conception two: public good as a system of checked power

Professionalism then benefits the public by promoting the good of individuals. The various goods of the many clients (A's health; B's legal justice) taken together constitute the public good in one sense of the term. However, being an effective protector of these goods often requires opposing attempts by the state or other powerful corporate bodies to harm individuals by ignoring or subverting their well-being. Therefore, the public good also needs to be understood as that system of checks designed to curtail attempts by the powerful to inappropriately and arbitrarily control the lives of individual citizens. Quasi-independent bodies, termed "intermediary institutions" by some political theorists,[27] have played a critical role in developing and preserving democratic institutions in the West. The professions, like unions and the church, have enabled citizens to act as a kind of counterweight to central government.[28] Professionals, in particular, have been able to oppose unjust state or corporate actions precisely because they derive their moral legitimacy from adherence to their legitimating public pledge to serve a particular good, and not from the will of the state or corporation or from whatever happens to be the dominant public opinion in some community at some point in time. Rather they are authorized by their pledge to do what they must to fulfill their promise to promote a particular client good such as legal justice or salvation.

Thus, although Camenisch is right that we generally do not require professionals to renounce citizenship as a condition of practice,[29] it is equally true that the professional ethic may dictate such a renunciation in some cases. Certainly history yields numerous examples of professionals standing apart from and against the will of the state on the ground that their pledge entitles and compels them to do so. The one German doctor who opposed killing Jewish and mentally impaired patients did so because such killing was inconsistent with his medical profession.[30] The Hutterite spiritual leader who spearheaded the Hutterite resistance to Hitler in 1933 appealed to his profession of faith. Furthermore, *pace* Camenisch, professionals have given up state-granted privileges of citizenship. They have done so if and when these privileges interfere with the ability to render trustworthy service to clients. For example, in swearing the Hippocratic Oath, Greek physicians voluntarily renounced the political privilege of every free Greek male to have intercourse with male or female slaves upon demand.[31] This renunciation is entirely appropriate because, as the argument has shown, sexual intercourse erodes physician trustworthiness.[32]

This independence from the state accounts for the professions' transnational character and their ability to hold state authorities responsible for harming individuals, even when the clients in question reside in a foreign country. Psychiatrists around the world condemned fellow Soviet psychiatrists when the latter, under pressure from the Soviet regime, started to treat political dissidents for the disease of political nonconformity. The condemnation was justified because the therapy in question could not possibly have been for the benefit of the sick. Disagreeing with the opinions of those in power does not signify a lack of health. The dissidents were not sick and did not deserve to be treated as such. Curiously enough, even the Soviet psychiatrists seemed to understand that the pledge, not the state's will, was the source of their moral legitimacy for they took great pains to try to show that their actions did in fact accord with the Hippocratic Oath.[33]

The professions are so far from deriving their authority from the state that attempts by the state to grant them authority have tended to delegitimate the professions. In Eastern Europe, the priests licensed by the state were the least trusted because they were perceived as serving the state's wishes rather than the client's good. Understanding the ground of professional legitimacy better, the West has been careful to acknowledge professions' independence from state control. The Greek polis never attempted to regulate medicine.[34] By and large the Roman regime did not meddle in professional practice either.[35] This separation of politics and the professions stemmed from their correct perception that the state does not give orders to medicine or law. The first lawyers, like physicians, evolved their own ethic;[36] it was not given to them by the state or polis. The United States has preserved this independence from state control. Here the courts (which are composed of lawyers) have the "inherent and exclusive power ... to regulate lawyers."[37] Medicine, too, regulates itself in light of its own publicly articulated understanding of the ground of its authority. Early Hippocratic physicians healed slaves, despite the polis' view that slaves were nothing more than living tools.[38] Today's doctors insist upon treating all wounded soldiers, including enemy personnel, brought into their presence.

This Western tradition of professional independence contrasts sharply with the lack of freedom in Ancient Egypt and Babylon where there was no idea of a pledge-based practice with its own intrinsic and distinctive character. In these two regimes, the political rulers controlled the interaction of doctor and patient, going so far as to prescribe terms of treatment.[39] The state could use doctors to further its own purposes. Even today we have Egyptians suggesting that prison doctors should get rid of troublesome political prisoners with diabetes by substituting lethal injections of glucose for medical shots of insulin.[40]

In the United States, numerous court rulings have rightly affirmed the existence and importance of a professional independence which is the natural consequence of professional legitimacy being grounded in a pledge rather than deriving from state or corporate sanction. The legal profession, for example, has successfully argued that, although an attorney is an officer of the court, he cannot be viewed as an officer or agent of the state akin to a policeman.[41] The attorney is bound to act as the second self of a client, even if that client is an official of a foreign government the state considers hostile to its interests. Because his profession makes him an agent of the client, rather than an "official of the government,"[42] the attorney does not take orders from the state. If the attorney were to do so, a client hated by the state might not get his case heard in court. In this manner, the attorney's public covenant to serve legal justice acts as a check on governmental power and the state's ability to deny legal justice to the client.

In addition, the court has held that a lawyer need not be a citizen of the United States to practice law in that country. A state may require that the attorney promise to uphold the Constitution. Such a regulation is justified because the lawyer professes to seek legal justice for clients within a constitutionally established system. However, since the lawyer is not present as a representative of the state, citizenship is irrelevant to the practice of law.[43] Imposing citizenship requirements violates counsel's professional independence. State regulations dictating what a physician must say to a patient may also violate professional independence.[44]

Finally, the court has suggested that professionals have a right
to act in accordance with their pledge, even when adherence to
this pledge pits them against a corporate employer. The courts
have held that the corporation's well-established right to fire an
employee at will may admit of a public policy exception when
the agent in question is a professional who has acted to protect
clients who are, of course, members of the public. The physician
who works for a company remains a physician as well as a company employee. If a corporation orders human testing of a drug
and a company physician balks because she fears the drug is
dangerous, the company may not simply be able to fire the physician at will, especially if she bases her opposition on a code of
ethics expressive of public policy. The professional may have
"a reasonably supportable ethical standard" on which to base
opposition to an employer's command and to thereby create
"an exception to the traditional employment-at-will rule, which
generally bars action for wrongful discharge, so as to permit
recovery where the employment termination contravenes a clear
mandate of public policy."[45]

Conception three: public good as the structure for effective citizen action

In insisting on the professional's independence from state or
corporate control, I do not want to be understood as pitting
professionals against the state or the organized community in any
simple-minded way. On the contrary, their adherence to the
pledge provides the structure in which we citizens of liberal
democracies pursue our individual projects. Professions practiced
in accordance with the relevant pledge are "disciplines" in the
strict Scholastic sense of the word. They are forms of practical
knowledge deriving their form and content from the object studied.[46] The object in all of the professions is the promotion of the
client's good. And as political philosopher Michael Walzer has
shrewdly observed, liberal democracies are distinguished by being
organized around such disciplines: "A liberal state is one that
maintains the limits of its constituent disciplines and disciplinary
institutions and that enforces their intrinsic principles."[47] Since
these limits and knowledge of them are prerequisites for the rule
of law, this structure of discrete disciplines is the public good.

To put the same point slightly differently: by insisting on their professional independence, professions do no more and no less than preserve the boundaries enforced by the rule of law. By providing a relatively fixed, stable, and predictable structure in which to operate, the liberal state with its rule of law enables people to form plans and to execute them without having to worry about the rules of the game changing overnight. One can go to a lawyer without worrying that she will behave as a doctor or gardener. Such a structure liberates us from chance and arbitrariness. We are more free than we would be without this stable and predictable structure. This freedom in turn permits us to pursue all of the goods, including health, legal justice, and salvation, which make our life worth living. I do not want to make professions into the source of all blessings. But we should not underestimate the extent of the contributions they make to a free and satisfying life within a liberal democracy.

Conception four: public good as balancing of individuals' competing goods

As I said at the beginning of this chapter, the most defensible understanding of the relation between professions and the public good has certain affinities with each of the three positions I have rejected. Professions do promote client-centered loyalty (first position) but only in a limited form. They also are an extension of public morality (third position), but not of majority consensus. Instead, the professional abides by the functional requirements for being worthy of moral trust. We must now address the second position's worries about excessive client loyalty.

The professions will lose their moral authority if they permit or require the individual professional to sacrifice another's well-being as part of promoting another's good. I say this not because such sacrifice is not morally permissible within liberal regimes in which all individuals are considered to possess equal rights to self-determination. I make the claim rather because this type of sacrifice cannot be justified within the framework of the pledge ethic which grounds professional authority to act to benefit the client. For insofar as the pledge is professed before the entire public, potential and actual clients are equally recipients of the professional's attention. The goods to be furthered, goods constitutive of a human life worth living, belong to potential and actual clients equally simply by virtue of their being persons who desire these goods. Consequently, to act legitimately, a pledge-based professional must show herself sensitive to the well-being of these other potential clients when serving the client at hand. While balancing the competing interests of individuals within the community is not the only meaning of the public good, it is an important one to which the pledge-based ethic must be sensitive. We must consider how, if at all, a pledge-based professional ethic accommodates the interests of persons other than the client at hand.

While there are many types of conflicting interests, I will explore how the ethic will tackle cases involving the professional responsibility to keep client confidence. I focus on this responsibility for two reasons. First, many critics have alleged that professionals wrongly see themselves as absolutely bound to keep clients' confidences, even at the expense of harming innocent third parties. While I will argue that this obligation is not absolute, the critics are properly concerned about client confidentiality. The issue of professional trustworthiness often does revolve around the question of what, if anything, a professional ought to reveal of what he has learned from an interaction with a client. For this reason, professional confidentiality provides a good test case for whether the pledge-based ethic can provide any sensible practical guidance to professionals.

Second, the issue of confidentiality forces the issue of exactly what is meant by acting as an agent worthy of client trust. When the client, already made vulnerable by disease or spiritual distress, discloses facts about himself, he makes himself more vulnerable. The attorney cannot defend me and present my case unless I am willing to submit to his interrogation, including his probing of matters which may not seem immediately relevant or which may implicate others whom I wish to protect. In confiding this information, I am giving the lawyer access to what is of value to me. I may be scared to start with and loath to trust anyone in an apparently hostile judicial system. Furthermore, I have only the profession of a stranger on which to rely for assurance that the information I provide will go no further. Interacting with the professional heightens client vulnerability. One cannot avoid seeing the professional as at least partially responsible for the client's extreme vulnerability. While some confidences should be disclosed, we are not entitled to talk as though professionals are simply human receptacles into which the client pours information to be subsequently discharged into the public realm with no questions asked. We must consider how, if at all, professionals can walk the ethical tightrope, maintaining their status as trust-worthy client helpers while simultaneously avoiding harming those who are potential rather than actual clients.

Limits to confidentiality in a pledge-based ethic

It is necessary to begin by being clear about what confidentiality is and why the professional owes it to the client. Keeping client confidence is the practice professionals observe of maintaining silence on matters about which they have learned through speaking with or observing the client. These matters are usually kept secret in the belief that the client wishes the information obtained to remain private. If and when a client authorizes a professional to make such matters public, disclosure by that professional is not a breach of client confidentiality.

Almost every ethicist writing about client confidentiality acknowledges its moral propriety. There are at least three reasons why it is a fitting practice. First, disclosure of what has been learned from the client would tend to jeopardize still further the client's already precarious ability to lead a fully human life. It is this precariousness the professional is supposedly helping to alleviate. Promising and keeping confidentiality helps offset this heightened vulnerability for which the professional is partially responsible and thereby assures clients that their belief in the professional's willingness to help has not been misplaced. Keeping confidence engenders the spirit of working together so critical to this participatory relation. So non-disclosure is a kind of func-tional requirement for being helpful.

In addition, keeping confidence is a condition imposed by the client's act of trust. Recall that trust is not absolute, but con-ditional. For the professional–client interaction to be legitimate, the professional must never presume to order the client's life priorities. The client's life story is the client's to disclose. By maintaining the conveyed information as private, the professional preserves the client's control over the unfolding of that story and, by implication, the unfolding of the client's life.

Finally, keeping confidence is a way of recognizing that the professional–client relation has a history. It is notoriously difficult to understand the conversation of two people who have evolved an intimate, trusting relation. One good reason for exempting spouses from testifying for or against one another in court lies in the problem of disentangling legally relevant meanings from the shorthand, inside-joke-ridden, history-laden conversation of intimates. While one's relation with a professional may not be as intense as with a spouse, conveying the nuances of what has been said to outsiders who have not been privy to the whole conversation is bound to be similarly problematic.[48]

There is then what could be termed a *prima facie* duty to keep confidence. That is, confidence should be kept unless one can discover some more compelling moral reason for not doing so. We now must consider whether there are any such reasons. Let me begin by stating what will not count as a compelling reason for overriding this *prima facie* duty. The duty cannot be legitimately overridden on utilitarian grounds. In the first place, if one is going to do a utilitarian calculation, one cannot consistently speak of a *prima facie* duty to preserve confidence. There can be no such duty since, in utilitarianism, nothing is binding apart from the result of the cost-benefit calculus. Nevertheless, there does seem to be a *prima facie* duty, for the reasons stated above.[49]

Second, though some modern ethicists have argued that when the benefits to the public of breaking confidence exceed the harms of doing so the obligation to keep confidence ceases to exist,[50] this argument is somewhat misleading. Before deciding on what harms result from a professional breach of confidence, we must first try to understand what function keeping confidence plays in a professional role and what kind of society we are choosing when we support or fail to support that role. It cramps our thinking to argue that, if we want to decide whether the medical profession should allow the police to run wanted posters in medical journals with a view to apprehending alleged criminals who come out of hiding for medical treatment, we need only weigh the harm of people not seeking medical treatment against the benefit of improved law enforcement and removing criminals from the street. These may indeed be harms and benefits we should consider. However, by focusing our attention on the mechanics of calculation, utilitarianism risks diverting us from the hard work of trying to articulate as fully as possible an adequate description of the action under consideration. Thus, in the above example, we should also consider whether, in breaching the promise to heal, the professional has not also wronged us by betraying the public trust. The initial formulation of what is to be calculated does not factor in the loss of trust between doctors and totally innocent patients made more vulnerable by doctors, who must now worry that these same doctors might turn them in because they happen to look like some alleged criminal. Nor does it capture one's sense that there is something like entrapment going on in this case. To put the point somewhat more contentiously: it seems as though utilitarianism cannot determine what is morally right or wrong in such a case since, to do the calculation well, we must appeal to some idea(s) of what is morally right or wrong if we are to be able to identify the factors that should go into the equation in the first place.[51]

Furthermore, the utilitarian calculation as it is usually performed is incorrect because it equates some *imagined* possible benefits (improved law enforcement) against the known actual harm of violating the client's trust. Comparisons of possible benefits/harms need to be weighted by their likelihood of actually occurring. A course of action that certainly produces a benefit is preferable to one that has only a small likelihood of yielding a slightly better outcome. When one has to balance the *known* harm of a breach of individual and public trust against the *possible* benefit of apprehending someone who has not yet stood trial or been convicted of any crime and who may not be dangerous, the case for disclosure looks much weaker.

We should also be somewhat wary of this utilitarian analysis because it will always be possible to invent some greater good(s) to offset the violation of trust. For example, one might posit that there will be better law enforcement if doctors are making citizens' arrests. But this is mere speculation since the opposite seems just as likely. If doctors do not turn in alleged criminal patients, more patients might be tempted to come out of hiding. The odds would therefore increase that they would be seen, identified, and apprehended. The utilitarian approach then should not be used to determine when to override a *prima facie* duty of professional confidentiality, for three reasons. First, it cannot, strictly speaking, override any *prima facie* duty because its methodology prevents one from meaningfully speaking of such a duty. Second, it does not give one a full sense of what is at stake in situations involving professionals because it does not think about the meaning of social roles but too quickly moves to calculating costs and benefits. Third, its cost and benefit calculations are themselves suspect because they usually are not weighted by probability of outcome and because pros and cons can be and are invented *ad nauseam*.

Nor does rights theory give us sound cause for overriding a *prima facie* duty to keep confidence. The rights theorist contends that a third party's "right to know" must often justifiably trump the client's right to have his disclosures remain private. But it does not seem as though there is any general public right to know. If there were such a duty, there would be a correlative duty to tell the public what one has learned. But journalists, perhaps the most vocal champions of the public's right to know, do not see their papers as bound to print all information that comes their way.[52] To take legal theorist Ronald Dworkin's example: the *New York Times* did not *have* to print the Pentagon Papers they obtained from Daniel Ellsberg.[53]

Furthermore, even if individuals have a right to know what affects them, confidentiality should not be violated for trivial reasons. Thus, if one is going to claim that the professional must disclose confidential information in order to protect the right(s) of some member(s) of the public, the right(s) in question must be of some significance. Consequently, one will need to argue that only when maintaining a secret poses a substantial, likely, and unavoidable risk to another party may the professional legitimately break confidence.[54] Yet these criteria are not very workable in practice, and they tend paradoxically to contribute to rights violations in numerous ways.

First, we will need something like a "reasonable person" standard here to decide when a risk is "likely" and "serious." Attorneys (psychiatrists, etc.) hear thousands of threats. While the threatened party might quake at hearing of the threat, the professional may not take it very seriously. Therefore, there must be additional criteria for the risk criteria – e.g. "likely" means "accompanied by threatening actions, or evidence of plotting, etc." Getting agreement on these criteria will almost certainly prove far more difficult than the rights theorists let on. While the rights theorist speaks confidently about what "reasonable" people think,[55] it increasingly looks as though there is not a single "reasonable" person standard that can be used in adjudication of rights disputes. In sex harassment cases, for example, courts are finding they have to distinguish between what reasonable men and reasonable women might think in various cases.

Second, if we are going to view the professional as having a general positive obligation to protect the rights of any and all members of the public, we are placing the professional in a terrible quandary. Moral rights are usually thought to underlie and result in legal rights. If we apply rights analysis to professional ethics, we surely will find ourselves operating under the reasonable/prudent person (or persons – see above) standards which pervade Anglo-American law. And, under these standards, professionals will be liable not only for disclosing what they in fact knew (e.g. a client's threat to kill a former girlfriend) but also for what they ought as a reasonable person to have known (e.g. that the client was the type of person who might kill a former girlfriend). Therefore, at law, "the obligation [will] exist to disclose information that may or may not actually be in the "hands" of the [professional]."[56] If we go this route we are asking the professional to become a public safety officer of the state who investigates clients and perhaps stereotypes them as part of a quest to protect the public from dangerous clients. Turning our professionals into quasi-police officers should give the rights theorists pause. Such an arrangement violates our democratic practice of protecting our rights by carefully maintaining clear and distinct boundaries between the various disciplines.

In addition, it is unclear how the professional could possibly be obliged to adopt an attitude of suspicion toward his clients, given that ordinary citizens are not bound to inform on one another.[57] Rights theorists would seem to be bound by their own logic to prove that it is not unjustifiably discriminatory to single out one group of citizens such as doctors or lawyers and require them to view their clients as criminal suspects.

Finally, it needs to be considered whether rules often thought to protect our rights, rules such as the one requiring doctors to break confidence and to report to the police anyone who seeks treatment for gunshot wounds, are not actually antithetical to both the practice of the professions and the protection of individual rights. The reporting requirement is intended to give police quick access to people who might have committed a crime by themselves or with accomplices. Yet police grilling of a critically injured patient might very well kill the patient who, in most rights theories, would have the right to be presumed innocent until proven guilty. Rights theorists cannot be happy with such an outcome; however, their position tends to result in this kind of erosion of client rights because it effectively turns the professional into an undercover police officer.

For all of the above reasons, neither the utilitarian nor the rights-based analysis provides a very satisfactory way of sensibly limiting clients' claim to confidentiality. The pledge-based ethic does provide a reasonable way of doing so. On the one hand, it recognizes a *prima facie* duty to keep confidence. On the other hand, it leaves the professional with the option of acting to protect others if and when the client ceases to be a client, as will tend to occur when the patient, defendant, or penitent becomes a serious threat to others. An example will help to reveal the relevant moral dynamic.

Let us assume that a parishioner has confessed to his priest a plan to commit a criminal act. In general, the professing cleric preserves confidence not out of respect for the client's "right of privacy" but rather as part of acting as a trustworthy agent pledged to assist penitents toward salvation. As long as the client qualifies as a member of the particular group the professional has pledged to serve, the latter is bound to do that which makes service possible and engenders client trust. However, from the point of view of the professing cleric, only that which has been revealed by a penitent in the course of his attempts to right himself in the eyes of God and of those against whom he has sinned is confidential. When the penitent is not present as a penitent, the priest is not present as a confessor. No relation has been established; confidence is irrelevant.

So, if the priest happens to see a member of the congregation shoot someone or overhears a plot by his parishioners to rob a local store, he is as free as any other citizen to report the matter to the police. The seal of the confessional applies only to what is revealed in confessional. Furthermore, a "confession" is not identical with "whatever is said within the confessional." If a person reveals within the confessional a plan to commit a crime, the revelation is not protected because the statement evidences no repentance. Where there is no repentance, no penance is possible. And where no penance is possible, the sacrament of confession does not exist.

Under the pledge ethic, the cleric is released from any obligation to keep matters secret when what is confessed is not confided as part of an interview in which the penitent is working with the cleric to attain spiritual salvation.[58] Note that the cleric is not some quasi-police officer masquerading as a minister. The cleric is through and through a professional. He is just very clear about what his function is and how it relates to professional– client speech. Communication which is salvific is "professional" and thereby protected. Non-salvific speech is not confidential and not protected. The priest or minister is not somehow bound by his ethic to violate the dictates of ordinary morality. The cleric is free to act to help others, including others threatened by the person before him, as long as he can do so without betraying the trust of someone who has come to him as a penitent.

A problem emerges only when the penitent, speaking as a penitent, reveals something of harm to a third party. Suppose a parishioner, while repenting of adultery, reveals to the minister that he has contracted a sexually transmitted disease as a result of his infidelity. Let us assume that the man indicates that he does not intend to inform his spouse of the disease, yet plans to continue having marital relations. Although the man might genuinely regret his adultery, he clearly exhibits no remorse over his intention to make his spouse ill. While the regretted adultery would be part of the protected confession, his proposed action of infecting his spouse would not so qualify. Since the latter is not part of the confession, it would not under the covenantal ethic be protected by the seal. The priest could therefore justifi- ably inform the wife (who is very likely also to be a member of the priest's congregation) of the threat her husband's disease posed to her health or, better still, invite husband and wife into his office and ask the husband whether he has some news to share with his wife. This response honors the organic dimension of the minister's clientele. The minister is not required to abandon the wife whom he also serves. But the response does not honor her at the expense of betraying the confessing penitent. His being as a penitent is also respected.

Again, the issue in a case like this is not whether the spouse's safety in some scheme of values outweighs the good of keeping the secret nor whether the penitent's "right to confidentiality" trumps a threatened third party's autonomous "right to avoid harm." The issue is rather whether or not what has been revealed qualifies as protected, salvific matter of a confession. If not, the minister who reveals the disease to the spouse has not broken confidence because trust has never really been invoked. The hus- band did not come seeking salvation but merely wanted to discharge his guilty conscience. As the argument of a prior chapter made clear, the cleric is not in the business of dispensing "cheap forgiveness"[59] and particularly not at the expense of other members of his flock who are striving to free themselves from outside forces and to reclaim their purposes as their own.

This limited form of keeping confidence, a far cry from the absolute duty always to protect the client which critics have imputed to professionals, maintains the latter's freedom to act appropriately within their role. As long as the client acts as a client, the professional keeps confidence. Should the client act in some other capacity, the professional is not present in the relation *qua* professional; the pledge is not invoked. Confidence need not be preserved because strictly speaking it has not been established. When the professional is not "in" a relation with the client as a professional, he or she is not bound by the professional ethic and is free to act in any other relevant role (as parent, citizen, friend, etc.).

In general, the hardest cases arise when the client confides something *as a client* which, if not divulged, will result in certain serious harm to a third party. For example, if a lawyer asks the client to discuss the events leading up to his arrest and if the client confesses to a prior murder for which an innocent party has been convicted and is about to be executed, the attorney faces a great dilemma. In this case, the confession has been elicited by the attorney quite naturally as a part of rendering service. As part of the relation, the interview falls within the protected domain. Yet a miscarriage of legal justice, the end the attorney is supposedly promoting, may result as a consequence of keeping confidence. The person about to be executed qualifies as a potential client of the attorney. As such, he too is entitled to a share of legal justice. What does the attorney do in such a case?

The answer cannot be simply: tell the court what you know. This answer will only satisfy persons who have not thought through the mechanics of breaking confidence. The attorney does not *know* the client is telling the truth. The client may be lying to protect a buddy in jail. Or, as we are now seeing in the Chicago prison system, the client may simply be claiming credit for many crimes in an attempt to appear more important. Moreover, although the lawyer believes the story, the judge cannot simply take what he reports at face value. The judge has a duty to look out for clients and protect them from unscrupulous attorneys.

The attorney, too, may have an axe to grind with the client. Should the attorney be believed? And should the attorney continue to represent the client in the present case after having informed on the same client? If so, how is the client to be protected against counsel, who is now perhaps a witness against him in a future trial for this second crime? If the original attorney should be dismissed, is the client then entitled to a new attorney? What does the judge do if the client decides to play an endless game of "Let's Jettison the Lawyer" by confessing the prior crime to his new attorney? The mind begins to boggle when one considers the mechanics of breaking confidence in the case of prior crimes.

Although the case is difficult, the pledging professional is not without options. One way out lies in the attorney refusing to claim any special knowledge of the prior case. Rather than proclaiming the client's confession before the court, the attorney could phone an anonymous tip to a newspaper questioning the prior conviction. Its journalists could investigate the evidence and determine whether a case existed for overturning the conviction. With this approach, the professional still keeps confidence but also acts to protect others seeking legal justice. The action does not undermine the process of legal justice; but it also does not require the professional to rush in where he justly fears to tread.

The above discussion does not exhaust problems associated with the practice of keeping client confidence. It does however show that the notion of a distinctive professional ethic is not the straw man it has been made out to be by some critics. Professionals have *prima facie* duties such as the duty to keep confidence. These obligations, stemming from their profession to serve a particular good, are not absolute but must themselves be continually rethought in each situation in light of the public promise to serve a specific good. The pledge ethic is an eminently practical, rich one with ample resources for balancing the competing claims of actual clients and the larger public.

CONCLUSION

The public good may be thought of as the sum of the good of individuals; as a system of checked state and corporate power; as a structure for effective action by citizens; or as an arrangement enabling us to balance the competing claims of actual and potential clients. The pledge-based professional ethic for which I have been arguing is consistent with and promotes the public good in all four senses of the term. When the public good is interpreted as an arrangement for weighing competing claims, the power of the pledge-based ethic becomes especially apparent. Since the pledgor commits to aid any and all members of the audience who hear the pledge and need the good which is being promoted, the pledgor must attend to the claims of all members of that audience. However, the pledgor is able to respect these claims because she limits what is owed to a client to what that client wills as a client. Rigorous application of this principle enables the professional to avoid many problems which necessarily arise if and when professionals falsely assume that they must act as the unconditionally loyal servant of the individual client at hand.

Chapter 9

Conclusion

Professionals possess and exercise legitimate authority in their own eyes as well as those of clients and non-clients when their activity accords with their solemn covenants to serve particular goods. Since the professional aims at the client's good, the individual client is necessarily the focus of professional attention. However, the professional is not exclusively client-centered. The client served is an individual who is part of a community before whom the doctor, lawyer, or cleric has made his or her "profession." The community is not, therefore, just an aggregate of people. Rather, it is a transnational group of people with a shared status: all are potential, if not actual, clients of the professionals whose pledges constitute a reason for coming into the presence of these covenanting agents. Even the professionals themselves are clients of a sort. For they are self-interested beings who derive their own share of their respected covenanted goods through service to their clients.

The covenanted goods are genuine goods in themselves, as well as being goods of the individual. Because the individual belongs to a community defined in part by its shared experience of professions, these true goods have an inherently public dimension. While professionals are under no obligation to serve some vague, amorphous good such as "public welfare" or "societal happiness," they do concern themselves with the well-being of other members of the community when promoting the good of an actual client. In fact, as we saw in Chapter 8, professions provide much of the disciplinary framework around which liberal democracies organize themselves. This public dimension of medicine, law, and the ministry is captured in our notions of the doctor as a promoter of the health of many individuals, the lawyer as an officer of the court, and the minister as a servant of the church. As we have seen, the public dimension conditions professional service in many ways, limiting the extent to which confidentiality is owed to the client whose actions will result in harm to another if kept secret; forbidding tactics which would deprive other potential clients of help or access to it; allowing for a termination of the professional–client relation when an uncooperative client is taking up time better spent with a different client; and so forth.

Professionals' genuinely good orientation (expressed as a pledge to promote a particular good), coupled with their obligation not to substitute their priorities for those of their clients, grounds their authority in the eyes of potential and actual clients by making practice trustworthy. Establishing this trust is critical because the professional–client relation is usually voluntary. Trust must be present, and it must be mutual for professional practice to exist. The client, often quite vulnerable, places health, liberty, and future happiness in the hands of a stranger. Professionals, in turn, know that their reputation and ability to derive their own share of the goods of health, justice, and salvation depend upon how the interaction with the client proceeds. Practices have died in the past when clients have lost faith in practitioners. In the case of medicine, law, and theology, power truly is a trust to be cultivated carefully. In these last few pages, I wish to bring together the themes that have run throughout this book, highlighting the many simple, elegant, mutually reinforcing ways in which the covenanting professions exhibit themselves as worthy of trust.

Professions merit our trust in part because they do not minimize the difficulties associated with cultivating it. Establishing and preserving mutual trust would be easy if we all shared identical opinions regarding what is of ultimate value, what various persons really intend, what events are possible. But we are not clones of one another. Professions rooted in pledges succeed in fostering trust precisely because they acknowledge and accommodate human individuality. This accommodation takes place on three fronts. First, while a businessman sells products to a typical consumer, the covenanting doctor, lawyer, and cleric recognize each client as atypical or unique. In the latter three cases, the interaction almost always starts with the professional listening to the client's story. People are, in part, what they experience. What they experience differs. The particular combination of actors, emotions, facial expressions, inflections, and sensations never repeats itself exactly. Consequently, what a litigant may have experienced at the place and time of injury cannot be divined by the attorney prior to hearing the client's tale. The lawyer may find the tale told by the client wildly improbable. Yet, as Mark Twain quipped, "Fiction must stick to the probable. Life need not." Lacking a god's-eye perspective, we look to our attorneys to ensure that the client's case, bizarre as it may seem, gets its day in court. The covenanting lawyer takes up the challenge, carefully avoiding substituting his will or his experience for that of the client.

The covenanting physician's willingness to seriously entertain patient reports of pain, even when there is no indication of organic dysfunction, and the open-endedness of the entire confessional approach (any troubling matter may be confessed, although not everything stated need be kept confidential) are equally signs of what could be termed the professions' "Socratic wisdom." The professions know that they do not know how a client is experiencing the world until that client speaks his or her mind. In general, covenanting professionals resist treating the client as a typical member of a "market segment." They insist upon hearing a story from its author – the client.

Individuality is also a consequence and expression of our life priorities. These affect how each of us assigns relative importance to the goods promoted by different professionals and how we determine whether we decide to seek the service on the terms proposed. Priorities, in turn, depend upon unique combinations of innate talents and habits and tastes acquired within a specific community. By accepting persons as clients solely on the basis of whether they lack a particular good, instead of discriminating among clients using racial, sexual, national, or socio-economic criteria, covenanting professionals position themselves to serve a widely diverse clientele. In the long run, experience with a broadly based clientele develops the professional's moral imagination. A supple mind, sympathetic to an ever larger array of human concerns, produces an agent increasingly attuned to human individuality. This respect for individuality manifested at the level of the single practitioner is further reinforced by the liberal, democratic environment professions help create and support. Communal and individual values mutually strengthen one another, thereby preserving people's freedom to order and successfully pursue goods within a framework dedicated to preserving distinct disciplines with their own internal goods.

We must not overlook a third reason why professions are particularly sensitive to differences among individuals. The very existence of professions itself creates differences between people. Professional and client often disagree in their assessment of problems and solutions because the former has been trained to anticipate and identify problems and formulate solutions while the latter has not. Lacking this training, the client sometimes will take issue with the professional's analysis. Covenanting professionals do not thereupon suspend critical judgment. Nor, however, do they force client compliance. Recognizing that the good at stake is ultimately the client's good, they let the client decline the offer of help. Moreover, covenanting professionals remember that, while they do have superior technical training, they do not possess a monopoly on knowledge concerning the good they serve. As a matter of *fact*, self-healing, self-representation, and self-ministering historically have all been recognized as real, though limited, options by medicine, law, and theology respectively. As a matter of *justice*, it is appropriate that the goods be viewed as potentially within the power of others to secure. For the professional depends upon clients' help when healing, defending, or ministering to them. Whether the client chooses to help depends, in turn, upon the client's ordering of life priorities. The client controls this ordering, not the professional. Thus, while covenanting professionals put themselves in service to the good, they do not thereby take sole title to it.

Professions, then, merit trust because they do not authorize the professional to subvert client values or to take over and manage the client's life. Clients retain the discretion needed for trust to exist and to thrive as individuals with their own opinions, priorities, and plans. Professions merit trust for a second reason as well: they do not purport to do what they cannot do. In particular, while professions pledge to adopt a client-centered orientation, they do not promise to produce a certain outcome. "Duty, not success, is the law of professions"[1] because success cannot be guaranteed. Human agents often act in an unpredictable fashion. For example, the human body will sometimes behave in a hitherto unobserved fashion. Honest physicians admit there is much about its working they do not understand. The living, choosing human with his or her own unique history is equally mysterious. For example, no professional knows, prior to working with a client, whether the client will co-operate or to what extent.

Moreover, sometimes a client's own condition places him beyond help. The doctor can do little for those whose health turns out to be irretrievably broken. Gerontologists inevitably will see many of their patients die. Some cases at law are hard to win. Few Palestinians have been acquitted in West Bank courts. Yet lawyers like the Israeli Leah Tsemel who take their cases and lose repeatedly are no more bad lawyers than gerontologists are bad doctors. As long as the professional adheres to the terms of the pledge, she is genuinely professional irrespective of whether the client likes the outcome of the service.

If the character of the relation, as well as the outcome, were unknown, clients would have no reason to trust professionals. However, the character of the relation is not uncertain. As I have been at pains to stress, the covenanting professional adopts a known, certain orientation – fidelity to a particular good. This fidelity establishes many practical constraints on professional activity of the sort summarized above. The orientation limits the outcome, but it neither guarantees nor predicts it. Nor need it do so. A proper orientation itself will suffice to legitimate professional authority as long as one remembers that fidelity to the pledge entails striving to acquire technical competence. The professional need not promise to deliver the technically best service. People's proficiency quite obviously will vary depending upon whether they are just starting out in the profession or have been practicing it for thirty years. Nevertheless, promising to serve does commit the professional to trying to acquire the skills necessary to be genuinely helpful. The attorney ought not to promise to win a case, but he should struggle to craft a well-argued brief. The client cannot be said to have obtained her day in court if only a fraction of her case is presented or if it is stated in an unintelligible form.

The moral commitment clearly affects the acquisition of technical proficiency. And it should and must do so if professional practice is to be legitimate. Pledge-adhering professionals rightly limit themselves to learning and doing that which genuinely aids clients. The covenanting professional neither knows nor bothers to learn techniques which do not belong to a trustworthy agent who serves a genuine good. Thus, the minister does not know how to get his parishioners to believe in false gods. Nor does the lawyer strive to perfect a sure-fire method for litigants to manufacture evidence. Covenanting professions do not glorify technique *per se*. Instead, they regulate the use and acquisition of technique in light of what furthers the specific good they serve. The prominence of the moral commitment explains why professionals tend to view moral error as more egregious than technical mistakes.[2] Technical errors are unavoidable, given the aforementioned uncertainties inherent in practice itself. One's moral orientation, though, is within one's control. The pledge-based ethic here proposed is sensitive to the distinction between the two types of error and focuses the practitioner's attention on what lies within the realm of the controllable. One can be praised or blamed for actions within one's control. The pledge ethic condemns moral error understood as the professionals' failure to exhibit the traits and behavior they must exhibit if they are to be worthy of the reasonable client's trust.

Although I have developed this argument for the pledge ethic through an analysis of the traditional three professions of medicine, law, and the clergy, it is clear that it can readily be extended to explore the meaning and nature of other activities. Thus, insofar as nurses, like doctors, promote the patient's good of health, nurses would, on the analysis here offered, possess moral legitimacy. If, however, nurses were to start conceiving of themselves as generalized "caregivers," we might expect this legitimacy to be called into question. For, as I have argued elsewhere, care, unlike health, legal justice, and salvation, is not a good in itself (or at least it is not such a good in any of the senses I was able to impute to the notion of care).[3] Care can have and sometimes does have a dark side, and to say that a relation is caring is not to say that it is necessarily moral.[4]

The analysis also suggests additional questions to ask others who would claim professional status. If, as others have contended, training, autonomy over work, group organization, and self-regulation suffice to constitute a profession, then plumbers will qualify as such. However, if, as I have argued here, what is truly distinctive about the professions is their distinctive moral commitment to serve a client good which is inherently individualistic and intrinsically good, then one may legitimately doubt whether plumbers are truly professional. It is both interesting and striking, for example, that the professions have been willing to innovate on behalf of their clients' good, even when such innovation tends to reduce the need for the professionals' help and therefore the professionals' income. One thinks, for example, of dentists' advocacy of water fluoridation and the resulting decline in tooth decay.[5] The Chicago plumbers' union, by contrast, has consistently opposed the introduction of plastic piping which is easier to repair and perhaps safer, because such piping would reduce the demand for plumbers in the long run. One might similarly wonder whether doctors will not lose moral legitimacy as they start trying to patent their discoveries. Again the issue is one of withholding innovations from clients when such innovations hold out great promise for furthering the specific goods the profession has pledged to promote. As MacIver has noted, the professions have traditionally refused to deny clients access to these goods precisely because their *raison d'être* lies in aiding their clients.[6] While such differences between and changes in agents' behavior may not decide the issue of professionalism once and for all, their moral import should at least be considered. It is one merit of the pledge ethic that it calls attention to such differences and to their relevance to the whole issue of the moral legitimacy of the professions.

I would end by observing that this legitimacy issue is not merely perdurable but is also likely to become more acute over the next decade. Precisely because it is professional pledges which encourage, sustain, and justify client trust in professionals, we would expect a loss of trust as "professionals" turn their backs on their covenants and try to justify their authority by appealing to their expertise or to a contract with the client. And in fact it increasingly looks as though the public is realizing that these other alleged grounds of legitimacy are not going to make professionals trustworthy in the public's eyes. Donald Schon has persuasively argued that we are witnessing a current crisis in professional knowledge. He attributes this crisis in part to the expert's love of technique which we explored in detail in Chapter 2. Instead of being sensitive to individual clients and their problems, the professional expert has shown a marked "disposition to employ his techniques, whatever the consequences."[7] We ought not, therefore, to be surprised at the escalating tension between the expert and those clients who dislike or even fear many of these consequences.

Nor is the fee-for-service model likely to remedy the damage done by experts. I cannot think it mere coincidence that prostitution has become known as "the most ancient profession" at the turn of this century,[8] the era in which professions exhibit every sign of becoming "the most recent prostitution." As we have seen, the fee-for-service approach undermines professionals' ability to oppose in a principled fashion the wishes of unreasonable or wicked clients who are, nevertheless, rational. As a result, the refusal to serve seems arbitrary or the product of a prejudice, while a decision to help looks like a calculated move to maximize income or power. Moreover, the model casts clients in the role of procurers who must negotiate for and buy the product that gratifies their desires. Mention of prostitution should remind us that desire gratification is perfectly consistent with self-disgust. The professions are bound to pay when clients take a closer look at the new and improved selves they have created with professional help. And pay dearly they will, if the rising tide of lawsuits against plastic surgeons and attorneys is any indicator of how the future will unfold.

Indeed, the current passion for charismatic ministers, healers, and leaders may reflect the public's growing lack of confidence in their hired experts. As the theologian James Gustafson notes, personal traits become supremely important precisely when the concept of the professional role loses definition and coherence.[9] It should surprise no one if the role has been obscured during the twentieth century. Decades of attacks on professional legitimacy are bound to take their toll. My attempt in these pages to develop a practical theory of the professions capable of grounding professionals' authority by making our trust in them reasonable will not in and of itself reverse this lack of confidence. But perhaps when we have collectively exhausted the appeal of the "expert" or the hired "service provider," we will be inclined to reconsider the significance of the longstanding motto of the learned professions: *Uberrima fides* ("Above all faithful"). When true to their covenants, professionals *do* merit the trust they proclaim themselves worthy of receiving. They will not abandon us. Let us hope that we will not continue to misconceive the ground of their moral legitimacy and desert them.

Notes

1 INTRODUCTION

1 The literature alleging and discussing professional lust for power, privilege, and wealth is truly enormous. For the consumerist perspective on this topic, see Richard Carter, *The Doctor Business* (Garden City, New York: Doubleday, 1958), 11–61; for that of a sociologist, Wilbert E. Moore, *The Professions: Roles and Rules* (New York: Russell Sage Foundation, 1970), 149–156; of economists, T. D. Hall and C. M. Lindsay, "Medical Schools: Producers of What? Sellers of Whom?," *Journal of Law and Economics* 23 (April 1980): 55–80; and of a historian, W. J. Reader, *Professional Men: The Rise of the Professional Classes in Nineteenth-Century England* (London: Weidenfeld and Nicolson, 1966), 146–166. Other indictments include those by Ivan Illich, "Disabling Professions," in *Disabling Professions*, (London: Marion Boyars, 1977) 27–39; Robert Jay Lifton, *The Nazi Doctors: Medical Killing and the Psychology of Genocide* (New York: Basic Books, 1986), Part 1 and Part 2 *passim*; and John McKnight, "Professionalized Service and Disabling Help," in *Disabling Professions*, 89.

2 "Physicians . . . , by way of building a towering reputation, are wont to diagnose insignificant troubles as greater ones and to exaggerate real dangers." Menander, *Phanium* 497K.

3 For discussions of professionals as public servants, see Louis Brandeis, *Business – A Profession* (Boston: Hale, Cushman, & Flint, 1933), 2; Paul Camenisch, *Grounding Professional Ethics in a Pluralistic Society* (New York: Haven, 1983), *passim*; Emile Durkheim, "Professional Ethics," in Durkheim, *Professional Ethics and Civic Morals*, trans. Cornelia Brookfield and preface by Bryan S. Turner (London: Routledge, 1992), 17–27. William Goode is clearly on strong ground when he states that no theme is more prevalent in speeches to members of the profession than the ideal of service to the community. William J. Goode, "Community Within a Community: The Professions," *American Sociological Review* 22 (April 1957): 194.

4 Ludwig Edelstein, *Ancient Medicine*, ed. Owsei Temkin and C. Lillian

Temkin, trans. C. Lillian Temkin (Baltimore: Johns Hopkins University Press, 1967), 319–324.

5 "Est einem sine dubio domus iuris consulti totius oraculum civitatis." Cicero, *De Oratore*, I.45.

6 For an argument to this effect, see Magali Sarfatti Larson, *The Rise of Professionalism: A Sociological Analysis* (Berkeley: University of California Press, 1977), *passim*. One increasingly encounters the equating of commerce and professions, including in contexts seemingly far removed from the marketplace. For example, in the arguments made before the court regarding Pennsylvania's law requiring wives to notify husbands prior to having an abortion, Attorney-General Peate treated the conversation between a doctor and patient as just another form of commercial speech, much to Justice Sandra Day O'Connor's dismay. See "Excerpts from Arguments on Pennsylvania's Abortion Law," *New York Times* 23 April 1992, pp. B10-B11.

7 Bates v. State Bar of Arizona, 443 US 350 (1976).

8 Eliot Freidson, *Professional Powers: A Study of the Institutionalization of Formal Knowledge* (Chicago: University of Chicago Press, 1986), 29.

9 See Michael D. Bayles, *Professional Ethics* (Belmont, California: Wadsworth, 1981), 18–19; Benjamin Freedman, "A Meta-Ethics for Professional Morality," *Ethics* 89 (October 1978): 1–19.

10 For instances of each of these three positions, see Bayles, *Professional Ethics*, 75; Peter Drucker, "What is 'Business Ethics'?" *The Public Interest* 63 (Spring 1981): 19; and Camenisch, *Grounding*, *passim* respectively. Drucker treats professional and ordinary ethics as identical; Bayles seems to see professional ethics as derived from and a further specification of ordinary ethics; Camenisch argues for professional ethics being an intensification of ordinary ethics.

11 For a variant of this sort of argument, see Professor Kenneth R. Andrews' seminal article "Toward Professionalism in Business Management," *Harvard Business Review* (March–April 1969): 49–60.

12 J. Cardozo, *Matter of Rouss*, 221 N.Y. 81, 84 (1917).

13 Camenisch, *Grounding*, 7.

14 No doubt some critics would dispute that they bear any responsibility for the evacuation of the moral content of the professions. Ethicist Lisa Newton, for example, questions whether there ever has been any vital connection between professions and a commitment to serve. She attacks professional norms expressed in publicly stated codes as nothing more than a means to establish and protect professional power and privilege. While the case remains to be made that professions are indeed legitimately entitled to act on behalf of clients, the vitriolic cast of such criticism suggests that professionals in fact do have special moral obligations to clients who have reposed trust in them. As others have noted, the denunciations of professional venality, insensitivity, and paternalism would not be so bitter if the accusers did not feel greatly betrayed.

15 For a discussion of this conceptual quagmire, see G. Turner and M. N. Hodge, "Occupations and Professions," in *Professions and*

Professionalization, ed. J. A. Jackson (Cambridge: Cambridge University Press, 1970), 23.

16 Dr Servatius, quoted in Hannah Arendt, *Eichmann in Jerusalem: A Report on the Banality of Evil* (New York and Harmondsworth: Penguin Books, 1964), 69.

17 Camenisch, *Grounding*, 1–3. Camenisch himself seems to be drawing his conception of ground from Immanuel Kant.

18 A client is "a person or company for whom a lawyer, accountant, advertising agent, etc. is acting." *Webster's New World Dictionary of the American Language*, 2nd edn, s.v. "client."

19 Camenisch, *Grounding*, 11. For further development of this line of argument, see Dorothy Mary Emmet, *Rules, Roles and Relations* (London: Macmillan, 1966), *passim*.

20 Karen Lebacqz, *Professional Ethics: Power and Paradox* (Nashville, Tennessee: Abingdon Press, 1985), 72–73; Everett C. Hughes, "Professions," in *The Professions in America*, ed. Kenneth S. Lynn (Boston: Beacon Press, 1967), 1–14.

21 Freidson, *Powers*, 32.

22 Sir Edward Coke, *The Reports* (Savoy: E. and R. Nutt and R. Gosling, 1738), 5, pt. 10, 142b.

23 The doctors may have made more money by revamping their techniques, but this possibility does not alter the fact that the logically prior question is: how must the physician act to preserve her practice? A desire to make money does not provide an answer to this question.

24 Of the liberal professions, "there were only three: divinity, physic, and law." Reader, *Professional Men*, 9. Physic refers to the practice of medicine.

25 Henri Bergson, *Two Sources of Religion and Morality*, trans. R. Ashley Audra and Cloudesley Brereton (New York: Henry Holt & Co., 1935), 66.

26 The literature on the practice of journalism reflects this ambivalence about the practice. See Penn Kimball, "Journalism: Art, Craft or Profession?" in Lynn, *The Professions*, 242–260.

27 Andrews, "Toward Professionalism", 49–60.

2 THE UNTRUSTWORTHINESS OF PROFESSIONAL EXPERTISE

1 See Geison's comments on the sociologist Larson's decision to simply exclude the ministry and military, two of the classic professions, as professions because they do not fit her capitalistic analysis of professions. Gerald Geison, *Professions and Professional Ideologies in America* (Chapel Hill, North Carolina: University of North Carolina Press, 1983), 6.

2 See, for example, William Schreiber's discussion of the qualifications of Mennonite leaders in his book *Our Amish Neighbors* (Chicago: University of Chicago Press, 1962), 130–131.

3 In the United States there is a statutory right to self-representation conferred by 28 USC. 1654. This right must be recognized if counsel

is validly waived, if the right is asserted in a timely fashion, and if self-representation is not likely to disrupt the trial. See *US v. Dougherty, Slaski, Begin, Maloney, O'Rourke, Melville and Malone* 473 F.2d 1113 (DCCir.1972).

4 *Bates v. State Bar of Arizona*, 443 US 386 (1976).

5 "The client is not a judge of the value of service he receives ..." Everett C. Hughes, "Professions," in *The Professions in America*, ed. Kenneth S. Lynn (Boston: Beacon Press, 1967), 5.

6 Wilbert E. Moore, *The Professions: Roles and Rules* (New York: Russell Sage Foundation, 1970), 111.

7 Quote is from Martin E. Marty, "The Clergy," in *The Professions in American History*, ed. Nathan O. Hatch (Notre Dame, Indiana: University of Notre Dame Press, 1988), 75.

8 Louis Brandeis, *Business – A Profession* (Boston: Hale, Cushman, & Flint, 1933), 2.

9 For an extended discussion of the nature and types of conflict of interest, see John Boardman, "Conflict of Interest: An Agency Analysis," in *Ethics and Agency Theory: An Introduction*, ed. Norman E. Bowie and R. Edward Freeman (New York: Oxford University Press, 1992), 187–203.

10 Paul Camenisch, *Grounding Professional Ethics in a Pluralistic Society* (New York: Haven, 1983), 4.

11 Richard P. McKeon, ed., *Selections from Medieval Philosophers*, 2 vols (New York: Scribner, 1930), 2:492.

12 Aristotle *Nicomachean Ethics* 1145a6–12.

13 McKeon, *Selections*, 2:492.

14 Brandeis, *Business*, 2.

15 Freidson, *passim*.

16 William F. May, *The Physician's Covenant: Images of the Healer in Medical Ethics* (Philadelphia: Westminster Press, 1983), 106–144.

17 See chs 4–8.

18 This responsibility is subject to some further caveats. The client must have accepted the promise for it to be morally valid. Furthermore, the person making the promise must have the power to honor it. A promise to fly to Pluto and back in a single day is not binding because the promisor cannot accomplish this feat.

19 I might try to help this man find a lawyer out of a sense of bonhomie or perhaps even out of a desire to see justice done. But life is short and individuals have other obligations to friends, to families, and to others to whom they have made pledges or promises. Consequently, I would contend that I have no obligation to help this man just because he is accused of a crime, although I might have a duty if he were my father or my best friend.

20 Dale Schaffer emphasizes a general professional duty to engage in research and to continue "formal education" in classrooms. Professional development occurs through study, not through interaction with the client. For the relevant discussion, see D. Schaffer, *Librarianship as a Profession* (Metachen, NJ: Scarecrow Press, 1968), 46–47. Moore assigns the professional only one "duty" – the duty to learn.

By "learn," Moore clearly means "master more technical knowledge." He too overlooks the possibility that the professional learns from his clients. Moore, *The Professions*, 241.

21 David Mellinkoff, *Lawyers and the System of Justice: Cases and Notes on the Profession of Law* (St Paul, Minnesota: West, 1976), 7–9.

22 F. Raymond Marks and Darlene Cathcart, "Discipline within the Legal Profession: Is it Self-Regulation?" *University of Illinois Law Forum* (1974): 218.

23 It would seem that the client could not disappear in the case of the ministry. After all, the cleric is a "servant of the church." In many faiths, it is the congregation that calls the minister to service. The minister preaches to the congregation one or more times a week. Yet even in the case of the ministry expertise threatens to make the client invisible. Speaking of "ministerial specialists," Robert Michaelson argues that the "danger exists that ministers become so specialized and so involved in administrative detail that they lose contact with the people." Robert S. Michaelson, "The Protestant Ministry in America: 1850 to the Present," in *The Ministry in Historical Perspectives*, ed. H. Richard Niebuhr and Daniel D. Williams (New York: Harper and Bros, 1956), 286.

24 Of course, surgery does exist as a division of medicine. But it, too, tends to be organized around parts of the body to be healed. Cardiac and otolaryngological surgery are specialties reflecting this ordering principle. However, the fact that surgery is a manipulative *technique* easily divorced from the healing of the body perhaps accounts in part for why physicians have historically been reluctant to accept surgeons as peers. For a discussion of this reluctance, see Leon Kass, *Toward a More Natural Science: Biology and Human Affairs* (New York: Free Press, 1985), 236; and Moore, *The Professions*, 153.

25 Plato *Gorgias* 464b2–465a8.

26 Plato *Gorgias* 465b1–6.

27 Mellinkoff, *Lawyers and the System of Justice*, 6, quoting the *Code of Professional Responsibility*.

28 *Code of Professional Responsibility*, Disciplinary Rule (DR) 6–101(A)(1). EC–214 forbids lawyers from holding themselves out as specialists.

29 Ibid.

30 *Code*, DR 6–101(A)(2) and DR 6–101(A)(3).

31 *Model Rules of Professional Conduct and Code of Judicial Conduct* (Chicago: American Bar Association, 1984), 15.

32 W. Tucker, "The Large Law Firm: Considerations Concerning the Modernization of the Canons of Professional Ethics," in *Wisconsin Law Review* (1965): 385.

33 Moore, *The Professions*, 138.

34 Court-provided counsel is commonplace in criminal trials and may become so in civil cases because lawyers are citing a lack of expertise as a ground for being absolved from representing a client. Linda Greenhouse, "Can Lawyers be Forced to Represent the Poor?" *New York Times*, 3 March 1989, p. B5.

35 Baier, "Trust and Antitrust," *Ethics* (January 1986): 231–260.
36 Marty, "The Clergy," 85.
37 Ibid.
38 Mark A. May quoted in ibid., 86.
39 Romans 12:5 (Revised Standard Version).
40 *OED*, s.v. "minister."
41 Karen Lebacqz, *Professional Ethics: Power and Paradox* (Nashville, Tenn.: Abingdon Press, 1985), 157.
42 Ibid., 158.
43 Ibid.
44 The professional responsibility to keep confidence is a complicated issue. I treat it at length in Chapter 8.

3 DELEGITIMATING CLIENT CONTRACTS

1 I draw my characterization of the contractual model largely from Robert Veatch who explicitly recommends use of such a contract. Robert M. Veatch, *A Theory of Medical Ethics* (New York: Basic Books, 1981), 108–138. The analysis also appeals to a lesser extent to the work of Alan Goldman. Goldman's traditional role-based view of professions and support of client autonomy seems to favor, if not require, something like a professional–client contract. Goldman clearly envisions that individuals will work out explicit "frameworks" in which all parties' equal right to autonomy will be respected. Alan H. Goldman, *The Moral Foundations of Professional Ethics* (Totowa, New Jersey: Rowman and Littlefield, 1980), 29.
2 I use the term "ateleological" instead of "value-neutral" because, as should be clear from Chapter 2, the substitution of expertise for *scientia* has been anything but value-neutral. To the extent that trust enables people to benefit from interactions designed to fulfill basic needs (e.g. health), trust may be said to be good. And if trust is good, any practice or process which destroys trust is *ceteris paribus* bad, not value-neutral.
3 Baier, "Trust and Antitrust", *Ethics* (January 1986): 231–260.
4 I am well aware that, as a matter of historical fact, the contract model has not arisen solely as a response to the perceived inadequacies of the expertise model. Many other factors have combined to make the model attractive. The rise of consumerism, increased suspicion of all authority, ever greater dependence upon legal solutions to moral problems are but a few trends reinforcing the model's appeal. Nevertheless, it makes sense to treat the theory as a reply to the claims of experts. This dialectical approach is theoretically sound because those who are propounding the contract model know that their theory can successfully legitimate professional authority only if the theory avoids those problems plaguing the expert model. This awareness accounts for why the contractualist is at pains to show that the client's desire to control the interaction has merit not because it is a private desire (as such, it would be no better than the expert's private desire) but because clients have claims as clients.

5 John Rawls invented the notion of a veil of ignorance. John Rawls, *A Theory of Justice* (Oxford: Oxford University Press, 1972), 136–142. Veatch, for example, uses a Rawlsian framework to develop his contractualist model of professional ethics. Veatch, *Theory*, 121–126.

6 Arguments for the contract model within the professional ethics literature draw heavily upon John Rawls' theory of justice, particularly upon his first principle of justice – the liberty principle. Veatch uses John Rawls' theory of justice to argue that abiding by the client's wishes is a demand of reason. Veatch, *Theory*, 108–138. However, not all arguments for contract use are Rawlsian. Goldman, for example, also contends that clients are morally entitled to state their wishes and then to have these wishes honored by the professionals whose aid they are seeking. Goldman grounds his liberty principle in human individuality, which is taken to be the ultimate good. Since people realize their individuality through initiating actions in accordance with their own value preferences, clients' wishes must be honored by the professional. Goldman, *Moral Foundations*, 4; 24–33.

7 See Hippocratic Oath in Ludwig Edelstein, *Ancient Medicine* (Baltimore, Maryland: Johns Hopkins University Press, 1967), 6.

8 Ibid., 89. One sees a similar emphasis upon deferring to client judgment in Aristotle's treatment of the architect–homeowner relation: "[T]here are some arts whose products are not judged solely, or best, by the artists themselves, namely those arts whose products are recognized even by those who do not possess the art; for example, the knowledge of the house is not limited to the builder only; the user ... of the house will be a better judge than the builder...." Aristotle *Politics* 1282a18–23 (Loeb edition).

9 *Model Rules of Professional Conduct and Code of Judicial Conduct.* As amended August 1984. (Chicago: American Bar Association, 1984), Rule 1.2.

10 Ibid.

11 This characterization of the laity somewhat understates the extent of their role in the process of salvation. The laity actually shares in the process of interpreting the inheritance or *klerikos* of their church or sect. The sense in which the laity exercises the power of the "clergy" is explored in Chapter 5.

12 Revelations 3:20 (Revised Standard Version).

13 "[W]e must assume that [professionals] are obliged to accommodate in some way the lay preconceptions and desires of all but their most incapacitated clients. Accommodation to lay ideas is in fact one of the elements leading them to deviate from the formal knowledge advanced by academics and researchers." Eliot Freidson, *Professional Powers: A Study of the Institutionalization of Formal Knowledge* (Chicago: University of Chicago Press, 1986), 218–219.

14 "Kervorkian-aided Suicide Investigated as Homicide," *New York Times*, 25 February 1993, sec.A, p.10.

15 Veatch, *Theory*, 327–330; Edelstein, *Ancient Medicine*, 6.

16 "The trial process simply does not permit the type of frequent and protracted interruptions which would be necessary if it were required

that clients give knowing and intelligent approval to each of the myriad tactical decisions as a trial proceeds." Chief Justice Burger in *Wainwright v. Sykes* US 72 (1977).

17 Veatch, *Theory*, 330.

18 John Rawls might be able to counter this objection with his second principle – the so-called difference principle. Rawls is willing to sacrifice liberty if the representative least advantaged person can be made better off through this sacrifice. In our example, the person who is critically ill is the least advantaged person and can obviously be made much better off by a small sacrifice of the cold-sufferer's liberty. However, those who favor contracts in professional ethics are not strict Rawlsians. Veatch and Goldman *are* subject to this objection largely because they place an even greater value on individual fulfillment than does Rawls and consequently make the will of the individual client more controlling.

19 Veatch, *Theory*, 127.

20 *Link v. Wabash Railroad Co.*, 370 US 626 (1962).

21 See, for example, the sample physician–patient contract in Veatch, *Theory*, 327–330.

22 Veatch assigns these two duties to the client, but then fudges on whether or not the professional owes service to someone who does not pay his bill. Veatch, *Theory*, 328.

23 William I. Schreiber, *Our Amish Neighbors* (Chicago: University of Chicago Press, 1962), 131.

24 I argue for this view of salvation on pp.84–87.

25 Calvin A. Kuenzel, "The Attorney's Fee: Why Not a Cost of Litigation?" *Iowa Law Review* 49 (1963): 75, 78.

26 Karen Lebacqz, *Professional Ethics: Power and Paradox* (Nashville, Tennessee: Abingdon Press, 1985), 103.

27 The American Medical Association's *Principles of Medical Ethics* states: "A physician shall, in the provision of appropriate patient care, except in emergencies, be free to choose whom to serve." Quoted in *Proceedings of the American Medical Association House of Delegates, 129th Convention, July 20–24, 1980* (Chicago: American Medical Association, 1980), 207.

28 This admission is made, for example, by law professor Stephen Gillers under questioning by Professor Charles Ogletree in *To Defend a Killer* (New York: Columbia University Seminars on Media and Society, 1989), videorecording.

29 See the numerous comments explicating this obligation in the footnotes to rule EC 2–2 in the *Code of Professional Responsibility* reproduced in Maynard E. Pirsig and Kenneth F. Kirwin, *Professional Responsibility: Cases and Materials*, 3rd edn (St Paul, Minnesota: West, 1976), 600–601.

30 David A. Lane, "Comments, Concurrences and Dissents: Pro Bono and Death Row," *Continuing Legal Education* 19 (1989): 5–6.

31 Pirsig and Kirwin, *Professional Responsibility*, 84.

32 Ibid.

33 William Blackstone, *Commentaries on The Laws of England* (New York: Collins and Hannay, 1832), Bk. 3, ch. 3, sec. 28.
34 *Code of Professional Responsibility*, as reproduced in Pirsig and Kirwin, *Professional Responsibility*, EC 2–23. All future references to the *Code* refer to this version.
35 Tithes have always been voluntary in the Protestant and the Eastern Orthodox churches. Mandatory tithing did exist during the Middle Ages within the Catholic church but, I would argue, these tithes are best understood as a form of state taxation since the church was the *de facto* state at that time.
36 Veatch, *Theory*, 329.

4 THE PUBLIC PLEDGE AS THE GROUND OF PROFESSIONAL AUTHORITY

1 Bayles refers to "scholarly professionals" who never interact with clients. Michael D. Bayles, *Professional Ethics* (Belmont, California: Wadsworth, 1981), 9. Freidson distinguishes practicing professionals from "researchers" whom he also treats as professionals. Eliot Freidson, *Professional Powers: A Study of the Institutionalization of Formal Knowledge* (Chicago: University of Chicago Press, 1986), *passim*.
2 Paul Camenisch, *Grounding Professional Ethics in a Pluralistic Society* (New York: Haven, 1983), 5.
3 *OED*, s.v. "client."
4 See Karen Lebacqz, *Professional Ethics: Power and Paradox* (Nashville, Tennessee: Abingdon Press, 1985), 144–150, for a discussion of how dependent ministers' power is on the good will of those they serve.
5 I add the caveat "on the expectation" because sometimes persons are brought by others into the presence of the professional on the strength of the pledge (e.g. persons in a coma; persons who are mentally disturbed, etc.).
6 Literally, "profession" means to "speak before." The "pro– " is used in its local sense, not temporally. In ancient Rome, the *professio* was made in the presence of or before a representative of the public. See the commentary concerning the term's local meaning in *The Correspondence of M. Tullius Cicero*, ed. Robert Yelverton Tyrrell and Louis Claude Purser (Dublin: Dublin University Press, 1915), 5:110. The word shares the same etymology as "prophet" where "pro– " is also used in local sense. *The Jewish Encyclopedia*, 1901 edn, s.v. "Prophets and Prophecy" by J. Frederic McCurdy.
7 Roman politicians had to make such a *professio*. In this case the public statement seems to have been designed to establish that the candidate met the property requirements for public office. Cicero, 5:110.
8 Ludwig Edelstein, *Ancient Medicine* (Baltimore, Maryland: Johns Hopkins University Press, 1967), 338–339.
9 See my discussion of medieval professors on pp. 20–22.
10 William Blackstone, *Commentaries on the Laws of England* (New York: Collins and Hannay, 1832), Bk. 3, ch. 3, sec. 26.

11 The client may have to co-operate with the professional in order to receive the promised benefit. However, the client is not bound by the profession to do so because the client need not seek the professional's help in the first place. The professional, by contrast, is generally bound by his "profession" to render service to those who qualify as clients. Whether and when he may refuse service or break confidentiality is a topic I discuss in Chapters 5–8.

12 The vows are also made as part of the professor's effort to perfect his or her life. I show in Chapter 7 how professionals benefit through adherence to the pledge. This benefit accrues as a non-accidental consequence of their own actions in accordance with the pledge and can thus be thought of as a perfection. Although ethicists and sociologists routinely note in passing that the original meaning of "to profess" was "to make a vow," this comment is both superficial and misleading. People do not make vows just for the sake of hearing themselves speak. Professional vows have been made to elicit the trust of the listener and to better the professors' lives. My argument is intended to establish that both of these purposes need to be considered if professional authority is to be grounded.

13 Emil L. Fackenheim, *What is Judaism?* (New York: Macmillan, 1987), 245.

14 For a short history of these pledges, see Camenisch, *Grounding*, 102–104.

15 "For many centuries the Oath was taken as the very model of medical conduct; it informed the attitude of generations of physicians. Indeed, until the present generation, it was sworn to by students of many if not most of our nation's medical schools on the occasion of completing their studies and entering their chosen profession." Leon Kass, *Toward a More Natural Science: Biology and Human Affairs* (New York: Free Press, 1985), 227.

16 Oath quoted in Edelstein, 6.

17 Kass, 241.

18 *Model Rules of Professional Conduct and Code of Judicial Conduct.* As amended August 1984 (Chicago: American Bar Association, 1984), Rule 1.2. Blackstone goes so far as to claim that the legal profession originated with those who continued to profess their respect for the law while others chose to "profess their contempt, nay even their ignorance of [the law] in the most public manner." Blackstone, *Commentaries*, Bk. 1, Introduction, sec. 25.

19 *Model Rules*, Rule 1.1.

20 Ibid., Preamble, Scope and Terminology, 1–3.

21 In addition, the American Bar's proud tradition of providing representation for an unpopular individual when local counsel refuses the case equally suggests that the lawyer has a covenantal obligation to aid those who seek justice for themselves. If the relation were simply contractual, the profession would not be able to assert that legal "representation should not be denied to people who are unable to afford legal services, or whose cause is controversial or the subject of popular disapproval." Ibid. The "should" would have no force except

for those who had already entered into a contract with the client in question.

22 Jacob Neusner, *Invitation to the Talmud: A Teaching Book* (New York: Harper and Row, 1973), 6.

23 Information obtained from interview with Rabbi Clifford Librach of Moses Montefiore Synagogue, Bloomington, Illinois, December 3, 1990.

24 Camenisch, *Grounding*, 102–104.

25 Hence the joke: "The lawyer's vacation is the space between the question put to a witness and the witness' response."

26 Elliot Krause is right to emphasize the crisis dimension of professional service. In its broadest sense, a crisis is a moment of and for judgment of significance to life. Since the goods which the professional promotes are life-constituting, professional service does involve the making of judgments which are actually or potentially altering of life. Elliot A. Krause, *The Sociology of Occupations* (Boston, MA: Little, Brown, 1971), 96.

27 The term "client" originally applied to vulnerable persons who depended upon the assistance of another for their very livelihood. *Oxford Classical Dictionary*, 2nd edn, s.v. "client." The stranger in Palestine "who had put himself under the protection of the people . . . among whom he had take up his abode" qualified as a "client" of the benefactor(s). *The Jewish Encyclopedia*, s.v. "Proselyte" by Emil G. Hirsch. This usage captures well the extreme vulnerability still present today among the clients of the learned professions (sick, injured or accused, and those who are spiritually or materially destitute).

28 Recall that Scribonius likens the professing doctor to a soldier who swears a loyalty oath. Such oaths of soldiers are clearly intended to convince the listener of the soldier's willingness to fight in the event of battle.

29 Peter Jennings, NBC Nightly News, February 6, 1992.

30 Everett C. Hughes, "Professions," in Kenneth S. Lynn and the editors of *Daedalus* (eds), *The Professions in America* (Boston: Beacon Press, 1965), 3.

31 Obituary for Dr Armand Hammer, *New York Times*, December 12, 1990, p.A16(N).

32 Alan H. Goldman, *The Moral Foundations of Professional Ethics* (Totowa, New Jersey: Rowman and Littlefield, 1980), 126.

33 Ibid., 128–132; 141.

34 It must not be forgotten that corporations are made up of people, and it is these people who appear in court. As the attorney Wesley Kinnear has argued, "People from corporations get caught up and sometimes ground up in legal suits against corporations. Corporate employees feel vulnerable not just because they are being attacked but also because they have pride in the corporation they work for and have helped to build. In this sense, the life of a corporate employee is just as much on the line as the life of any other litigant." Interview with Wesley Kinnear in Chicago, Illinois on September 20, 1992.

35 For example, in a tax dispute between the US Internal Revenue

Service and the Sundstrand Corporation, the judge severely repri-
mands the Internal Revenue Service for "cryptic" and unfair practices
and for "flagrantly" changing its responses whenever asked to state
and defend its claim against the company. *Sundstrand Corp. v. Com-
mission, Reports of the United States Tax Court*, 96 T.C., 226, 410.

36 Kass, *Toward a More Natural Science*, 242.

37 For a discussion of the increasing hostility towards attorneys and its
relation to the public perception that lawyers distance themselves
from clients and act as though they are superior to them, see Shulamith
Gold, "Lawyer-bashing? Objection!", *Chicago Tribune*, July 23, 1993,
sec. 5, 1–2.

38 Harry Stack Sullivan, *The Psychiatric Interview* (New York: W. W.
Norton, 1970), 238–239.

5 THE LEGITIMACY OF THE PROFESSIONS' ENDS

1 Henceforth I shall use the term "clergy" to refer to Jewish rabbis,
Catholic priests, Protestant ministers, Anabaptist leaders, or anyone
who is thought of as especially skilled in interpreting the word of God
for the benefit of others. The term "clergy" derives from the Greek
word *klerikos*, meaning an allotment or inheritance. The word of God
can be thought of as an allotment or inheritance granted to a certain
group of people. Judaism and Christianity may differ as to who has
inherited the word of God. It is sometimes claimed, for example, that
for Jews, God's word (the Oral and Written Torah) is accessible to
the whole community, while Christians restrict accessibility to those
who have experienced the grace of God. Both agree, however, in
treating the word of God as a gift from God to humans. Moreover,
as I shall argue, both religions use their inheritance with its promise
of salvation to ground the roles of their spiritual leaders, divergent
though the roles may be. Finally, the term "clergy" has been used in
the past to refer to non-Christian, as well as Christian, spiritual leaders.
For this last usage, see *OED*, s.v. "clergy." So there is also historical
precedent for the usage I am here adopting.

2 For example, it is argued that medicine *creates* illness: "It is part of
being a profession to be given the official power to define and
therefore create the shape of problematic segments of social
behavior." Eliot Freidson, *Profession of Medicine* (New York: Dodd,
Mead 1975), 206. Hughes also contends that physicians "consider it
their prerogative to define the nature of disease and of health." Everett C. Hughes, *Men and their Work* (Glencoe, Illinois: The Free Press,
1958).

3 Freidson, *Medicine*, 251.

4 The quote from the American Society of Plastic and Reconstructive
Surgeons appears in Ellen Goodman, "Time to Announce Equal
Rites Honors," *Bloomington (Illinois) Pantagraph*, August 18, 1992,
sec. A, 7.

5 Stanley Hauerwas, *Suffering Presence: Theological Reflections on*

Medicine, the Mentally Handicapped, and the Church (Notre Dame, Indiana: University of Notre Dame Press, 1986), 58.

6 My discussion of "organism" draws heavily upon Aristotle's treatment of the body–soul relation in Aristotle *De Anima* 2 and 3 and upon Kass' suggestive treatment of health. See Leon Kass, *Toward a More Natural Science: Biology and Human Affairs* (New York, Free Press, 1985), 164–174.

7 *The American Heritage Dictionary*, 8th edn, s.v. "kailo- " in the appendix "Indo-European Roots."

8 The Greeks were highly attuned to the "wholing" properties of the organism, properties which we moderns seem to be rediscovering. Greek physicians did no systematic dissecting of the body, perhaps because they thought the body's parts were best understood when they were "at work" as part of a functioning whole. For a discussion of Greek dissecting procedures, see Ludwig Edelstein, *Ancient Medicine* (Baltimore, Maryland: Johns Hopkins University Press, 1967), 248.

9 Austin H. Riesen, "Arrested Vision," *Scientific American* 183, no.1 (July 1950): 16–19.

10 Edmund D. Pellegrino, MD, "Health Care: A Vocation to Justice and Love," in Francis Eigo, ed., *The Professions in Ethical Context: Vocations to Justice and Love* (Villanova, Pennsylvania: Villanova University Press, 1986), 101.

11 Obituary for Jacqueline du Pré, *Chicago Tribune*, October 20, 1987, sec. 2, 11.

12 Panin quoted in Phillipa Foot, *Virtues and Vices* (Berkeley: University of California Press, 1978), 37.

13 Jesus suffered great pain while on the cross, but I am unwilling to say that he became mentally or physically unhealthy. Suffering sometimes gives new purpose to life. It may sharpen an agent's awareness of the shape of his career, giving him a sense of his "whole" life which, in turn, enables him to make his life even more purposeful and whole. Jesus' final surrender, so in keeping with his life's insistence upon trusting God, may be viewed as the act of a supremely healthy man. Not pain but rather the absence of the judging and thinking powers presupposed by "balancing" bodily and transbodily purposes would signal unhealthiness. Jesus seems to have had those powers until the last moment.

14 The Hippocratic Oath clearly envisions the physician promoting health through both preventive and remedial measures. The oath opens with the physician appealing to Hygieia and Panaceia as witnesses to his professionalism (or lack thereof). Edelstein, *Ancient Medicine*, 5. Hygieia is the goddess of health maintenance; Panaceia is the goddess of curative treatment.

15 Plato *Republic* I.351c6-e1.

16 St Augustine *The City of God against the Pagans* IV.4.

17 H. L. A. Hart, *The Concept of Law* (Oxford: Oxford University Press, 1961), 153–154.

18 I leave open the vexing question of whether one can be unjust to

one's self-in-the-making, a self which might be thought of as "another" person since one is not yet fully that new person.

19 I also leave open the question of whether a robbery by a repeat offender and a first offense by a leading citizen of the town are the "same" crime.

20 Hart, *Concept of Law*, 155. The precept also implies that different cases should be treated differently.

21 Judge Dorothy S. Nelson quoted in Christopher F. Mooney, "Law: A Vocation to Justice and Love," in Eigo, *The Professions*, 83.

22 Example taken from James W. Nickel, "Dworkin on the Nature and Consequences of Rights," *Georgia Law Review* 11 (1977): 1115–1137.

23 Kant first elaborated this notion. Immanuel Kant, *Groundwork of the Metaphysics of Morals*, trans. H. J. Paton (New York: Harper and Row, 1964), 95–99.

24 For an elaboration of this gloss on Kant's formulation, see ONora O'Neill, *Constructions of Reason: Explorations of Kant's Practical Philosophy* (Cambridge: Cambridge University Press, 1989), 115.

25 For an excellent discussion of how our self-perception depends upon hearing the voices of others, see Nancy Sherman, *The Fabric of Character: Aristotle's Theory of Virtue* (Oxford: Clarendon Press, 1989), 27–28; 138–144.

26 For a discussion of this point, see Aristotle, *Nicomachean Ethics* 1130a30–b35; 1131a10–b24.

27 See the extensive discussion of Gilmore's fight to persuade the court to honor his decision not to appeal against the death sentence in Robert M. Cover, Owen M. Fiss, and Judith Resnick, *Procedure* (Westbury, New York: Foundation Press, 1988), 429–445.

28 "And on Yom Kippur the whole house of Israel stands nakedly before its God, confessing, 'We have no merit.' " Emil L. Fackenheim, *What is Judaism?* (New York: Macmillan, 1987), 116.

29 God's blessing to the people of Israel ends in the promise of peace: "The Lord lift up his countenance upon you, and give you peace." Numbers 6:26. "Peace, peace, to the far and to the near, says the Lord; and I will heal him." Isaiah 57:19. This and subsequent quotes are from the Revised Standard Version.

30 Leo Baeck, *The Essence of Judaism* (New York: Schocken Books, 1961), 191.

31 Malachi 2:10.

32 Rabbi Simeon ben Yohai, quoted in Baeck, *Essence of Judaism*, 173.

33 Eternal confidence comes from acting rightly. Acting rightly means loving thy neighbor. The commandment to love is ultimately a commandment of justice where "justice is not merely the avoidance or prevention of interference with the rights of others." Loving justice is "rather a positive and social commandment, the sincere and willing acknowledgment of our fellow man, the realization of his equality" as a fellow human being. Ibid., 195.

34 Although "negative" rights of non-interference are often distinguished from "positive" rights to the receipt of some benefit or privilege, I would reject any hard and fast distinction between the two. The

"negative" right to speak without interference to be meaningful requires a "positive" right of access to a court system in which to sue police or other parties who attempt to interfere with the right's exercise.

35 "[T]he task of this nation ... is to bring the blessing of God upon the families of the earth despite all obstacles. ... We must truly become disciples of Aaron, loving humanity and bringing them closer to Torah, so that the God of Israel will be the God of the whole world." Rabbi Shlomo Riskin, "Three Biblical Covenants," *Jerusalem Post International Edition*, October 27, 1990, p. 23.

36 Baeck, *Essence of Judaism*, 275.

37 Paul Tillich, *Systematic Theology*, 3 vols (Chicago: University of Chicago Press, 1951–1963), 2: 165–166.

38 Ibid.

39 Ibid.

40 *OED*, s.v. "salvation."

41 Pascal quoted in Etienne Gilson, "The Intelligence in the Service of Christ," in *The World Treasury of Modern Religious Thought*, ed. Jaroslav Pelikan with a foreword by Clifton Fadiman (Boston: Little, Brown, 1990), 221.

42 Matthew 19:24.

43 Mark 2:17.

44 "You also must be ready: for the Son of man is coming at an hour you do not expect." Luke 12:40.

45 Isak Dinesen's description of true faith quoted by Hannah Arendt in *Men in Dark Times* (San Diego: Harcourt Brace Jovanovich, 1983), 104.

46 Matthew 27:46.

47 Psalms 22:1–4.

48 Luke 22:42.

49 Luke 23:46.

50 One might certainly object that the notion of salvation I am defending is far too existential, making man into a self-savior. However, even those Christians who emphasize the saving help of the holy spirit must acknowledge that man saves himself "even if only by calling on the divine name for help." Mircea Eliade, ed. *The Encyclopedia of Religion* (New York: Macmillan, 1987), s.v. "Soteriology," by Ninian Smart.

51 Dietrich Bonhoeffer, "Letters from Prison," in Pelikan, *World Treasury*, 473.

52 For example, Aristotle would see Jesus' time on the cross as of little ethical interest. Like the man lashed to the mast of a ship, Jesus has no ability to originate actions. Our character (or ethos) derives not from what we suffer but from the actions we initiate and from those we could initiate but choose not to originate. In the case of Jesus on the cross, voluntary, and hence ethically significant, action is not an option. See Aristotle, *Nicomachean Ethics* 1109b30–1111b3.

53 *OED*, s.v. "martyr."

54 The power of ministry or of the clergy resided in the whole church in

the beginning. John Knox, "The Ministry in the Primitive Church," in *The Ministry in Historical Perspectives*, ed. H. Richard Niebuhr and Daniel D. Williams (New York: Harper and Bros., 1956), 9–23. And as Marty points out, the Christian church to this day resists a hard and fast distinction between clergy and laity. Martin E. Marty, *Protestantism* (New York: Harper and Bros., 1956), 9–23, argues that "[t]houghtful Christians have always been uneasy about [the laity–clergy distinction] and have pleaded for a recovery of New Testament realities. They regularly remark that authentic rebirth in the life of the church comes with the recovery of the laity."

55 Not even the Pope is free simply to proclaim salvific dogma. The Pope is bound to abide by the sense of the living faith, the faith of church members at large. *New Catholic Encyclopedia*, s.v. "Infallibility" by F. X. Lawlor.

6 THE LIMITS OF PROFESSIONAL DISCRETION

1 Annette Baier, "Trust and Antitrust," *Ethics* (January, 1986): 236–237.

2 Paul Camenisch, *Grounding Professional Ethics in a Pluralistic Society* (New York: Haven, 1983), 121.

3 Alasdair MacIntyre, "Patients as Agents," in *Philosophical Medical Ethics: Its Nature and the Significance*, ed. H. T. Engelhardt, Jr and S. F. Spicker (Dordrecht, Holland: Reidel, 1977), 197–212.

4 Of course, some priests have arrogated to themselves a power of enforcing compliance to which they are not entitled. See, for example, Sissela Bok's discussion of the Catholic priests who, in arranging for a young female parishioner to undergo an exorcism, violated the church's own checks on coercive treatments. In particular, Bok sees the priests as violating church requirements that the girl have the option of communicating with other persons, including physicians. Bok, *Secrets* (New York: Pantheon Books, 1982), 132–133.

5 *OED*, s.v. "doctor."

6 Douglas Rosenthal, for example, seems to take this technical reasoning as archetypically professional, although it is unclear why he does so given his belief that the "traditional" model of the paternalistic professional never corresponded to the reality of legal practice. One can be forgiven for wondering whether it ever really corresponded to the reality of the medical profession either. Douglas Rosenthal, *Lawyer and Client: Who's in Charge?* (New York: Russell Sage Foundation, 1974), 7–16, 148.

7 For representative arguments which try to establish a client right to know or a client right of autonomy with a correlative physician duty to disclose, see Robert M. Veatch, *Theory of Medical Ethics* (New York: Basic Books, 1981), 200–213; Alan H. Goldman, *The Moral Foundations of Professional Ethics* (Totowa, New Jersey: Rowman and Littlefield, 1980), 173–229; Bok, *Secrets*, 59–71, 254–258; Mike Martin, "Rights and the Meta-Ethics of Professional Morality," *Ethics*

91 (July 1981): 625. The need for disclosure of diagnoses and prognoses has been brought home to me every time I have taught
professional ethics to classes with nurses as students. I have taught the
class for a number of years and have never had a nursing student
who favors withholding a diagnosis or prognosis from a patient. All
have said that they cannot work effectively with a patient to help
that person toward health if the patient does not understand what
the problem is with his or her body and what sort of limitations a
disease may impose.

8 Gerald Dworkin outruns his data when he asserts that anyone who
questions the legitimacy of a patient's right not to hear certain kinds
of information about his disease or treatment must do so "on the
grounds that it is better for the patient not to act in this manner."
Gerald Dworkin, *The Theory and Practice of Autonomy* (Cambridge:
Cambridge University Press, 1988), 118. One can simply argue that
communication of diagnoses is an essential part of the therapeutic
process. Doctors are not obliged to conform to patients' desires for
procedures which either do not aim at healing the person or actually
tend to destroy health (e.g. writing a patient's will; prescribing ster-
oids for someone who desires to be a bodybuilder). Therefore, doctors are not obliged to honor a patient's right to know nothing about
their own condition if and to the extent that this "right" prevents
healing from occurring. Indeed, people whose behavior makes it
impossible for a physician to heal them need not be taken on by
physicians as patients in the first place.

9 Hippocratic physicians told patients, albeit sometimes too bluntly,
that they were about to die. Some remedies were prescribed only
after the patient had been told to make his will. Ludwig Edelstein,
Ancient Medicine (Baltimore, Maryland: Johns Hopkins University
Press, 1967), 384. Since the 4th Lutheran Council in 1215, Catholicism
has required physicians to disclose a patient's fatal condition so that
the patient who might be in mortal sin, or in need of setting his
affairs in order, could make the appropriate arrangements. Immanuel
Jakobovits, *Jewish Medical Ethics: A Comparative and Historical
Study of the Jewish Religious Attitude to Medicine and Its Practice*
(New York: Bloch, 1975), 121. So disclosure continued to be the
norm even as religion involved itself in medical ethics. In short,
physicians have a long history of treating approaching death, the
ultimate limiting factor, as an integral part of the patient's life, not
as something shameful or upsetting to be hidden from the patient.
Doctors have seen that healing requires disclosure of diagnoses and
prognoses to the patient. So, it is more than a little misleading to
claim, as the sociologist Emile Durkheim does, that "it is the doctor's
duty on occasion to lie, or not to tell the truth he knows." Emile
Durkheim, *Professional Ethics and Civic Morals* (London: Routledge,
1957), 5.

10 When this case was discussed by a panel of male and female doctors,
judges, and philosophers, all agreed that the woman could rationally
prefer the life of the child to her own and that the physician should

respect this decision. *Autonomy: Does Doctor Know Best?* (New York: Columbia University Seminars on Media and Society, 1989), videorecording.

11 I would include within the class of the untreatable that large number of persons who, despite often protracted stays in intensive care, die within a year of being discharged from intensive care units (ICUs). I have no problem with attempts to study the mortality rates of patients entering ICUs with a view to ascertaining whether the high degree of interventionist medicine practiced in such units is warranted. Health is broken at some point. Intervening to heal irretrievably unhealthy persons is not therapy and therefore is not professional.

12 Goldman, *Moral Foundations*, 202.

13 Dworkin, *Theory and Practice*, 114–120.

14 Ibid., 116.

15 For one of the few discussions I have seen of this problem, see the dissent in *NAACP v. Button*, 371 US 415 (S.Ct., 1963).

16 What counts as ample notice needs to be carefully explored in light of current notification practices, people's reading and listening habits, and practical constraints on notification. Many of the problems plaguing attempts to specify the conditions under which consent is informed will resurface in this debate. The current practice of law firms appears designed to minimize the likelihood of persons' learning they are party to class action suits. One notice announcing a class action suit run one Sunday in the back pages of a few of a country's newspapers would not meet most philosophers' stringent standards for informed consent.

17 "Standing traditionally has been regarded as an access barrier concerned with one's credential to bring suit." Lee A. Albert, "Standing to Challenge Administrative Action: An Inadequate Surrogate for Claim for Relief," *Yale Law Journal* 83 (1974): 425.

18 David Mellinkoff, *Lawyers and the System of Justice: Cases and Notes on the Profession of Law* (St Paul, Minnesota: West, 1976), 23.

19 Once the defendant has decided how to plead, the client's lawyer must accept it, despite reservations the lawyer may have concerning the plea. If the client has decided to plead guilty, "it would be improper for the lawyer to inform the court that his client is innocent, thereby compelling the defendant to stand trial." Law professor Monroe Freedman quoted in Maynard E. Pirsig and Kenneth F. Kirwin, *Professional Responsibility: Cases and Materials* (St Paul, Minnesota: West, 1976), 466. Professor H. Richard Uviller, LLD, agrees with Freedman. See comments by Uviller in Nina Moore Galston, ed., *Professional Responsibility: The Murky Divide between Right and Wrong* (Dobbs Ferry, New York: Oceana Publications, 1977), 56–57.

20 For a fascinating discussion of how the author Isak Dinesen came to judge her youthful self guilty of a kind of moral cannibalism, see Hannah Arendt, *Men in Dark Times* (New York: Harcourt Brace Jovanovich, 1955), 108.

21 US law confirms this conclusion, protecting "the client from unauthorized release of his adversary from liability, unauthorized submission to dismissal, with prejudice, of his claim, as well as from other unauthorized compromises or settlements of his claim." Rosenthal, *Lawyer and Client*, 120.

22 Mellinkoff, *Lawyers*, 22–25.

23 There is no general right to be provided with counsel. Ibid.

24 *Morris v. Slappy*, 461 US 1 (1983).

25 In general, the client's "chance to have his day in court loses much of its meaning if his case is handicapped from the outset by the very kind of prejudgment our rules of evidence and procedure are intended to prevent." "Professional Responsibility: Report of the Joint Conference," *American Bar Association Journal* 44 (1958): 1159, 1216.

26 A "lawyer should not draw a will under circumstances which give rise to the inference of undue influence" upon the client he is advising. *State v. Horan*, 21 Wis 2d 66 (1963).

27 Wills distributing property serve as a kind of litmus test for professional ethics. We do think it is generally right that people be allowed to distribute their property as they see fit. Goldman, who argues that lawyers must never serve an immoral purpose, has great difficulty coping with wills. Some wills are unjust by his standards. So in order to preserve the right to draw up one's will as one sees fit, Goldman must invent a special class of rights (e.g. the right to draft an unjust will) which it is not right to exercise. But if rights are morally legitimate claims to be able to do or to have something, this class of rights is legitimately illegitimate. This morass signals that Goldman's right-based legal ethics has gone badly wrong. Goldman, *Moral Foundations*, 147–148.

28 The *Model Rules* rightly require lawyers to inform clients of all offered settlements, "unless prior discussions with the client have left it clear that the proposal will be unacceptable." *Model Rules of Professional Conduct and Code of Judicial Conduct*. As amended August, 1984 (Chicago: American Bar Association, 1984), Rule 1.4. The lawyer is not permitted to pursue a settlement that he, the lawyer, happens to prefer.

29 What counts as evidence is complicated. But I would further distinguish work product which does not need to be shared from physical evidence which may have to be provided to the other side. If, for example, a client gives his defense attorney the murder weapon, the attorney cannot suppress such a material piece of evidence. To do so would be to substantially impair the other side's ability to make a strong case on its behalf. This impairment denies access to the court and thus becomes a breach of legal justice according to the concept of access developed in the subsequent paragraphs.

30 "Discovery was hardly intended to enable a learned profession to perform its function either without wits or on wits borrowed from the adversary." Supreme Court Justice Robert H. Jackson's concurring opinion in *Hickman v. Taylor* 329 US 495 (1947).

31 *Model Rules, passim.*
32 Durkheim, for example, seems to take the priest as professionally bound to do whatever church dogma or representatives tell him to do: "Passive obedience, within prescribed limits, may for [the priest and soldier] be obligatory." Durkheim, *Professional Ethics*, 5.
33 Karl Rahner, S.J., *Theological Investigations* (Baltimore: Helicon, 1963), 135–74.
34 Bok, *Secrets*, 77.
35 Richard A. McCormick, S.J., *Notes on Moral Theology 1965–1980* (Lanham, Maryland: University Press of America, Inc., 1981), 65.
36 This point would seem obvious but I have been party to a conversation in which it was argued that doctors are in fact bound to castrate a patient who demands this service and who is willing to pay for it. The conversation cannot be dismissed as just silly since the claim is a natural outgrowth of the service provider model to which many subscribe and which binds the professional to consent to unusual agendas of the layperson as long as the person has paid for the service and the service does not infringe upon any other person's autonomy. If we assume that the patient has no wife and never intends to marry, these conditions would seem to be met and the professional, therefore, bound to castrate the patient.
37 For a discussion of a forced exorcism, see Bok, *Secrets*, 131–133.
38 Guy Oakes, "The Sales Process and the Paradoxes of Trust," *Journal of Business Ethics* 9 (1990): 671–679.
39 Whether or not Demosthenes actually wrote speeches for both sides is a matter hotly debated. What is not in question is that such a practice, when it occurred, was recognized by the public and writers like Plutarch as a breach of the client's trust. Robert J. Bonner, *Lawyers and Litigants in Ancient Athens: The Genesis of the Legal Profession* (New York: Barnes and Noble, 1969), 221–223.
40 Michael D. Bayles, *Professional Ethics* (Belmont, California: Wadsworth, 1981), 131.
41 We hear, for example, the psychoanalyst Jeffrey Masson "on tape saying of a fellow psychoanalyst, 'We were going to pass women on to each other and we were going to have a great time together when I lived in the Freud house.' " He also "on tape cavalierly remarked that the way to really discover a woman's childhood problems was to have sex with her." Both quotations are from Jane Meredith Adams, "Articles of War," *Chicago Tribune* May 28, 1993, sec. 5, 1–2.
42 "Bad Doctors Hide in a Vast Maze," *Chicago Tribune*, November 5, 1993, sec. 1, 1,6.
43 Example is from Bayles, *Professional Ethics*, 130.

7 THE PROFESSIONAL'S GOOD

1 I am here alluding to the problem of conflict of interest. What precisely constitutes a conflict of interest is a fascinating and difficult topic. Despite differences of opinion among philosophers, there seems to be some consensus that conflicts of interest are problematic precisely

because they give the public of potential/actual clients a good reason to believe that the client's welfare has ceased to be the primary focus of the professional–client interaction. Since the client comes to the professional precisely because the client trusts that his welfare will be at the moral center of the relation, conflicts of interest can be thought of as akin to a breach of promise.

2 See the introduction by Warner Wick to Immanuel Kant, *The Metaphysical Principles of Virtue* trans. by James Ellington (Indianapolis: Bobbs-Merrill, 1964), lviii.

3 Daniel Calhoun, *Professional Lives in America: Structure and Aspiration 1750–1850* (Cambridge, Massachusetts: Harvard University Press, 1965), 4–9, 26; Magali Sarfatti Larson, *The Rise of Professionalism: A Sociological Analysis* (Berkeley: University of California Press, 1977), 56–63.

4 In the UK, barristers cannot sue for fees; in the United States, they may do so. But again there is no guarantee they will win their suit.

5 Hippocratic physicians were very clear on this point from the beginning. They did not see themselves as lovers of men but rather as agents who wanted to perform the specific activity of healing very well. See Ludwig Edelstein, *Ancient Medicine* (Baltimore, Maryland: Johns Hopkins University Press, 1967), 324.

6 Yves Simon, *A General Theory of Authority* with introduction by A. Robert Caponigri (Notre Dame, Indiana: University of Notre Dame Press, 1962), 25–26.

7 Lebacqz is one of the few other ethicists to worry about the connection between professional authority and professionals' motives. She argues that the client cares not just that the professional performs well but that the professional brings a certain integrity to her performance. Karen Lebacqz, *Professional Ethics: Power and Paradox* (Nashville, Tennessee: Abingdon Press, 1985), 73.

8 For example, rabbis are increasingly seen not as practitioners of a distinctive ministry but rather as just another job holder or administrator. "The rabbi is decreasingly a man apart. Like many of his congregants he is in a *service profession*" (emphasis mine). Arthur Hertzberg, *Being Jewish in America: The Modern Experience* (New York: Schocken Books, 1979), 99–100. See also J. A. Jackson, ed., *Professions and Professionalism* (Cambridge: Cambridge University Press, 1970), 14.

9 The psychiatrist Sullivan, for example, argued that patient behavior itself reflected group behavior. It was the psychiatrist's participation in that group as well that enabled the psychiatrist to help the patient. See introduction by Otto Allen Will, MD to Harry Stack Sullivan, *The Psychiatric Interview* (New York: W. W. Norton, 1970), xv.

10 Dr Bernie Siegel, MD quoted in interview with Bruce Felts, "An Interview with Bernie Siegel," *Solutions Quarterly* (Summer 1990): 32.

11 See the brief discussion of Dr Cassell's work in Elizabeth Schneider, "Professor Finds Limit to Human Lifespan," *Chicago Maroon*, November 20, 1990, 4.

12 Of course, not all physicians will address this question. Those who are

unwilling to confront their own mortality and to admit limitations to their skill will abandon patients whom they cannot cure. See Janice Norton, MD's moving account of her conversations with a woman who was left to die alone by her physicians (and her clergyman) who were made uncomfortable by her impending death. Norton's account is reprinted in James B. White, *The Legal Imagination: Studies in the Nature of Legal Thought and Expression* (Boston: Little, Brown, 1973), 174–180.

13 Luke 4:23 (Revised Standard Version).

14 Religious healers have long understood this shared identity of interest: "To pray for the healing of one's neighbour, that is to say for a complete restoration of his whole being, his soul as well as his body, leads inevitably to the discovery that this Biblical healing is just what one needs oneself." Bernard Martin, *The Healing Ministry in the Church* (Richmond, Virginia: John Knox Press, 1960), 121.

15 For a discussion of this tendency among professionals, see Douglas E. Rosenthal, *Lawyer and Client: Who's in Charge?* (New York: Russell Sage Foundation, 1974), 173–174.

16 The exact number of such abortions in the United States is not known precisely because, if doctors and patients were to talk openly about sex-selection abortions, they would find themselves condemned by many, including some women who favor abortion rights. For a discussion of the American bias toward male children and the likely percentage of sex-selection abortions performed, see Nora Frenkiel, "Planning a Family, Down to Baby's Sex," *New York Times*, November 11, 1993, B1, B4.

17 This dynamic was once clearly understood by the women's movement. Early defenders of women's rights were opposed to abortions on the ground that pregnancy *per se* was not the problem facing the woman. The woman's problem was perceived instead as one of finding an appropriate balance in life. Killing the child does not produce a balance; choosing well leads to balance. Contraception, with its promise of better family planning, was thus the original focus of the movement. For a brief description of the original position, see letters by Mary Krane Derr and Rachel MacNair in Letters to the Editor, *Utne Reader* 42 (November–December 1990): 16, 18.

18 Daniel Callahan, *What Kind of Life: The Limits of Medical Progress* (New York: Simon and Schuster, 1990), 55.

19 The inherent conflict between healing and abortion accounts for why, although many Roman and Greek philosophers approved of abortion, ancient physicians were opposed to dismemberment of an embryo unless the fetus was already dead or unless an abortion was necessary to save the woman's life. Abortions of the second sort qualify as therapeutic insofar as they enable the woman to achieve balance or health in her life. Obviously no balance will be possible for the woman who is dead. A brief overview of ancient Greek, Roman, Indian, Jewish, and Christian thinking about abortion appears in Immanuel Jakobovits, *Jewish Medical Ethics: A Comparative and Historical*

Study of the Jewish Religious Attitude to Medicine and Its Practice (New York: Bloch, 1975), 170–173.

20 Leon Kass, *Toward a More Natural Science: Biology and Human Affairs* (New York: Free Press, 1985), 179. In Vermont and Montana, so many doctors have refused to do abortions that non-physician abortion technicians now perform the majority of abortions. Peter Jennings, NBC Nightly News, Special Report, November 29, 1990.

21 Alan H. Goldman, *The Moral Foundations of Professional Ethics* (Totowa, New Jersey: Rowman and Littlefield, 1980), 213.

22 James Boswell, *Life of Samuel Johnson*, ed. Herbert Vaughan Abbott (Chicago: Scott, Foresman, 1923), 144–145.

23 J. Bleckley, *Warren v. Purtell*, 63 Ga. 428, 430 (1879). Or as another jurist put it: "The improbable – by definition being not impossible – sometimes does occur." J. Frank, *Old Colony Bondholders v. N.Y., N.H. & H.R.Co.*, 161 F.2d 413, 443 (1947).

24 Edward Levi, *An Introduction to Legal Reasoning* (Chicago: University of Chicago Press, 1949), *passim*.

25 Sir Frederick Pollock, *Oxford Lectures and Discourses* (Buffalo, New York: W. S. Hein, 1970), 111.

26 Ibid.

27 For an eloquent defense of this point, see James F. Neal's contribution in *To Defend a Killer* (New York: Columbia University Seminars on Media and Society, 1989), videorecording.

28 Shlomo Riskin, "Pluralism and the Sinai Umbrella," *Jerusalem Post International Edition*, August 25, 1990, 22.

29 Goldman concedes the problem with his ethic: "It must be admitted also that the moral perceptions of lawyers may be mistaken even when they take them to be clear. They might overestimate the moral case for the other side and refuse to aid clients without objectively sufficient reason." Goldman, *Moral Foundations*, 151. Goldman suggests that the client just look elsewhere for help. One wonders though just how the unpopular client is to find counsel, since Goldman's moral right ethic, unlike the pledge ethic, imposes no obligation upon the lawyer to see that the client's case does get represented. Unpopular clients have difficulty finding counsel even *with* the Bar's public commitment to defending them. Their plight will probably become more desperate in this new "moral" order.

30 This latter fear is not unjustified. Some lawyers have accused peers who appeal against death sentences against the will of those sentenced to die of using clients to further their own objective of having the death penalty ruled unconstitutional. To date American courts have been reluctant to allow the anti-death-penalty lawyers standing when the client's wish not to appeal against the sentence is well established. For a discussion of when and whether lawyers should be permitted to argue against the death penalty, see the discussion of the Gary Gilmore case in Robert M. Cover, Owen M. Fiss, and Judith Resnick, *Procedure* (Westbury, New York: Foundation Press, 1988), 429–445.

31 "[A]n otherwise valid conviction should not be set aside if the reviewing court may confidently say, on the whole record, that the consti-

tutional error was harmless beyond reasonable doubt." *Delaware v. Van Arsdall*, 475 US 673 (1986).

32 "Under the doctrine of *res judicata*, a judgment on the merits in a prior suit bars a second suit involving the same parties or their privies based on the same cause of action." Justice Potter Stewart in *Parklane Hosiery Company, Inc. v. Leo M. Shore*, 439 US 322 (1979).

33 The "moral lawyer" view tends to place the court at the beck and call of the individual lawyer. The lawyer must, one surmises, constantly seek to drag the court's attention back to the case he is pursuing because his morality has deemed the cause "right." How this behavior is to be reconciled with the court's need to hear other clients' cases is, to my knowledge, never discussed by proponents of the "moral" lawyer view.

34 "There is no salvation outside the church." This view, though by no means accepted by all Christians, is held by those sects offering "exclusivist interpretations of the sacred myth (echoing Jesus' 'I am the Way')." *The Encyclopedia of Religion*, ed. Mircea Eliade, s.v., "Soteriology" by Ninian Smart, 420.

35 Rabbi Joel Blau quoted in Charles E. Shulman, *What It Means to be a Jew* (New York: Crown Publishers, 1960), 13.

36 Immanuel Kant, "What is Enlightenment?" ed. Lewis White Beck, in *Kant: Selections* (New York: Macmillan, 1988), 465.

37 Jacob Neusner, *Invitation to the Talmud: A Teaching Book* (New York: Harper and Row, 1973), 12–13.

38 Ibid., 9.

39 Ibid., 244.

40 Peter Berger's phrase for describing the religious framework in which the pious live appears in Leo Driedger, *Mennonite Identity in Conflict* (Lewiston, New York: Edwin Mellen Press, 1988), 37–38.

41 Riskin, "Pluralism," 22.

42 "Catholic Education," *New York Times*, September 30, 1990, sec. E, 7. Literate Catholics know that church orthodoxy itself has been far from static. See James Gustafson, *Protestant and Roman Catholic Ethics* (Chicago: University of Chicago Press, 1978), 80–94. One might add that under canon law, priests cannot be suspended by a bishop without "due cause." Their authority, like that of the laity, ultimately derives from "their union with Christ their Head." It might be argued that nothing about their authority prevents them from criticizing a particular dogma. The Second Vatican Council explicitly recognized "the human frailty and sinfulness of the church," thereby legitimating "criticism of the church and its bishops and the questioning of [their] decisions." Charles Dahm and Robert Ghelardi, *Power and Authority in the Catholic Church: Cardinal Cody in Chicago* (Notre Dame, Indiana: University of Notre Dame Press, 1981), 77, 85.

43 *New Catholic Encyclopedia*, s.v. "Ecumenical Movement" by B. Leeming.

44 Paul Tillich, *Systematic Theology*. 3 vols (Chicago: University of Chicago Press, 1951–1963), 3: 193, 195.

45 Ibid., 3: 194–195.

46 For a slightly different development of a similar point, see David Tracy, "Defending the Public Character of Theology, " in *Theologians in Transition*, ed. James M. Wall with an introduction by Martin E. Marty (New York: Crossroad, 1981), 113–124.

47 This point becomes quite clear in Rosenthal's defense of informed consent. The client is even permitted to contract to be informed of nothing. Rosenthal, *Lawyer and Client*, 154–161.

48 See my discussion on pp. 40–43 of a client's desire not to permit a professional to attend to another client in need of emergency assistance.

49 See, e.g., Sullivan, *Psychiatric Interview*, 24–25.

50 When the patient has done so will always be a judgment call. I would argue that the physician should make three attempts to persuade the sick person to do what is healthy. The first refusal to comply may be the result of a misunderstanding or a chance oversight on the patient's part. A second act of non-compliance, though, suggests intentional disregard: the patient is willfully not complying. A third refusal means the patient's unwillingness is habitual. When up against such entrenched unwillingness, the professional doctor may justifiably conclude that his time is better spent with other patients.

51 Rosenthal considers additional restrictions limiting what the lawyer may do without the prior consent of the client. Rosenthal, *Lawyer and Client*, 158–161.

52 *Model Rules of Professional Conduct and Code of Judicial Conduct*. As amended August 1984 (Chicago: American Bar Association, 1984), Rule 1.4.

53 *Link v. Wabash Railroad Co.*, 370 US 626 (1962).

54 Geoffrey Hazard seems to have standing in mind when he claims that the central value of the Anglo-American legal system is client autonomy, not as some have asserted, a commitment to the truth. Geoffrey Hazard, *Ethics in the Practice of Law* (New Haven, Connecticut: Yale University Press, 1978), 129.

55 For example, one could argue that lawyers ought to be legally as well as professionally responsible for telling clients that *by law* the client has the ultimate responsibility for what the lawyer does. Most clients do not know the law very well. Discussing it should be part of a conversation aimed at involving the client to the extent possible in the conduct of the case. Knowing that they are ultimately responsible for what their attorney undertakes on their behalf, clients would almost certainly tend to guard their interests more vigilantly.

56 "Once a verdict is returned, there are limited bases for impeaching it." Cover, Fiss, and Resnick, *Procedure*, 1189–1190.

57 James M. Gustafson, *Ethics from a Theocentric Perspective: Theology and Ethics* (Chicago: University of Chicago Press, 1981), 19.

58 Ibid., 18.

59 Ibid., 19.

60 See p. 82 for an amplification of this point.

61 To "believe that there is 'no judgment and no judge' is ... the root

of all sin." Leo Baeck, *The Essence of Judaism* (New York: Schocken Books, 1961), 160.
62 "The Ministerial Covenant in the United Methodist Church Today," *Quarterly Review* 10 (Spring 1990): 25.
63 See p. 87.
64 "The Ministerial Covenant", 25.
65 Ibid., 27.
66 Calhoun, *Professional Lives*, 1–2.
67 The courts must remain accessible. Yet they also must be able to judge and dispose of cases in a timely fashion if they are to be legitimate. Judges are increasingly managing trials with a view to getting cases settled expeditiously. For a discussion of the relation between such judicial activism and legitimacy, see Cover, Fiss, and Resnick, *Procedure*, 398–427.
68 Hazard, *Ethics*, 211.
69 Ibid., 147.
70 Bayles argues for such a patient entitlement. Michael D. Bayles, *Professional Ethics* (Belmont, California: Wadsworth, 1981), 77.
71 Sir Isaiah Berlin, "Two Concepts of Liberty," in *Four Essays on Liberty* (New York: Oxford University Press, 1969), 131.
72 Ibid.

8 THE PROFESSIONAL AND THE PUBLIC GOOD

1 William F. May, "Notes on the Ethics of Doctors and Lawyers," in *Moral Responsibility and the Professions*, ed. Bernard Baumrin and Benjamin Freedman (New York: Haven Publications, 1983), 104.
2 Monroe Freedman, *Lawyers' Ethics in an Adversary System* (Indianapolis: Bobbs-Merrill, 1975), *passim*.
3 William Blackstone, *Commentaries on the Laws of England* (New York: Collins and Hannay, 1832), 1:139.
4 See Greek version of Hippocratic Oath in Ludwig Edelstein, *Ancient Medicine* (Baltimore, Maryland: Johns Hopkins University Press, 1967), 5.
5 Alan H. Goldman, *The Moral Foundations of Professional Ethics* (Totowa, New Jersey: Rowman and Littlefield, 1980), 103;146–147.
6 Ibid., 195–197.
7 Ibid., 218–219.
8 Ibid., 4–5; Jeffrey Blustein, "Family Obligations," in *Virtue and Values: An Introduction to Ethics*, ed. Joshua Halberstam (Englewood Cliffs, New Jersey: Prentice-Hall, 1988), 192–197.
9 Goldman, *Moral Foundations*, 139.
10 For the benefit lawyers reap, see pp. 126/128, 134–143.
11 Goldman, *Moral Foundations*, 141.
12 Ibid., 139–140.
13 Karen Lebacqz, *Professional Ethics: Power and Paradox* (Nashville, Tennessee: Abingdon Press, 1985), 82. The Supreme Court too has held that a defendant cannot manipulate defense counsel into helping the defendant commit perjury. Defendant's case is not prejudiced by

counsel's non-cooperation in such a case because any right of a defendant to testify on his own behalf does not include the right to testify falsely. *Nix v. Whiteside* US 1986.

14 Paul Camenisch, *Grounding Professional Ethics in a Pluralistic Society* (New York: Haven, 1983), 102–104.

15 Ibid., 105–109.

16 We have seen that the pledge ethic meets these necessary conditions for moral promising. The promise is voluntarily given by the promisor, is understood by the promisee in roughly the same terms as it is made by the promisor; is accepted by the promisee; and is of benefit to both the promisee and promisor. I have also argued that an act of promising to be moral must also preserve the promisor's discretion and that the pledge ethic does so. As Henry Sidgwick has observed, a promise does not mechanically bind the promisor under all circumstances. If circumstances have materially changed since the promise was made, we are entitled to reconsider the force of the original promise. Henry Sidgwick, *The Methods of Ethics* with foreword by John Rawls (Indianapolis, Indiana: Hackett, 1981), 311.

17 Camenisch, *Grounding*, 125–126.

18 Ibid., 120–126.

19 Perhaps Camenisch would respond that the relevant moral community is larger than the boundaries of one's own country. He is less clear than one would wish regarding who or what forms the relevant moral community.

20 Camenisch acknowledges the difficulty here. *Grounding*, 136–137. This case is of more than merely hypothetical interest because the Holocaust depended so crucially upon the help of lawyers and doctors. The doctors suggested the gassing; the lawyers devised the laws for transfer of the property of the Jews to the Nazis. This co-opting of professionals in Germany might be a natural outgrowth of the unusual way in which the Germans have understood professions. They have not seen professions as being grounded in a public statement or a profession. Unlike the pledge-based professions of Greece, Rome, England, and America which are not creatures of the state and do not derive their limits from it but rather from the pledge, the traditional professions were regulated from without in Germany at least until the beginning of the nineteenth century. For support of this last claim, see Charles E. McClelland, *The German Experience of Professionalization: Modern Learned Professions and Their Organizations from the Early Nineteenth Century to the Hitler Era* (Cambridge: Cambridge University Press, 1991), 3. In Germany, a profession has been more or less just another occupation. Indeed, "beruf," the German word for profession, "without qualifiers simply means occupation." McClelland, *German Experience*, 15.

21 St Thomas Aquinas quoted in Paul De Jaegher, S.J., *The Virtue of Trust: Meditations* (New York: P. J. Kennedy and Sons, 1949), 1.

22 I disagree with Annette Baier's claim that one trusts one's fellow library users. Baier, "Trust and Antitrust," *Ethics* (January, 1986), 259. One may hope for the best in chance encounters *if* a structure is

in place to give one some reason to expect fellow library users to appropriately care for what one values. But if these persons are stealing shoes from underneath cubicles; setting fires in stairwells; or spending hours poring over the books on sex in the second floor stacks, one will not repose trust in people casually encountered in the library. Only if one has good reason to hope one will be well treated and then has that hope confirmed will trust exist and develop. The fact that the users in the library where I work never leave their books, papers, much less wallets or purses, unattended shows that users do not trust one another.

23 Larson notes that professions developed their most distinctive characteristics in England and the United States. Magali Sarfatti Larson, *The Rise of Professionalism: A Sociological Analysis* (Berkeley: University of California Press, 1977), xvii.

24 This phrase is the one Homer uses to describe the physicians in *Odyssey* XVII, 383–385.

25 Poem quoted in Edelstein, *Ancient Medicine*, 344.

26 Geoffrey Hazard, *Ethics in the Practice of Law* (New Haven, Connecticut: Yale University Press, 1978), 92; 95.

27 Mary Ann Glendon, *Rights Talk: The Impoverishment of Political Discourse* (New York: Free Press, 1991), 14.

28 In fact, one of the worrying trends in modern political affairs and political theorizing is the trend toward ignoring the importance of these intermediary institutions and focusing instead on the citizen versus the state or upon liberal individualism versus communitarianism. For a fascinating discussion of the importance of intermediary institutions in the development of civil society, see Adam Seligman, *The Idea of Civil Society* (New York: Free Press, 1992), *passim*. Stephen Carter's concern about the left's contempt for religion can also be read as a critique of the current lack of understanding of the need for intermediary institutions, or "nose-thumbers," capable of questioning and fighting the tyranny by the majority. Stephen L. Carter, *The Culture of Disbelief: How American Law and Politics Trivialize Religious Devotion* (New York: Basic Books, 1993).

29 Camenisch, *Grounding*, 53.

30 Robert Jay Lifton, *The Nazi Doctors: Medical Killing and the Psychology of Genocide* (New York: Basic Books, 1986), 88–89.

31 Norman F. Cantor, "Privacy in Greece" (New York: The Bar of the City of New York, 1963), 10, typescript.

32 See pp. 118–119 for a further discussion of this point. See also Leon Kass, *Toward a More Natural Science: Biology and Human Affairs* (New York: Free Press, 1985), 238–240.

33 Robert M. Veatch, *A Theory of Medical Ethics* (New York: Basic Books, 1981), 53–55.

34 Edelstein, *Ancient Medicine*, 376.

35 Ibid., 375.

36 Robert J. Bonner, *Lawyers and Litigants in Ancient Athens: The Genesis of the Legal Profession* (New York: Barnes and Noble, 1969), *passim*.

37 Charles C. Wolfram, *Modern Legal Ethics* (St Paul, Minnesota: West, 1986), 17.

38 For a discussion of slaves as living tools, see Aristotle *Politics* 1253b28–36.

39 "Not that the Egyptian or Babylonian physicians were unethical or necessarily devoid of sympathy or love for their patients. But as far as standards of treatment were generally acknowledged, they were . . . imposed by the state." Edelstein, *Ancient Medicine*, 376. See also Aristotle *Politics* III 1286a12–15.

40 Chris Hedges, "The Sheik Will Be Staying Put, For Now," *New York Times*, July 11, 1993, sec. 4, 1.

41 "But a lawyer is not an employee of the State. He does not have the responsibility of an employee to account to the State for his actions because he does not perform them as agent of the State." Concurring opinion of Justice Abe Fortas, *Spevack v. Klein*, 17 L.Ed.2d 574 (S. Ct. 1967).

42 Although lawyers are licensed by the states, "they are not officials of the government by virtue of being lawyers." In re Griffiths, 93 S.Ct. 445, 450.

43 See discussion of citizenship requirements in Robert H. Aronson and Donald T. Weckstein, *Professional Responsibility* (St Paul, Minnesota: West, 1990), 47.

44 Or such seems to be thrust of Justice Sandra Day O'Connor's resistance to collapsing professional speech into government-regulated commercial speech. "Excerpts from Arguments on Pennsylvania's Abortion Law," *New York Times*, April 23, 1992, B10–B11.

45 *Pierce v. Ortho Pharmaceutical Corporation*, 399 A.2d, Superior Court of NJ, Appellate Division. See also *Warthen v. Toms River Community Memorial Hospital*, 433 A. 2d, Superior Court of NJ (1985).

46 See pp. 20–22.

47 Michael Walzer, "The Politics of Michel Foucault," in *Foucault: A Critical Reader*, ed. David Couzens Hoy (Oxford: Basil Blackwell, 1986).

48 In one way or another, each of the above reasons derives the obligation to keep confidence from the character of the professional–client relation. History supports this derivation. For example, in the Catholic church, the priest must keep a confession secret "because it is almost (quasi) of the essence of the sacrament to keep secret the confession." Quote is from the fifteenth century canonist Lyndwood cited in *The Catholic Encyclopedia*, s.v. "Seal of Confession" by R. S. Nolan.

The seal of the confession originates in demands imposed by trustworthily ministering to a confessee in distress. The obligation is not the result of secular legislation. In fact, clerical immunity against having to reveal what a confessee has said in a court of law (so-called "testimonial privilege") entered common law through ecclesiastical law, not the reverse. See Sir Frederick Pollock and William Maitland, *The History of English Law*, 2nd edn, with an introduction by

S. F. C. Milson, 2 vols (Cambridge: Cambridge University Press, 1968), 1:94–95.

I know of no historical evidence to support philosopher Benjamin Freedman's odd speculation that the obligation to preserve confidence stems from the state's desire to have professionals pursue the client's cause with zeal, even if this means sacrificing the well-being of a third party. Benjamin Freedman, "A Meta-Ethics for Professional Morality", *Ethics* 89 (October 1978), 14–17.

49 Jeremy Bentham, who as the father of utilitarianism might be expected to have a just appreciation of the theory's mode of analysis, was aware that professional confidentiality posed a problem. He went beyond the notion of a *prima facie* duty, insisting instead upon an *absolute* duty to keep confidence. He contended that, insofar as the calculus could be done, the moral benefits conferred by trusted priests through the practice of confession probably more than offset any benefit to be gained by breaking confidence on behalf of a particular person or cause. Jeremy Bentham, *The Works of Jeremy Bentham*, ed. John Bowring (New York: Russell and Russell, 1962), 98–99.

50 Benjamin Freedman offers a rule-utilitarian defense of professional morality, including the obligation to keep confidences. Freedman, "A Meta-Ethics for Professional Morality," 14–19.

51 I am inclined to agree with Charles Taylor that utilitarianism tacitly appeals to human goods which its calculus does not explicitly acknowledge. Charles Taylor, *Sources of the Self: The Making of the Modern Identity* (Cambridge, Massachusetts: Harvard University Press, 1989), 22–24.

52 Sissela Bok, *Secrets* (New York: Pantheon Books, 1982), 254–258.

53 Ronald Dworkin, "Does the Public Have a Right to Know?" in US Department of Health and Human Services, Ethics Advisory Board, *Appendix: The Request of the National Institutes of Health for a Limited Exemption from the Freedom of Information Act*, 1979.

54 Bok, *Secrets*, 124–131.

55 Michael D. Bayles, *Professional Ethics* (Belmont, California: Wadsworth, 1981), 19.

56 John E. Beach, "Code of Ethics: The Professional Catch 22," in *Ethical Theory and Business*, ed. Tom L. Beauchamp and Norman E. Bowie (Englewood Cliffs, New Jersey, 1988), 499.

57 In a case involving deceptive advertising, Justice Hugo Black observed: "There is no duty resting upon a citizen to suspect the honesty of those with whom he transacts business." *FTC v. Standard Education Society*, 86 F.2d. 692 (2nd Cir., 1936).

58 I might add that the limited obligation of clerics to keep confidence I am here defending dovetails nicely with the common and statutory law granting clerics immunity from being forced to testify against persons whose confession they have heard. In the United States, state legislation grants the cleric testimonial privilege but only regarding confessions made to the latter in his or her professional character while conforming to the relevant denomination's rules of confession. Nolan gives a description of each state's legislation as it pertains to

testimonial privilege of the clergy. Nolan, *The Catholic Encyclopedia*, s.v. "Seal of Confession."
59 Chapter 7, p. 138.

9 CONCLUSION

1 Edward G. Ryan, *Address*, University of Wisconsin Law School, June 1880.
2 Stanley Hauerwas, *Suffering Presence: Theological Reflections on Medicine, the Mentally Handicapped, and the Church* (Notre Dame, Indiana: University of Notre Dame Press, 1986), 55.
3 Daryl Koehn, "The Dark Side of Care," unpublished essay.
4 For a discussion of the morality of Carol Gilligan's notion of care, see Daryl Koehn, "With a Different Ear: Hearing Gilligan Anew," forthcoming in *Southwest Philosophical Quarterly*, 1994.
5 The example of changes in conveyancing and loss of professional income is considered by MacIver, "The Social Significance of Professional Ethics," in Maynard E. Pirsig and Kenneth F. Kirwin, *Professional Responsibility: Cases and Materials*, 3rd edn (St Paul, Minnesota: West, 1976), 15.
6 Ibid.
7 Donald A. Schon, *The Reflective Practitioner: How Professionals Think in Action* (New York: Basic Books, 1984), 12.
8 The first reference to prostitution as a profession appears to be Rudyard Kipling's line: "Lalun is a member of the most ancient profession in the world" from *Soldiers Three* (1888), quoted in *The Oxford Dictionary of Quotations*, 3rd edn (Oxford: Oxford University Press, 1979), 304. Now such terminology is commonplace – e.g., "The prostitute . . . is expected to preserve a rigorous attitude of psychological noninvolvement, precisely such as is required *of other professionals*" (emphasis mine). *Encyclopedia Britannica*, 15th edn, s.v. "Prostitution" by Paul Henry Gebhard.
9 James Gustafson, "The Clergy in the United States," in Kenneth S. Lynn, and the editors of *Daedalus* (eds), *The Professions in America* (Boston: Beacon Press, 1967), 82.

Bibliography

BOOKS

Arendt, Hannah. *Eichmann in Jerusalem: A Report on the Banality of Evil*. New York and Harmondsworth: Penguin Books, 1964.
—— *The Human Condition*. Chicago: University of Chicago Press, 1958.
—— *Men in Dark Times*. New York: Harcourt Brace Jovanovich, 1955.
Aristotle. *The Basic Works of Aristotle*. Edited and with an introduction by Richard McKeon. New York: Random House, 1941.
Aronson, Robert H. and Donald T. Weckstein. *Professional Responsibility*. St Paul, Minnesota: West, 1990.
Augustine, Saint. *The City of God against the Pagans*. Vol. 2: *Books IV–VII*. Translated by William M. Green. Cambridge, Massachusetts: Harvard University Press, 1963.
Baeck, Leo. *The Essence of Judaism*. New York: Schocken Books, 1961.
Baumrin, Bernard and Benjamin Freedman. *Moral Responsibility and the Professions*. New York: Haven Publications, 1983.
Bayles, Michael D. *Professional Ethics*. Belmont, California: Wadsworth, 1981.
Bayles, Michael D. and Kenneth Henley, eds. *Right Conduct: Theories and Applications*. New York: Random House, 1989.
Beauchamp, Thomas L. and Norman E. Bowie, eds. *Ethical Theory and Business*, 4th edn. Englewood Cliffs, New Jersey: Prentice Hall, 1993.
Beck, Lewis White. *Kant: Selections*. New York: Macmillan, 1988.
Bensman, Joseph. *Dollars and Sense: Ideology, Ethics, and the Meaning of Work in Profit and Nonprofit Organizations*. New York: Macmillan, 1967.
Bergson, Henri. *Two Sources of Religion and Morality*. Translated by R. Ashley Audra and Cloudesley Brereton. New York: Henry Holt, 1935.
Berlin, Isaiah. *Four Essays on Liberty*. New York: Oxford University Press, 1969.
Blackstone, William. *Commentaries on the Laws of England*, 2 vols, with Foreword by Christian, Chitty, Lee, Hovenden, and Ryland. New York: Collins and Hannay, 1832.
Bok, Sissela. *Secrets*. New York: Pantheon Books, 1982.

Bonner, Robert Johnson. *Lawyers and Litigants in Ancient Athens: The Genesis of the Legal Profession.* New York: Barnes and Noble, 1969.

Brandeis, Louis. *Business – A Profession.* Boston: Hale, Cushman and Flint, 1933.

Brennan, Troyen. *Just Doctoring: Medical Ethics in the State.* Berkeley: University of California Press, 1991.

Calhoun, Daniel. *Professional Lives in America: Structure and Aspiration 1750–1850.* Cambridge, Massachusetts: Harvard University Press, 1965.

Callahan, Daniel. *What Kind of Life: The Limits of Medical Progress.* New York: Simon and Schuster, 1990.

Camenisch, Paul. *Grounding Professional Ethics in a Pluralistic Society.* New York: Haven Publications, 1983.

Carney, William J. *The Changing Role of the Corporate Attorney.* Lexington, Massachusetts: D. C. Heath, 1984.

Carter, Richard. *The Doctor Business.* Garden City, New York: Doubleday, 1958.

Chapman, Carleton B. *Physicians, Law, and Ethics.* New York: New York University Press, 1984.

Cicero. *The Correspondence of M. Tullius Cicero.* Edited and introduced by Robert Yelverton Tyrrell and Louis Claude Purser. Dublin: Hodges, Figgis, 1915.

Cooper, David, *Value Pluralism and Ethical Choice.* New York: St Martin's Press, 1993.

Cover, Robert M., Owen M. Fiss, and Judith Resnick. *Procedure.* Westbury, New York: Foundation Press, 1988.

Dahm, Charles and Robert Ghelardi. *Power and Authority in the Catholic Church: Cardinal Cody in Chicago.* Notre Dame, Indiana: University of Notre Dame Press, 1981.

DeGeorge, R. *Business Ethics.* New York: Macmillan, 1982.

Disabling Professions. London: Marion Boyars, 1977.

Driedger, Leo. *Mennonite Identity in Conflict.* Lewiston, New York: Edwin Mellen Press, 1988.

Dworkin, Gerald. *The Theory and Practice of Autonomy.* Cambridge: Cambridge University Press, 1988.

Dworkin, Ronald. *Taking Rights Seriously.* Cambridge, Massachusetts: Harvard University Press, 1977.

Edelstein, Ludwig. *Ancient Medicine.* Edited by Owsei Temkin and C. Lilian Temkin and translated by C. Lilian Temkin. Baltimore, Maryland: Johns Hopkins University Press, 1967.

Eigo, Francis, ed. *The Professions in Ethical Context: Vocations to Justice and Love.* Villanova, Pennsylvania: Villanova University Press, 1986.

Ellul, Jacques. *The Technological Society.* New York: Vintage Books, 1964.

Fackenheim, Emil L. *What is Judaism?* New York: Macmillan, 1987.

Farmer, Richard N. and W. Dickerson Hogue. *Corporate Social Responsibility.* Chicago: Science Research Associates, 1973.

Foot, Philippa, ed. *Theories of Ethics.* Oxford: Oxford University Press, 1967.

—— *Virtues and Vices.* Berkeley: University of California Press, 1978.

Foucault, Michel. *Discipline and Punish: The Birth of the Prison*. New York: Pantheon Books, 1977.

Freedman, Monroe. *Lawyers' Ethics in an Adversary System*. Indianapolis: Bobbs-Merrill, 1975.

Freidson, Eliot. *Profession of Medicine: A Study of the Sociology of Applied Knowledge*. New York: Dodd, Mead, 1975.

—— *Professional Powers: A Study of the Institutionalization of Formal Knowledge*. Chicago: University of Chicago Press, 1986.

Galston, Nina Moore, ed. *Professional Responsibility: The Murky Divide between Right and Wrong*. Dobbs Ferry, New York: Oceana Publications, 1977.

Geison, Gerald L., ed. *Professions and Professional Ideologies in America*. Chapel Hill, North Carolina: University of North Carolina Press, 1983.

Glendon, Mary Ann. *Rights Talk: The Impoverishment of Political Discourse*. New York: Free Press, 1991.

Goldman, Alan H. *The Moral Foundations of Professional Ethics*. Totowa, New Jersey: Rowman and Littlefield, 1980.

Greenleaf, Simon. *A Treatise on the Law of Evidence*. Boston: Little, Brown, 1856.

Gustafson, James M. *Can Ethics be Christian?* Chicago: University of Chicago Press, 1975.

—— *Ethics from a Theocentric Perspective: Theology and Ethics*. Chicago: University of Chicago Press, 1981.

—— *Protestant and Roman Catholic Ethics*. Chicago: University of Chicago Press, 1978.

Halberstam, Joshua. *Virtues and Values: An Introduction to Ethics*. Englewood Cliffs, New Jersey: Prentice Hall, 1988.

Hart, H. L. A. *The Concept of Law*. Oxford: Oxford University Press, 1961.

Hauerwas, Stanley. *Suffering Presence: Theological Reflections on Medicine, the Mentally Handicapped, and the Church*. Notre Dame, Indiana: University of Notre Dame Press, 1986.

Hazard, Geoffrey. *Ethics in the Practice of Law*. New Haven, Connecticut: Yale University Press, 1978.

Hertzberg, Arthur. *Being Jewish in America: The Modern Experience*. New York: Schocken Books, 1979.

Hick, John, ed. *Classical and Contemporary Readings in the Philosophy of Religion*. Englewood Cliffs, New Jersey: Prentice Hall, 1970.

Hostetler, John Andrew. *Amish Society*. Baltimore: Johns Hopkins University Press, 1968.

Hughes, Everett C. *Men and their Work*. Glencoe, Illinois: Free Press, 1958.

Hume, David. *Commentaries on the Law of Scotland, Respecting Crimes*. Edinburgh: James Neill for Bell and Bradtute, 1819.

Jackson, J. A., ed. *Professions and Professionalization*. Cambridge: Cambridge University Press, 1970.

Jakobovits, Immanuel. *Jewish Medical Ethics: A Comparative and*

Historical Study of the Jewish Religious Attitude to Medicine and Its Practice, new edn. New York: Bloch, 1975.

Jaspers, Karl. *Socrates, Buddha, Confucius, Jesus*. San Diego: Harcourt Brace Jovanovich, 1957.

Jones, Anthony, ed. *Professions and the State: Expertise and Autonomy in the Soviet Union and Eastern Europe*. Philadelphia: Temple University Press, 1991.

Kant, Immanuel. *Groundwork of the Metaphysics of Morals*. Translated by H. J. Paton. New York: Harper and Row, 1964.

—— *Religion within the Limits of Reason Alone*. Edited and translated by Theodore M. Greene and Hoyt H. Hudson. New York: Harper Torchbooks, 1960.

Kass, Leon. *Toward a More Natural Science: Biology and Human Affairs*. New York: Free Press, 1985.

Keane, John, ed. *The Power of the Powerless: Citizens against the State*. London: Hutchinson, 1985.

Larson, Magali Sarfatti. *The Rise of Professionalism: A Sociological Analysis*. Berkeley: University of California Press, 1977.

Lebacqz, Karen. *Professional Ethics: Power and Paradox*. Nashville, Tennessee: Abingdon Press, 1985.

Levi, Edward. *An Introduction to Legal Reasoning*. Chicago: University of Chicago Press, 1949.

Lifton, Robert Jay. *The Nazi Doctors: Medical Killing and the Psychology of Genocide*. New York: Basic Books, 1986.

McCormick, Richard A. *Notes on Moral Theology 1965–1980*. Lanham, Maryland: University Press of America, 1981.

McKeon, Richard, ed. *Selections from Medieval Philosophers*, 2 vols. Vol. 2, *Roger Bacon to William of Ockham*. New York: Scribner, 1930.

Martin, Bernard. *The Healing Ministry in the Church*. Richmond, Virginia: John Knox Press, 1960.

Marty, Martin. *Protestantism*. New York: Harper and Bros., 1956.

May, William F. *The Patient's Ordeal*. Bloomington, Indiana: Indiana University Press, 1991.

—— *The Physician's Covenant: Images of the Healer in Medical Ethics*. Philadelphia: Westminster Press, 1983.

Mellinkoff, David. *Lawyers and the System of Justice: Cases and Notes on the Profession of Law*. St Paul, Minnesota: West, 1976.

Model Rules of Professional Conduct and Code of Judicial Conduct. As amended August 1984. Chicago: American Bar Association, 1984.

Moore, Wilbert E. *The Professions: Roles and Rules*. New York: Russell Sage Foundation, 1970.

Neusner, Jacob. *Invitation to the Talmud: A Teaching Book*. New York: Harper and Row, 1973.

Newton, Lisa. *Ethics in America: Study Guide*. Englewood Cliffs, New Jersey: Prentice-Hall, 1989.

Niebuhr, H. Richard and Daniel D. Williams. *The Ministry in Historical Perspectives*. New York: Harper and Bros., 1956.

Niebuhr, Reinhold. *An Interpretation of Christian Ethics*. New York: Harper and Bros., 1935.

O'Neill, ONora. *Constructions of Reason: Explorations of Kant's Practical Philosophy*. Cambridge: Cambridge University Press, 1989.

Pelikan, Jaroslav, ed. *The World Treasury of Modern Religious Thought*. With a Foreword by Clifton Fadiman. Boston: Little, Brown, 1990.

Pirsig, Maynard E. and Kenneth F. Kirwin. *Professional Responsibility: Cases and Materials*, 3rd edn. St Paul, Minnesota: West, 1976.

Plato. *The Republic of Plato*. Translated by Allan Bloom. New York: Basic Books, 1968.

Pollock, Sir Frederick. *Oxford Lectures and Discourses*. Buffalo, New York: W. S. Hein, 1970.

Pollock, Sir Frederick and William Maitland. *The History of English Law*. 2nd edn. With an introduction by S. F. C. Milsom. Cambridge: Cambridge University Press, 1968.

Rader, Melvin and Jerry H. Gill. *The Enduring Questions: Main Problems of Philosophy*. Fort Worth, Texas: Holt, Rinehart and Winston, Inc., 1991.

Rahner, Karl. *Theological Investigations*. Baltimore: Helicon, 1963.

Rawls, John. *A Theory of Justice*. Oxford: Oxford University Press, 1972.

Reader, W. J. *Professional Men: The Rise of the Professional Classes in Nineteenth-Century England*. London: Weidenfeld and Nicolson, 1966.

Robison, Wade L., Michael S. Pritchard, and Joseph Ellin. *Profits and Professions: Essays in Business and Professional Ethics*. Clifton, New Jersey: Humana Press, 1983.

Rogerson, Kenneth F., ed. *Introduction to Ethical Theory*. Fort Worth, Texas: Holt, Rinehart, and Winston, Inc., 1991.

Rosenthal, Douglas E. *Lawyer and Client: Who's in Charge?* New York: Russell Sage Foundation, 1974.

Rosner, Fred, MD. *Modern Medicine and Jewish Ethics*. New York: Yeshiva University Press, 1986.

Rosner, Fred, MD and J. David Bleich., ed. *Jewish Bioethics*. Brooklyn, New York: Hebrew, 1979.

Sandel, Michael. *Liberalism and the Limits of Justice*. Cambridge: Cambridge University Press, 1982.

Sandel, Samuel. *We Jews and You Christians*. Philadelphia: J. B. Lippincott, 1967.

Schaffer, Dale. *Librarianship as a Profession*. Metachen, New Jersey: Scarecrow Press, 1968.

Schon, Donald A. *The Reflective Practitioner: How Professionals Think in Action*. New York: Basic Books, 1984.

Schreiber, William I. *Our Amish Neighbors*. Chicago: University of Chicago Press, 1962.

Seligman, Adam. *The Idea of Civil Society*. New York: Free Press, 1992.

Service is My Business. Chicago: Rotary International, 1948.

Shulman, Charles E. *What It Means to be a Jew*. New York: Crown Publishers, 1960.

Spurrier, William A. *Ethics and Business*. New York: Scribner, 1962.

Sullivan, Harry Stack. *The Psychiatric Interview*. New York: W. W. Norton, 1970.

Taylor, Charles. *Sources of the Self.* Cambridge, Massachusetts: Harvard University Press, 1989.

Tillich, Paul. *Systematic Theology.* 3 vols. Chicago: University of Chicago Press, 1951–1963.

Veatch, Robert M. *Case Studies in Medical Ethics.* Cambridge, Massachusetts: Harvard University Press, 1977.

—— *A Theory of Medical Ethics.* New York: Basic Books, 1981.

Wall, James M., ed. *Theologians in Transition.* With an Introduction by Martin E. Marty. New York: Crossroad, 1981.

Walton, Clarence. *The Ethics of Corporate Conduct.* Englewood Cliffs, New Jersey: Prentice Hall, 1977.

White, James B. *The Legal Imagination: Studies in the Nature of Legal Thought and Expression.* Boston: Little, Brown, 1973.

Wolfram, Charles C. *Modern Legal Ethics.* St Paul, Minnesota: West, 1986.

ARTICLES

Baier, Annette. "Trust and Antitrust," *Ethics* (January 1986): 231–260.

Bayles, Michael. "National Health Insurance and Noncovered Services," *Journal of Health Politics, Policy and Law* 2 (1977): 335–348.

Boatright, John R. "Conflict of Interest: An Agency Analysis," in *Ethics and Agency Theory: An Introduction*, ed. Norman E. Bowie and R. Edward Freeman, 187–203. Oxford: Oxford University Press, 1992.

Buchanan, Allen. "Medical Paternalism," *Philosophy and Public Affairs* 7 (1978): 370–390.

Deneke, Arno H. "The Dilemma of the Virtuous Lawyer or When Do You Have to Blow the Whistle on Your Client?" *Arizona State Law Journal* (1979): 245–252.

Donaldson, Thomas. "The Language of International Corporate Ethics," *Business Ethics Quarterly* (June 1992): 271–282.

Freedman, Benjamin. "A Meta-Ethics for Professional Morality," *Ethics* 89 (October 1978): 1–19.

Friedman, Milton. "The Social Responsibility of Business Is to Increase Its Profits," in *Right Conduct: Theories and Applications*, ed. Michael D. Bayles and Kenneth Henley, 316–321. New York: Random House, 1989.

Gaylin, Willard. "What's an FBI Poster Doing in a Nice Journal Like That?" *Hastings Center Report* 2 (April 1972): 1–3.

Gert, Bernard and Culver, Charles M. "Paternalistic Behavior," *Philosophy and Public Affairs* 6 (1976): 45–57.

Hall, T. D. and C. M. Lindsay. "Medical Schools: Producers of What? Sellers of Whom?" *Journal of Law and Economics* 23 (April 1980): 55–80.

Jackson, J. A. "Professions and Professionalization: Editorial Introduction," in *Professions and Professionalization*, ed. J. A. Jackson, 5–10. Cambridge: Cambridge University Press, 1970.

Luban, David. "Professional Ethics: A New Code for Lawyers?" *Hastings Center Report* 10 (June 1980): 11–15.

Martin, Mike W. "Rights and the Meta-Ethics of Professional Morality," *Ethics* 91 (July 1981), 619–625.

Marty, Martin E. "The Clergy," in *The Professions in American History*, ed. Nathan O. Hatch, 73–91. Notre Dame, Indiana: University of Notre Dame Press, 1988.

Masters, Roger D. "Is Contract an Adequate Basis for Medical Ethics?" *Hastings Center Report* 5 (December 1975): 24–28.

May, William F. "Code, Covenant, Contract, or Philanthropy?" *Hastings Center Report* 5 (December 1975): 29–38.

Mooney, Christopher F. "Law: A Vocation to Justice and Love," in *The Professions in Ethical Context: Vocations to Justice and Love*, ed. Francis Eigo, 86. Villanova, Pennsylvania: Villanova University Press, 1986.

Newton, Lisa. "Virtue and Role: Reflections on the Social Nature of Morality," *Business Ethics Quarterly* 2 (July 1992): 357–366.

Oakes, Guy. "The Sales Process and the Paradoxes of Trust," *Journal of Business Ethics* 9 (1990): 671–679.

Oken, Donald. "What to Tell Cancer Patients: A Study of Medical Attitudes," *Journal of the American Medical Association* 175 (1961): 1120–1128.

Parsons, Talcott. "Professions," in *International Encyclopedia of the Social Sciences*, ed. Daniel L. Sills, 2nd edn. New York: Free Press, 1968.

Pound, Roscoe. "What is a Profession?" *Notre Dame Lawyer* 19 (1944): 203–204.

Schudson, Michael. "The Profession of Journalism in the United States," in *The Professions in American History*, ed. Nathan O. Hatch, 145–161. Notre Dame, Indiana: University of Notre Dame Press, 1988.

Turner, C. and M. N. Hodge. "Occupations and Professions," in *Professions and Professionalization*, ed. J. A. Jackson, 17–50. Cambridge: Cambridge University Press, 1970.

VIDEORECORDINGS

Ethics in America. Columbia University Seminars in Media and Society, 1989. Videocassettes.

Index

McClelland, Charles E. 208
McCormick, Richard A. 201
McCurdy, J. Frederic 190
MacIntyre, Alasdair 91, 197
MacIver 180, 212
McKeon, Richard P. 185
McKnight, John 182
MacNair, Rachel 203
Mafia 69, 140–1
Maitland, William 210
Marks, F. Raymond 186
Martin, Bernard 203
Martin, Mike 197
Marty, Martin E. 29, 185, 187, 197, 206
Masson, Jeffrey 201
May, Mark A. 29, 187
May, William F. 22, 144–6, 185, 207
medicine: in Babylon 160; in Egypt 160; in Germany 208; in Greece 1, 159, 194; in Rome 1, 159
Mellinkoff, David 23, 186, 199, 200
Menander 182
methodology 6–7, 9–12
Michaelson, Robert S. 186
Milson, S. F. C. 210–11
monopoloy and the professions 2, 3, 150
Mooney, Christopher F. 195
Moore, Wilbert E. 18, 182, 185–6

Neal, James F. 204
Nelson, Dorothy S. 77, 195
Neusner, Jacob 192, 205
Newton, Lisa 182
Nickel, James W. 195
Niebuhr, H. Richard 186, 197
Nolan, R. S. 210–11
Norton, Janet 203

O'Connor, Sandra Day 183, 210
O'Neill, ONora 195
Oakes, Guy 110, 201
Ogletree, Charles 189
ordinary morality and professional ethics 3, 4, 6, 147–53

Panin 194
Pascal, Blaise 196

Pelikan, Jaroslav 196
Pellegrino, Edmund D. 194
Pirsig, Maynard E. 189–90, 199, 212
Pius XII, Pope 133
Plato 26, 77, 80, 186, 194
Plutarch 201
Pollock, Frederick 127, 204, 210
privilege and status of professionals 2, 4; see also fame; fees
profession(s): attacks upon 1–5; as chosen mechanism of service 6, 161–2; as commerce 2, 183; as intensification of public trust 153–5; nature of 7, 11, 15, 54–68, 188; skill 11; three liberal 12–13; non-traditional 12–13, 179–80; see also professional oath/pledge; professionalization; professionals
professional oath/pledge: binding quality 63–4; as ground of client trust 42, 54–68; objections to as legitimating ground 69–173; as ordering principle 42–3, 55, 65; and public expectations 62–4; use of in liberal professions 60–1, 191; see also promises
professionalization 5–6
professionals: altruism of 19–20; disciplining 24, 109–15; discretion of 39–43; education of 23–5, 52–3; ends of 70–88; good of 117–43; legitimacy of ends of 69–88; motivation of and trust 19–20, 49–50, 117–43, 202; and public good 144–73; specialization of 25–7; vulnerability of 66–7; see also contract with client; expertise
promises 4, 185, 208; see also profession(s); professional oath/pledge
public good: meanings of 154–73; served by professions 154–73
Purser, Louis C. 190

Rahner, Karl 201